Praise for *Up in Arms*

"A tale of the modern American frontier, told by one of our great independent journalists."

—SAM QUINONES, **author of** *Dreamland:*
The True Tale of America's Opiate Epidemic

"With *Up in Arms*, John Temple delivers another fierce and searching portrait of an American subculture. His last book, *American Pain*, opened up the vault on painkiller pill mills, delivering a prescient harbinger of the opioid crisis. Now, his new and piercing look at the Bundy clan and the wider Patriot militia culture is a must-read for anyone trying to understand the continuing schism between rural and urban America."

—ANTHONY SWOFFORD, *New York Times* **bestselling author of**
Jarhead: A Marine's Chronicle of the Gulf War and Other Battles

"John Temple's depth of reporting is nothing short of remarkable. Reading *Up in Arms*, I was truly immersed, as if I was witnessing the bizarre series of events unfolding in real time. Most Americans only experienced a fraction of the saga through mass media's parachute journalism. Temple's in-depth approach propels you into the unbelievable story with extraordinary details, characters, history, and riveting scenes."

—ELAINE MCMILLION SHELDON, **Academy Award–nominated**
documentary filmmaker of *Heroin(e)*

UP IN ARMS

How the Bundy Family Hijacked
Public Lands, Outfoxed the Federal
Government, and Ignited America's
Patriot Militia Movement

JOHN TEMPLE

BenBella Books, Inc.
Dallas, TX

BenBella Books, Inc.
10440 N. Central Expressway,Suite 800
Dallas, TX 75231
www.benbellabooks.com
Send feedback to feedback@benbellabooks.com

Printed in the United States of America
10 9 8 7 6 5 4 3 2 1

Library of Congress Cataloging-in-Publication Control Number: 2018058469
ISBN 9781946885951 (trade cloth)
ISBN 9781948836289 (electronic)

33614081435918

Editing by Laurel Leigh
Copyediting by Scott Calamar
Proofreading by James Fraleigh and Kim Broderick
Text design and composition by Katie Hollister
Cover design by Ty Nowicki
Cover image by Reuters/Newscom
Printed by Lake Book Manufacturing

Distributed to the trade by Two Rivers Distribution, an Ingram brand
www.tworiversdistribution.com

Special discounts for bulk sales (minimum of 25 copies) are available.
Please contact bulkorders@benbellabooks.com.

To my tribe . . . Hollee, Gideon, Hank

CONTENTS

AUTHOR'S NOTE

This book is based on notes and recordings of interviews conducted by the author with the participants as well as public statements and records. No details are invented, and no names are changed. In passages containing dialogue, quotation marks are used only when the author was reasonably sure that the speaker's words were verbatim, such as exchanges taken from court testimony or captured on audio recordings. When a source recounted a conversation from memory, the author did not use quotation marks in that dialogue. These quotes are introduced by a colon and are italicized. Occasionally, a quotation was lightly edited for clarity.

ZION CANYON

I n November 1994, a young Mormon woman from Orderville, Utah, asked Ryan Bundy to a dance. Ryan was age twenty-two at the time, the eldest son of a rancher named Cliven Bundy. The Bundys lived in Bunkerville, Nevada, two and a half hours away from the dance, a journey that would require Ryan to traverse three states and some of the most perilous hairpins, gorges, and drop-offs in the West.

Ryan said yes. It didn't matter that Bunkerville and Orderville were in different states. They were sister cities of a sort, sharing a common history, culture, religion. Both straddled the Virgin River, and both were founded by Mormons as communal settlements, where all work, products, and land were shared. Also, both towns were part of the region called Dixie, an isolated slice of eastern Nevada, northern Arizona, and southern Utah, cut off by canyons and deserts, where state lines didn't matter much and the old Wild West seemed not so long ago. So it wasn't strange for a nice Mormon girl from Orderville to arrange to meet a nice Mormon boy from Bunkerville who'd recently come home from his two-year religious mission.

Ryan set out on a Saturday morning. It was chillier than usual—blustery, gray skies. He wore a white cowboy hat and drove a powder-blue 1976 Ford F150 pickup truck, a battered and angular two-seater. He was planning to help a rancher near Orderville move some cattle before the dance, so he threw some gear into the cab: a saddle, a rope, and a change of clothing. He carried a rifle, too, and a carton of .22-caliber shells in the glove box.

He got on Interstate 15 and drove northeast, up and out of the flat desert and into Arizona, threading through cramped, shoulderless mountain passes and into Utah, all the way to Hurricane, where he filled up at a Chevron station and faced a decision. He could loop south, back through Arizona, taking a few extra minutes but navigating much easier desert terrain, or he could head straight through the canyons of Zion National Park, a route renowned for its beautiful, treacherous passes.

But Zion Canyon was faster. And Ryan wasn't thinking about which route would be the easier drive. Bundys didn't take the easiest route. They took the route they believed in.

And maybe Ryan was looking for a fight. An opportunity to test his newfound beliefs.

He pulled up to the pay booth at the entrance to Zion National Park. A ranger said it cost five dollars to enter.

Ryan said, no, he wouldn't pay the entrance fee. He drove into the park, not too slow, not too fast.

The ranger called the national park dispatcher: *We got a gate runner.*

DIXIE RESIDENTS TEND TO LOATHE THE FEDERAL GOVERNMENT'S GRASP ON local lands, and Ryan Bundy and his twelve siblings had a deeper connection than most to Zion Canyon.

Way back in 1858, just a few years before the American Civil War, Ryan's adoptive great-great-grandfather, Nephi Johnson, was the first white man to brave the rugged Zion Canyon. After his arduous climb into the gorge, which descends a half-mile deep in spots, Johnson reported back that it looked like good farmland. Over the next half century, the Mormons cultivated and grazed the fifteen-mile-long canyon, and a trickle of non-Mormon photographers and painters visited to document its beauty. The arches and chasms of Zion National Park are stacks of sandstone, shale, and volcanic rock, ablaze with deep reds and purples and brilliant whites. Blossoming wildflowers and ferns hang from seeping spring walls. Knotty pinyon pines and junipers cover the mountainsides, and Douglas firs tower above the high plateaus.

The pictures and photos made their way back to Washington, DC, and newly elected President William Howard Taft decided the canyon was too valuable to leave to a bunch of cows. In 1909, he declared the canyon a national monument. A decade later, the fledgling National Park Service designated more land and established Zion National Park. Park Service leaders were ambitious, driven by the alluring vision of a vast system of American national parks. Dixie ranchers who were used to open-range cattle ranching didn't much like the idea, fearing that grazing would be curtailed. Mormons generally believed the land was here to be used by them, not gawked at by visitors.

The conflict over Zion Canyon is the story of the West. Look at a map of the United States that identifies federal land, and the disparity is clear. The eastern two-thirds of the country contains only sprinklings of federal property, mostly national forests. East of the Mississippi, the federal government controls only 4 percent of the land. A swath of the Appalachian Mountains. A chunk of Florida Everglades. Patches of upper Wisconsin and Michigan. Moving west, the middle north/south stripe of the country, the so-called Corn Belt from the Dakotas to Texas, is nearly free of federal control.

At the Rocky Mountains, everything changes. From Colorado to California, Washington to Arizona, the map is a swirl of national forests, national parks, national monuments, and millions of acres that lack those distinctions but are managed by a federal agency. Forty-seven percent of the West belongs to the federal government, regulated mostly by four agencies: the National Park Service, the Fish and Wildlife Service, the Forest Service, and the biggest landholder, the Bureau of Land Management. Every square foot of those western vistas is accounted for, part of an entangled system of federal, state, and private rights that dictate how the land is grazed and mined, how its vegetation is used, how its water is extracted and doled out.

Nevada is the epicenter of this phenomenon. The federal government controls almost 80 percent of Nevada, the highest percentage of any state.* From above, the delineation of western federal lands resembles the bands of a giant hurricane on a meteorological map, and Nevada is the swirling nucleus of the storm. Aside from a few splotches of privately owned land—the Las Vegas Valley and a serpentine strip following Interstate 80 as it heads from Reno toward Salt Lake City—the state is a near-solid block of federal land.

The reason so much western territory remained in federal hands is mainly because, for many years, nobody else wanted it. Throughout its history, the US government bought or took land as it expanded westward. It also transferred land to states and individuals through homesteading and land grants. In the agriculture-friendly Midwest, settlers snapped up millions of 160- to 640-acre homesteads.

But the eleven western states are marked by soaring mountains and arid desert, land where growing crops is impossible without massive irrigation. Settlers locked up the agricultural valleys, and the most

---

* This percentage refers to 2017. In 1990, the federal government
   controlled approximately 86 percent of Nevada's lands.

beautiful and striking vistas were turned into national parks, including crown jewels like Yellowstone, Yosemite, the Grand Canyon, the Sierra Nevada, the Rockies. But vast stretches of the West were essentially unfarmable. So as the frontier closed in the 1890s, the federal government was left holding millions of acres of western land it couldn't give away. For decades, ranchers enjoyed grazing their herds on this open range for relatively minor fees. But starting in the 1960s, ranchers were increasingly forced to share public lands with other users, including outdoors enthusiasts, the military, miners, and energy projects. In addition, as scientists learned more about how overgrazing damaged public lands, ranchers chafed under increasing environmental regulation. By the 1990s, the relationship between western ranchers and the federal government was spiraling into outright rebellion. Cattlemen began to adopt views similar to those of "Patriot" militias that believed they were the last bulwark against a too-powerful federal government.

Dixie was a hot zone in the range wars, full of ranchers who believed the federal government had become an abomination. Ryan's father, Cliven Bundy, was one of them.

Ryan had spent two years away from the family serving as a missionary in Colorado for the Mormon Church, more formally known as The Church of Jesus Christ of Latter-day Saints (or, simply, the LDS Church). While Ryan was spreading the gospel, his father had refused to sign a new contract with the federal government, which meant the Bundy cattle were illegally grazing on public land. Ryan returned home in December 1993 to find that his father had gained a certain notoriety through his defiance of the Bureau of Land Management.

Ryan enrolled in classes at nearby Dixie State University in St. George, Utah, though he was increasingly busy with the construction business he'd founded and knew that he was not long for college. He was solidly built, favored boots and jeans and a Stetson, and was clean-shaven with neatly trimmed hair. His voice was an assertive bray, and even standing still, he bore himself with a certain hip-cocked cowboy swagger. Ryan had inherited the Bundy good looks, and he resembled his father and younger brother Ammon: big square head, strong jaw, and high cheekbones. But a week after his seventh birthday, an accident left Ryan with a lopsided face. A Ford LTD had run over him, breaking his arm and cracking his skull. Young Ryan recovered, but a bone splinter had sliced into a motor nerve that operated the left side of his face. Eight years later, the sliver of bone was removed, and his paralysis improved a little, but half of his face still sagged. This left him with a squinty eye and pursed lips on the right side of his face, and an aloof staring eye and downturned frown on the left. It was hard to read his facial expression, hard for some to even look him in the eye, though Ryan himself had no trouble returning a level gaze.

Ryan tried not to offend without reason, but he did not fear confrontation any more than his father did. He couldn't deny that he took some pleasure in antagonizing those who, in his opinion, deserved it. Still, he wanted to live virtuously, and his stint as an LDS missionary had only strengthened his faith. So Ryan wondered whether his father was doing the right thing in firing the BLM. Ryan had always been a daddy's boy, following Cliven as he worked the ranch, gathered cattle, fixed fences. Ryan wanted his own ranch someday, whether that meant inheriting Bundy Ranch or buying his own. Both Ryan's father and grandfather had always paid grazing fees to the BLM. Now Cliven's name was in the *Washington Post*, accusing the government of a "land grab." It was a bold move. But was it self-serving or was it righteous? Ryan prayed for wisdom.

The answer had come during a different trip to Orderville, coincidentally, some ten months before Ryan ran the gate at Zion National Park. Cliven had been invited to speak to a group of a few dozen men about what he'd learned and knew about the proper form of government. Ryan accompanied him and listened as his father spoke.

Cliven said the King of England hadn't protected the life, liberty, and property of the thirteen original colonies, so the colonists had rebelled and won independence. They became thirteen sovereign states, united by the US Constitution. States that joined the union later were supposed to exist on an equal footing. But how could Nevada and Utah be considered sovereign states if the federal government owned the majority of their lands? How could Nevada and Utah be free if the federal government ruled them as colonies? The federal government, Cliven told the ranchers, was acting unconstitutionally. The authors of the Constitution, he said, had not intended for the federal government to own land, except for a very few specific purposes, and the powerful bureaucracies that had grown up around the administrative branch had become a vast dark cloud over the country.

If the land was public, Cliven said, its management was the responsibility of the county government, the government closest to the people. Which was why Cliven was planning to mail a check for his grazing fees—$1,961.47—not to the federal BLM, but to Clark County, Nevada.

Ryan watched and listened, and a powerful and familiar sensation swept through him. The spirit of the Lord was delivering him a revelation, the answer he'd been looking for. What his father was teaching on this day was true.

From that day forward, Ryan vowed, he would never back down from this truth.

ABOUT A MILE AND A HALF INTO ZION NATIONAL PARK, A RANGER CAUGHT up with Ryan's truck and switched on his lights and siren. Ryan pulled over.

The ranger approached, asked for Ryan's name and driver's license.

Ryan refused to hand over the documents.

He said: *Do you have documentation that gives you the authority to stop me?*

The ranger gave him his badge and identification. Ryan read them, gave them back.

Ryan said: *The federal government has no right to stop me. You don't have the authority.*

The ranger recognized this kind of talk. He knew he was dealing with a constitutionalist. He told Ryan to wait, then called for backup. Ryan said he wasn't going to wait. The ranger asked again for his license, and this time Ryan showed it to him but kept it in his hand. Ryan told the ranger that the federal government couldn't charge an entrance fee to the canyon because it didn't own the land.

The ranger said: *You have three choices. Pay the five dollars. Turn around and take the alternate route to Orderville. Or, go to jail.*

Ryan said: *I don't like any of those options.*

He put the truck in drive, pressed the accelerator, and one of the most scenic police chases in history began.

The ranger jumped back to avoid getting hit, ran to his vehicle. Another ranger had arrived, and the two of them sounded their sirens, flashed their lights, and followed the pickup. It wasn't much of a chase. Ryan stuck to the twenty-five-mile-per-hour speed limit on the hairpin turns. He wasn't trying to escape. He simply didn't believe these men had the authority to stop him.

The road through Zion Canyon, completed in 1930, was a marvel of engineering that had taken three years to build. It included the mile-long Zion–Mount Carmel Tunnel with six scenic "windows" blasted through the sandstone walls. A couple miles in, at the mouth of the famed tunnel, another ranger had stopped traffic so an oversized truck could pass through the narrow shaft. Ryan thought the rangers were trying to pull him over, so he veered into the oncoming traffic lane, zipped by the standing cars, and plunged into the dim tunnel. The rangers followed.

At the east exit of the national park, Utah Highway Patrol troopers blocked the entrance lane with a patrol car and unrolled a spike strip on the road. Ryan yanked the pickup into the opposite lane again, dodging the spikes. A trooper ran into the road to block him and then jumped out of his way. The ranger chasing Ryan tried to pass him but drove over the spike strip, shredding all four of his tires.

Ryan kept driving for fifteen more miles, until his path was completely blocked by two Kane County Sheriff patrol vehicles. Dozens of lawmen—state, local, federal—had gathered, guns drawn. Ryan didn't believe he'd broken any laws, but he recognized the sheriff's law-enforcement authority as the highest in the land. He stopped. Three officers took him into custody, while others trained their guns on him.

Ryan missed his date in Orderville. He sat in the Kane County Jail for a couple of days, and the state charged him with failing to stop for a peace officer, a third-degree felony. He entered into a diversion agreement, and the state eventually dropped the charges.

The National Park Service never pursued the case at all. Maybe they didn't believe it was worth making a federal case over a five-dollar toll. Ryan chose to believe the feds knew he was going to challenge their ownership of the land, and they didn't want to engage with him on that question. He believed they didn't want to fight that battle with an informed and resolute opponent.

But Ryan knew he'd have another chance. It was just a matter of time until the Bundys and the federal government went to war.

Part I

Chapter 1

A CALL TO ARMS

For decades, when Cliven Bundy was asked what he would do if the feds came for his cattle, the rancher gave the same answer: *Whatever it takes.* The phrase was pure Cliven—vaguely challenging, maddeningly ambiguous. Cliven liked to test people.

In March 2014, two special agents with the Bureau of Land Management traveled to Bunkerville to tell Cliven that the BLM was finally ready to seize his herd, twenty-one years after first threatening to do so. The herd was made up of some nine hundred head of cattle that roamed a vast stretch of rugged desert backcountry called Gold Butte, all of it public land managed by the BLM. The BLM agents went to the rancher's house near the banks of the Virgin River and knocked on the door. Nobody answered. They drove into the Gold Butte range and found Cliven's son-in-law, who worked the ranch. At their request, the son-in-law called Cliven, who answered but refused to speak to the federal agents. For the rest of the day, the BLM agents tried to track down various Bundy sons to discuss the impending roundup and gauge the family's level of antagonism. Doors were slammed and phones hung up. That evening, they finally got ahold of Ryan Bundy and talked for forty-six minutes.

"We really want to know if we're gonna have any type of physical problems with you guys," the agent said. "Because we want to avoid that at all costs."

Ryan didn't hesitate.

"I'll tell you the best way to avoid that is to start adhering to the Constitution, recognize that there are rights here that you are violating, and simply do not show up," Ryan said.

"I have to be honest, have to inform you, that that's not an option," the agent said.

Things had heated up from there. Cliven sent a letter to Clark County sheriff Doug Gillespie, who headed up the joint city-county Las Vegas Metropolitan Police Department. The rancher demanded that the sheriff protect Bundy Ranch from the feds. The family called friends, neighbors, and others they'd met over two decades of land-rights meetings and protests and asked them to back the Bundys when the BLM came to Gold Butte. Cliven boasted to reporters that people would come from hundreds of miles away, because they knew if the Bundys fell, they'd be next. In truth, the family had no idea whether people would show up at all.

Ten days after the phone call with Ryan, the BLM began closing chunks of the entire 578,000-acre Gold Butte area, a swath of desert and mountain nearly the size of Rhode Island's landmass. For six weeks, there'd be no climbing on the Mormon Mesa. No off-roading in Gold Butte. No loading boats into Lake Mead from Overton Beach.

It was finally happening. The feds were coming for Cliven's cattle. And not like the small-time rustlers who'd risked getting hanged to grab a calf or two from Cliven's forefathers. The BLM had hired dozens of cowboys and brought several platoons to guard them—law-enforcement rangers and agents decked out in tactical gear, with rifles and ballistic vests and German shepherd dogs. On a deserted dry streambed called Toquop Wash, the BLM began constructing corrals and hauling in mobile offices and supplies to build a sprawling command post.

A band of men that included Cliven, Ryan, and the youngest Bundy sibling, Arden, age sixteen, rode out to Toquop Wash on horseback to investigate the federal operation. Arden wore a GoPro camera on his head, recording jouncy video of the scene. They encountered a long caravan of heavy-duty pickup trucks and big rigs hauling livestock trailers, campers, water tanks, flatbeds with stacks of portable metal fencing, hay bales, and livestock chutes. The trucks were pulling off Interstate 15 and heading toward the flat spot a half-mile north where crews would erect pens to corral the cattle before shipping them to auction. The mounted Bundy men mingled with the trucks like cowboys confronting an armored battalion. They dogged the vehicles to the fenced-off compound, where guards let the caravan vehicles inside, one by one. Arden mostly stayed out of their way, but Ryan moseyed his horse right in front of the trucks, staring down the drivers through their windshields, snapping photos with a cell phone.

THE FEDS PAID ATTENTION. APPARENTLY THE BUNDY FAMILY WASN'T ALL talk. The roundup hadn't even begun, and the Bundys had shown they were willing to disrupt it. The commander of the roundup, a gung-ho BLM agent named Dan Love, decided to beef up the security operations, to counter force with force.

Tall and muscular, with wraparound shades and a thick black beard, Love was known to be arrogant but articulate, funny but aggressive. In 2009, Love had led an investigation into the illegal trading of Native American artifacts taken from federal lands. The case culminated in a massive raid in which 150 agents in tactical gear hauled away twenty-three suspects in shackles. Most of the defendants considered themselves collectors, not criminals. Two ultimately committed suicide, including a well-respected doctor from Utah. Locals resented the BLM's heavy-handed tactics and said Love was too forceful to navigate the politics of the range wars, that his raid of the artifact traders would have been more suitable for the takedown of violent drug kingpins. But Love had ardent backers high in the BLM's law-enforcement branch. After the operation, he was named "agent of the year" and promoted to special agent in charge of law enforcement for all of Utah and Nevada.

Now he was leading the Bundy roundup, a massive operation that the BLM expected to take at least a month to carry out. The scale of the roundup was partially determined by the vastness of Gold Butte. By now, Cliven's cattle ranged far beyond his original permitted grazing area, which was called the Bunkerville Allotment. They had drifted far and wide over approximately one-fifth of Clark County. They nibbled golf-course turf in Mesquite and gulped water from Lake Mead, thirty-five miles away.

Under Dan Love, the roundup had taken on the flavor of a military campaign. One hundred and thirty-four rangers and agents from the federal land agencies and the Federal Bureau of Investigation volunteered or were assigned to the operation. Eighty-three of them were BLM rangers or special agents, which was about a quarter of the nation's BLM law-enforcement personnel. Two FBI SWAT teams would be standing by with a helicopter, a mine-resistant armored vehicle, and two hostage negotiators. However, while working the roundup, law-enforcement officers were told to wear more casual uniforms, to keep the heavy-duty firepower and tactical uniforms out of sight.

The BLM was set to pay a private livestock contractor in Utah $966,000 to collect up to 1,100 head of cattle. The BLM didn't want to tear up undisturbed land, so all off-road activity would be conducted on foot or horseback. Helicopters would run the clusters of cattle toward three temporary holding pens. The cattle would be hauled in trailers from the temporary pens to the command post in Toquop Wash before being shipped to a livestock auction house in Utah. The command-post location was chosen partly because it was a full seven miles from the Bundy property. It contained larger pens and dozens of white mobile trailers parked in a rectangle to form an impromptu office park. Portable spotlights lit up the area at night.

The plan covered hazards, too, including approximate travel times to nearby hospitals by ambulance and helicopter. By chopper, Mesa View Regional in Mesquite was five minutes away; University Medical Center in Las Vegas was fifty-five minutes, but it could handle more serious cases. Stay hydrated, the plan advised personnel. Seek high ground if it rained—the Virgin River's meandering, ankle-deep waters could turn deadly in flash floods. Watch hands and feet. Snakes, scorpions, and Gila monsters were everywhere. Be cautious around the ornery Bundy bulls. Most of all, the plan said, beware the ornery Bundys themselves. If confronted, don't lose your cool or venture further into their space.

Over the years, various law-enforcement agencies had evaluated the Bundy family to determine just how dangerous a roundup might be. In 2011, the FBI's Behavioral Analysis Unit in Quantico, Virginia, had concluded that Cliven Bundy, though "hyper-sensitive" and "prone to anger-filled rants," was unlikely to commit violence, mainly because there was no evidence he'd ever physically harmed anyone in his sixty-plus years. In its own 2014 assessment, BLM analysts had interviewed some eighteen relatives and associates and concluded that the Bundys posed a moderate threat.

> The threats (Cliven) has made to "do whatever it takes," appear to be more reactive than proactive, leaving BLM to assess that, although Bundy may support a violent reaction to a perceived threat to his property, family or person, he is not likely planning any preemptive strike against our operation. That being said, BLM does not have enough information to determine his threshold for this perceived threat or the precise trigger point that would elicit a violent response.

Of the family members, the analysts concluded, Ryan Bundy was the most radical and most likely to take action against law enforcement. The report mentioned the long-ago police chase through Zion Canyon and also described a 2007 traffic stop in Utah that ended with police using a Taser gun on an "extremely agitated" Ryan.

The BLM analysts determined there was little chance that the Bundy roundup would attract the attention of "violent, anti-government, anti-law enforcement extremist groups."

> At this time, there is no intelligence available indicated that any of the groups are aware of this operation or specifically interested in Bundy's cause. However, Bundy's rhetoric and the nature of his argument against the BLM may resonate with a violent Sovereign Citizen-esque organization.

The BLM was keeping a close eye on the Bundy family. During the day, plainclothes special agents rode dirt bikes on the roads and land around Gold Butte. After dark, they set up observation posts on high ground and used night-vision goggles to watch the Bundy house.

Love also had a video camera erected on the public land across the road from the house, but hours after it was put up, the camera captured Ryan Bundy approaching on a yellow all-terrain vehicle. The live feed went black, and agents who went to investigate found the camera and tripod on the ground, knocked over.

Early in the planning process, Sheriff Gillespie had agreed to provide security for the BLM operation. Gillespie had gotten to know Cliven two years earlier, when the BLM was preparing a previous roundup operation that was eventually aborted. The sheriff knew Cliven's views but had no luck convincing the old rancher to comply with a federal court order directing him to remove his cattle from public lands. Gillespie advised Love to wait until fall to do the roundup instead of conducting it during calving season, when the cows were more vulnerable. Love ignored the advice. To Gillespie, the BLM commander seemed needlessly aggressive. The sheriff decided he didn't want any part of the operation—the BLM was on its own.

Love shrugged it off. Local sheriffs rarely had the stomach for controversial operations like this one. Like the artifacts bust in Utah, the Bundy roundup was a job for federal agents.

WHEN THE BLM FINALLY BEGAN ROUNDING UP CATTLE ON SATURDAY, April 5, 2014, some Bundy family members captured video of a convoy of six livestock trailers hitched to heavy-duty pickup trucks pulling onto the interstate in Mesquite. They could see livestock inside at least one of the cars. A caravan of white government SUVs flanked the shipment, police lights flashing.

"They got lights," one of the onlookers said wonderingly. "It's like the president of the United States."

The family posted the video to the Bundy Ranch blog they had created two years earlier to document the festering conflict. The blog's early posts had been nothing more than cut-and-pasted articles about the dispute from the *Las Vegas Review-Journal* and the St. George *Spectrum*. The posts had grown more heated as the BLM had begun planning the roundup. The Bundys posted contact information of state and county officials, asking readers to call in protest. When the Bundys discovered the identity of the livestock contractor the BLM had hired to round up the cattle, they posted his name and phone number under the headline: "Cattle thieves! Should be hung!" In early March 2014, the family started a YouTube channel and posted more than a dozen short educational videos starring Cliven and bearing titles such as "Range Improvements" and "Is Cliven Trespassing? NO he is NOT!" In the videos, Cliven drove around the ranch, pointing out examples of federal conservation folly, or explaining how his cattle adapted to the desert, or discussing his views on constitutional rights. Grandchildren, dogs, and prize bulls made appearances. Offscreen, roosters crowed.

The day after the roundup began, Dave Bundy, age thirty-seven, a fleshier, milder replica of Cliven, had dropped by the ranch to see how things were going. Midafternoon, he and Ryan headed out to see what the BLM was doing. They took Riverside Road, the narrow state highway the Bundys traveled to get from the ranch to Bunkerville and further east to Mesquite. The road cuts through range after range of small, dusty, nearly identical hills, roughly parallel with the Virgin River. Dave and Ryan stopped on the roadside where they had a view of a contingent of BLM vehicles gathered on Gold Butte land to the south, away from the river. Ryan had two daughters with him in his white van. Dave leaned against his sedan on the narrow shoulder of the road, holding up an iPad to film the khaki-clad feds. They didn't have any cattle, but Dave was determined to get a picture if they did.

Ryan saw a black vehicle depart the BLM contingent and climb up a dirt road to the top of a hill. Two men got out and set up a rifle facing the Bundy brothers, and Ryan felt odd and uncomfortable seeing those men looking at him through a scope.* Ryan took a picture of the men: two black, featureless bumps peeking over the ridge, only their heads and shoulders showing.

The rest of the feds barreled toward the Bundys, raising a cloud of dust. Through a loudspeaker, they ordered the family members to disperse. Ryan turned his van in the direction of the ranch and began to drive off. Dave stayed put on the side of the road. The BLM vehicles stopped, and nine or ten men got out. They approached Dave cautiously. Dave put his iPad on the hood of his car. Ryan saw this and stopped. Then backed up to watch more closely.

The officers told Dave to leave, that Gold Butte was closed for the roundup. Dave replied that the road he was standing on was a state highway. The land surrounding it might be under federal control, but Nevada had an easement for Riverside Road itself. He said he was exercising his First Amendment rights by taking pictures in a public space. He dialed 911 on his cell phone and asked that the Mesquite police report to the scene.

Foot on the brake, Ryan sat in the driver's seat of his van, rooted in the middle of the road, and stared hard at the two federal lawmen edging closer to his brother. A BLM agent came up alongside Ryan's passenger window and told him he was "free to leave." Other rangers surrounded the van in a semicircle, their feet wide, knees flexed, like linebackers waiting for the snap.

"I *am* free to leave," Ryan agreed. His voice was calm, measured, determined. "But I will not leave without him."

Backing down wasn't Ryan Bundy's style. But there were factors to consider. The men with the rifle on the bluff above them. His two

---

* In an email to his superiors the next day, a BLM ranger on the hill said he looked through the scope of an AR-15 rifle to "see what was happening" inside Ryan Bundy's van.

daughters in the van. But most of all, his father's instructions from earlier in the day. Cliven had told his sons and daughters to take pictures, track what the BLM was doing—but to not engage. Ryan didn't consider himself a leader like his younger brother, Ammon. Ryan was a loyal and dogged foot soldier. An able disciple. He would follow his father's orders.

Still, Ryan couldn't bring himself to leave. The agents crept closer to Dave.

"He's a grown man," the agent outside Ryan's window said.

"He is," Ryan agreed. "And he's my brother."

"He's being dealt with," the ranger said. "Sir, this is the last time I'm gonna ask you. Your first choice is to leave."

Ryan idled his van on the highway, watching his brother and the hovering agents. Help his brother? Or obey his dad?

The ranger on Dave's left made his move, grabbing Dave's arm. Then the one on the other side moved in. But Dave was strong, and the rangers had a moment of tug-of-war before a third and fourth piled on, wrestling him to the gravel. Another ranger rushed in with a German shepherd on a leash, the dog barking, over and over, eager to join the scrum.

The ranger at Ryan's window spoke again, trying to command Ryan's attention, his voice higher than before, more strained.

"Your first choice is to leave. To leave. Sir . . . sir. Leave now. Leave now."

Ryan said nothing, just watched his brother struggling facedown on the ground, two agents kneeling on him, a couple more clustered around the throng.

Ryan's foot eased off the brake, then pressed it again. Off, and on again.

"We've been playing this game all day," the ranger said, his voice growing firmer. "Leave the area. I'm gonna drag you out of the car, okay? Here in a second."

Ryan let off the brake, and the van traveled a few feet, then he braked again.

The ranger took two big side steps to stay even with Ryan's window. "You have children in the car," he said. "Don't act like this."

There was nothing to do. Cliven had told Ryan to stand down.

Ryan finally spoke.

"I am leaving," he said. "I'm in the process of leaving."

Ryan drove away, leaving his brother behind.

UP TO NOW, AMMON BUNDY, CLIVEN'S FOURTH CHILD, HAD NOT BEEN deeply involved in his father's dispute. In fact, the BLM threat assessment report had labeled Ammon as the least dangerous of the male Bundys.

Ammon lived in Phoenix, Arizona, and led a more worldly life than Ryan and Dave and his other siblings. But Ammon had checked in regularly with Cliven as the feds had closed the lands around Bundy Ranch. The old man was frantic with worry and anger, his high-pitched voice sounding raw and creaky over the phone. But every time Ammon had asked his father what he should do, Cliven told him to stay in Phoenix. Cliven believed the feds would back down only if large crowds showed up to support Bundy Ranch. With thirteen kids and some fifty grandchildren, plus plenty of cousins and aunts nearby, the family alone would be a multitude, but they needed many more. Still, Cliven didn't want everybody to gather at the ranch until it was necessary. His children had jobs, families of their own.

Always the planner, Ammon asked what he could do to prepare. Cliven said the Lord had given him one insight, that the family would need to feed an army of supporters. And he knew the exact amount of provisions.

Cliven told Ammon: *I want you to get ready to feed a lot of people—two hundred people for seven days.*

That, too, was pure Cliven. He'd issue a commandment but give little thought about how to pull it off. Still, Ammon was glad to have a job to do. He and his wife, Lisa, calculated how much food they'd need to feed that many people. They came up with a simple menu: spaghetti one day, hamburgers the next. Ammon stayed put in Phoenix and waited for his father's call.

Then Dave got arrested. All Cliven knew was what Ryan had told them, that federal officers had grabbed Dave and wrestled him down to the gravel road and knelt on him. This enraged the Bundys, who were horrified by the idea of the gentlest Bundy brother caught in the maw of a corrupt and inexorable federal judicial system. Cliven began calling anyone he could think of—the sheriff, local lawmakers—and he still couldn't figure out where the feds had taken Dave.

At 9:30 PM, Cliven's wife, Carol, sat down at the family computer and logged onto the Bundy blog. She switched the font color to a bright, angry red, hit the all-caps button, and pounded out a furious call to arms, not bothering to check the post for typos:

YOU HAVE BEEN ASKING WHAT YOU CAN DO!
AND NOW ITS TIME!!!!!!
They have my cattle and now they have one of my boys. Range War begins tomorrow at Bundy ranch at 9:30 a.m. Bring your signs and horses, and plan to stay as long as you can!
We are going to get the job done!

Later that night, Cliven called Ammon again, and this time he sounded different, grimmer.

Cliven said: *It's time. It's time to get the family together.*

WHEN THE BUNDY BROTHERS AND SISTERS ARE ASKED ABOUT THEIR MANY siblings, they sometimes rattle off the chronology, rapid-fire in one breath, reducing the whole family to an alphabet-like simplicity: Shiree-Ryan-Mel-Ammon-Dave-Lance-Katie-Molly-Hanna-Rachel-Bailey-Stetsy-Arden.

Thirteen kids, which doesn't include Duane, a decade or so older than all of them, who wasn't Cliven's biological son but had come to live at Bundy Ranch when he was a teenager. So sometimes the family said Cliven had thirteen children, sometimes fourteen.

But the family is still more complicated than that. There are three waves of Bundy siblings. The first was the one girl and five boys Cliven had with his first wife, Jane. She left the family when Ammon was five years old. For a decade, Cliven raised the kids by himself, and then, in 1991, he married Carol, who brought her four daughters into the family. Cliven and Carol had three more children together. All thirteen siblings call Carol "Mom."

The Bundys lived in the low-roofed house near the Virgin River that Cliven's father built in 1951, a simple 1,200-square-foot structure with no air conditioning, where every surface bore a film of desert dust. Between his marriages to Jane and Carol, Cliven and the five boys sometimes slept in one bedroom, and Shiree had the other to herself. Then Carol and her girls joined the family, and things got really crowded before the older ones began graduating from high school and going on missions, one by one. Afterward, they mostly came back to Dixie and did not venture far from the Virgin Valley. They found jobs, found wives and husbands, and began producing their own large families, though none quite as large as the one they'd grown up in. Shiree, the oldest, married a cattleman and livestock auctioneer and moved to Orderville. Cliven's sons mostly did the kinds of things their father and grandfather had done: They ran cattle and heavy equipment, built roads and houses. Ryan and Dave started their own construction outfits. Mel worked in a gold mine.

In the older wave of Bundy brothers, Ammon stood out. As a boy, he'd skipped a lot of school, which was easy to do because Cliven was often away working construction jobs in Las Vegas, and his mom was long gone, bouncing around southern Utah and Salt Lake City. When mail came from the junior high school, Ammon intercepted it so his dad wouldn't know he was ditching class. Cliven was generally too busy to notice, caught up in being a single father of five, ranching, and making a living. And Ammon kept busy around the ranch, which was a young mechanic's dream, strewn with junker cars, heavy machinery, farm equipment. Ammon took apart machines to figure out how they worked, and then tried to put them back together.

The Bundy boys learned ranching as they went. They rode horses, roped, chased cows, mended fences and water pipes. They drove tractors and trucks on the ranch from the time they could reach the pedals. By sixteen years old, driving was routine. When Cliven worked the ranch, the five older boys labored alongside him and were expected to carry a man's load. At nightfall, if someone hadn't returned from the mountains, the family would go out searching. In those days, before they had cell phones, if their truck broke down, the boys were in for a long walk or a cold night in the hills. They learned to carry big jugs of water with them on the range, plus beef jerky and cans of food, also a blanket. Ammon wanted to be a rancher, but when he was around fifteen years old, Cliven sat him down and told him that he couldn't count on the ranch. The ranch didn't even really support his single family, especially now that the Bureau of Land Management was really shrinking the Bundy herd. There was no way it would support the families of Ammon and his siblings.

But Ammon believed his father wasn't maximizing the ranch's full potential, and he let Cliven know it. Nothing worked properly. To harvest the hay, Ammon couldn't just hook up the tractor to the swather. He'd have to dig a battery out of a truck and hook it to the tractor, then fix a flat tire, and then roll-start the machine. To loosen a bolt, he'd have to search through a dusty toolbox in a dim barn for twenty minutes to find the right socket. Finally, Ammon bought himself a pretty nice tool set, and before long Cliven was taking Ammon's tools if his son forgot to lock the box. Ammon had yelling matches with Cliven, butting heads more often than the other sons. But Ammon understood when his father said he wasn't going to be able to make a living off the ranch, and he began looking to a future beyond the Virgin Valley, beyond Dixie.

All the boys played sports at Virgin Valley High School, but Ammon was the best athlete. A sturdy playmaker at running back, he played both sides of the ball on occasion. He regularly made the St. George newspaper and earned all-league honors his senior year. He started fabricating his own fence panels in the school's machine shop, selling them to teachers who had livestock, and he restored a 1966 Ford pickup. He graduated and went on a mission to Minneapolis, then returned home and began college at Southern Utah University in Cedar City. He met Lisa, who was immediately impressed by his self-assured maturity. Ammon started a traveling auto-maintenance business in the summer of 1998. He and Ryan outfitted a service truck with everything it needed for them to go to a customer's home or work and top off their fluids, air up their tires, wash their windshields. The business was so successful that Ammon dropped out of college to pursue it. He focused on doing maintenance for truck fleets, naming the company Valet Fleet Service. He and Lisa married in July 2001 and found that Dixie was too small for his ambitions. Chasing larger fleets, the couple moved to Phoenix.

Ammon finally controlled his own operation, one he could run in a methodical, organized way. He put in eighteen-hour days at the red-white-and-blue warehouse on a busy corner in an industrial sector of the city. He created a tracking system designed to predict and service the fleets' maintenance needs in order to prevent breakdowns. The company gradually grew to twenty employees, and Ammon also started a truck leasing business that operated out of the same location. He posed for the company website's team photo, arm around one of his mechanics, in front of a white truck cab. His family grew also. He and Lisa had five kids. Life was busy. Too busy for any conflicts with the law, other than a speeding ticket in Gila County, Arizona, in 2005.

In this way too, Ammon was unlike some of his brothers. Cliven had run a traditional Mormon household—no alcohol, no tobacco. But Mel drank and chewed tobacco when he was young and generally raised a little hell. Younger brother Lance got hooked on narcotic pain-killers and had been charged with serious crimes: passing bad checks, stealing guns, and selling methamphetamine, though the meth charges were later dropped. Ryan didn't drink or smoke, but he did have a tendency to get into minor skirmishes with authorities that then escalated, much like his long-ago run through Zion Canyon. These incidents had nothing to do with intoxication or hell-raising. These were matters of principle, of liberty. Ryan clashed with school board members (they wouldn't let his daughter carry a pocketknife to school), with city officials (he was burning brush without a permit), with animal control officers (he allegedly trespassed on an animal shelter to take back his horse). Ryan considered these disputes the price he paid to live free.

Theoretically, Ammon's outlook wasn't so different than Ryan's. He believed people were unhappy without freedom, and that governments generally wound up striving to take away the agency of their citizens. But he'd gained a different status than Ryan and their father. At thirty-eight years old, Ammon wasn't scratching out a living as a desert cowboy. He lived in the city and had remodeled his sprawling ranch house with a big yard for the kids. Valet Fleet Service was booming, and Ammon was busy developing his own fleet-management software. He was respected in Phoenix, in the church. It was not a life that put him in conflict with authorities. Most of the time, Ammon *was* the authority.

AMMON WAS NAMED AFTER TWO MEN. CLIVEN GAVE HIM THE MIDDLE NAME of his father, David Ammon Bundy, who died in 1996. Ammon's other namesake was a prominent figure in the Book of Mormon, "a strong and mighty man" who journeyed on a mission around 121 BC to spread the word of the Lord. He worked as a shepherd and gained respect when he drove enemy shepherds away from a water hole. Ammon's bravery convinced his fellow shepherds that his teachings about God were true.

The Book of Mormon was first published in 1830 by Joseph Smith, the founder of the religion, who said he'd translated the text from inscribed golden plates buried east of Rochester, New York. To the LDS Church, the Book of Mormon possesses equal or even greater weight than the Holy Bible, because Mormons believe that God never stops revealing principles and commandments to humanity.

Like Joseph Smith, the Bundys believe the Constitution of the United States is also a divinely inspired document, nothing short of a miracle given the chaos and discord of the period when it was written. In speeches and writings and sermons, Joseph Smith repeatedly predicted that a time would come when the Constitution would "hang by a thread." At this moment, the prophet said, it would fall to the

Mormon people to save the Constitution. This prophecy is an article of faith among many Mormons. In Ammon Bundy's home, a framed image of a torn Constitution sewed together with a thread hangs in the main room.

The Bundys pay close attention to what others call gut feelings. Those notions, they believe, are the Lord's way of communicating. These might be an answer to a prayer or an unprompted moment of guidance. As he prepared to set out for Bundy Ranch on that April morning in 2014, a few hours after his father's urgent call, Ammon became aware of one of those divine nudges. He was loading up his travel trailer, which he was going to tow to Bunkerville behind his Chevy pickup, when he suddenly felt he should leave his firearms behind, even though he believed his family might face violence.

He said to his wife: *I just feel very strongly that we're not to be armed in any way. I don't know why I'm feeling this way, but I want you to know.*

LEAVING A NONPLUSSED LISA AND THE KIDS IN PHOENIX, AMMON DROVE north, crossing over the Colorado River and entering Clark County, Nevada. In Las Vegas, he stopped at a Sam's Club and filled the trailer's stowage space with a week's worth of food for two hundred people, as Cliven had commanded.

Clark County is the southernmost county in Nevada, where the tip of the state's broken arrowhead plunges into Lake Mead. The county butts up against California to the west, Arizona to the east. Utah is fifteen minutes away. Ninety-two percent of Clark County's land is controlled by the federal government and managed by numerous agencies. The other 8 percent is owned by the state of Nevada and private landowners.

Even in the expansive West, Clark County is big. It's the twenty-second largest county in the United States, a little smaller than New Jersey, a little larger than Connecticut. It takes an hour and forty-six minutes to drive the 123 miles across it on Interstate 15, from Primm through the sprawl of the Las Vegas Valley and all the way to Mesquite. Clark County contains 7 percent of the state's landmass, but two-thirds of its people. The county is home to the Hoover Dam, to the pulsating Las Vegas Strip, to Nellis Air Force Base and its gigantic bombing range, to snowcapped mountains, to scorching desert. And increasingly, it's home to lots of people. More than two million residents, almost three times as many as there had been twenty-five years earlier.

Clark County is also home to Bundy Ranch, seventy-five miles northeast of Las Vegas. When Cliven says "Bundy Ranch"—pronounced "rainch"—he sometimes is referring to the land his family actually owns, a 160-acre rectangle that straddles the Virgin River. But more often than not, he means the hundreds of thousands of Gold Butte acres that surround his property, from the top of Virgin Peak through the Virgin Valley to the Mormon Mountains. Cliven doesn't own this range itself—it's public land—but his family has held claims on the water and forage. It's some of the sorriest rangeland in the US—parched and barren—but to Cliven, it's home.

Gold Butte's landscape isn't as dramatic as the canyons and mountains of southern Utah and the Arizona Strip, but up close it has a powerful presence. The reddish gravel underfoot is actually a spectrum of hues: blues, roses, oranges, olives. The vegetation is equally varied: indigo bush, Nevada jointfir, buckhorn cholla, beavertail, Arizona cottontop, barrel cactus, desert trumpet, desert globemallow, Mormon tea. At daybreak and twilight, the air glows. And the desert's immense hush is its own sound.

Viewed from above, the Bundy property is a jumble of geometric green fields surrounded by a vast expanse of sere grays and tans. Those fields are irrigated by a wide man-made ditch of brown water, diverted from the Virgin River, that courses through the property. Horse pastures and cattle corrals and junked vehicles and other ranch detritus surround the Bundy house, which is tucked into a green cottonwood grove scattered with grandchildren's playthings.

On the surrounding fields, the Bundys raised heirloom casaba melons. The seeds had been passed down through the family for 140 years. Cliven flooded the fields before planting and covering the seeds with dry soil. When the melons were white and sweet, the family put a coffee can by the gate and a sign directing folks to pick their own, three for ten dollars. Honor system, cash in the coffee can.

Cliven also raised cattle. He got his first cow when he was five years old. He traded the cow for two heifer calves and was on the way to growing his own herd. Cliven revered the old cowboy ways. He'd build a fire by dropping a dried yucca plant onto dirt and covering it with wood, and then strike a kitchen match on a rock. He held authentic Bundy-raised steaks over the fire on forked sticks until they sizzled. He'd bring sourdough that the family had passed down for generations, wrap the dough around a stick and cook it, squeezing his own tamarisk honey and homemade butter onto the bread.

Cliven's cows were mutts, a mix bred to range the harsh Mojave without much assistance from humans. Part Hereford for their efficiency at turning forage into size. Part Angus for their quality beef. And part Brahman for their highly developed sweat glands, which gave the herd the durability to trudge miles without water in the scorching 115-degree summer. They were spread over so many thousands of acres that Cliven only had a general idea as to how many head he had at a particular time. The cattle grazed on desert grasses, chaparral, and burrow sage, plants so spindly and scarce that it took more than one hundred acres of desert to sustain a single cow.

The Bundys branded any cattle they could gather with a V over an O, seared into the rump. Some of the cows also bore signature Bundy earmarks, a pointed notch snipped out of the left ear, a rectangle lopped from the lower half of the right. When the calves were close to a year old, Cliven and the boys would round up as many as possible. Because of their independence and because they were partly hot-blooded Brahmans, they were more wild beasts than livestock. They didn't like humans, weren't used to human contact. Get within a quarter mile, and the entire herd would turn their heads and stare fixedly at you. Get closer, and they'd trot away. Harvesting the undomesticated Bundy herd resembled hunting more than ranching. Cliven rigged up temporary trapping corrals, metal portable fences baited with hay and water. The gate had a spring lock that would swing shut when the cattle were inside. Or, on horses or vehicles, the cowboys herded the cattle into the temporary pens and closed the gates, about as easy as driving a wild herd of elk.

Cliven gathered a few calves at a time, working different parts of the range, and hauled them to Bundy Ranch to "grain-finish" them, fattening them on hay until they were ready for market. The beef wasn't technically organic, but the very hands-off nature of Cliven's ranching meant that the beef was free of hormones and antibiotics. Cliven called it "natural." A year-old calf might weigh five hundred pounds and fetch a dollar per pound, an amount that fluctuated depending on drought and demand. If spring brought one hundred calves, that was $50,000. But that revenue was eaten up in a thousand ways. When Cliven hauled a livestock trailer behind his pickup into the desert, that meant gravel chewing away at eight tires. Hay for the feeder calves either cost money or had to be grown at the ranch, cutting down on the melon fields. Bulls over five years old tended to lose vigor, and the herds needed new blood, so Cliven had to buy new bulls every so often, which cost thousands. Equipment costs were never-ending—fences, vehicles, tools, pipes, on and on. Profit margins were thin.

The entire operation flowed, literally, from the snowmelt-fed waters emerging here and there from the base of Virgin Peak. Some springs, like Nickel Creek, were year-round gushers that put out as much as three hundred gallons per minute. Others, like Key West Spring and Juanita Spring, were just seeps, like a sluggish tap faucet turned on halfway—they took a minute or two to fill up a gallon jug. But even a pencil-thin trickle could water hundreds of cattle, if properly captured and distributed. Like his father and generations of desert cowboys before him, Cliven built and monitored a system of "range improvements." This could mean fences or corrals, but in Gold Butte, it mostly meant water systems. Dozens of structures collected water from the springs and distributed it to troughs located miles downslope. A few ancient head boxes dated back to the 1800s. One was a bathtub-sized concrete box that had been broken apart by the years, cattle brands carved into the rim tank by the original cowboys. Over time, Cliven had pieced it back together.

Cliven tried to reduce the distance between watering holes so that the herds would cluster and not overgraze large areas. He believed he was improving the environment, not to mention the hunting opportunities. He enjoyed seeing the chukar birds, deer, quail, and jackrabbits that gathered near the water troughs. And the desert tortoises. He liked those little critters, despite all the trouble they'd caused him.

Monday morning, as Ammon hauled his travel trailer toward Bundy Ranch, Cliven drove to Las Vegas to meet with Sheriff Gillespie.

At the sheriff's office, Cliven demanded protection from the feds who were stealing his cattle and had arrested his son. The BLM was reporting the roundup's progress on its website: Their contract cowboys had gathered seventy-six cattle on Saturday, and another sixty on Sunday, the day they arrested Dave. Those cattle were worth as much as $1,000 per head. It was the sheriff's job, Cliven said, to protect his property and family. Gillespie acted sympathetic but made it clear that he wasn't going to intervene in a federal operation. And, the sheriff said, no cow was worth spilling a drop of human blood.

In Vegas, Cliven bought some pallets of drinking water for the supporters he was hoping would show up at the ranch. Then he headed toward home. Ammon called and said he was on his way, bringing food. Cliven said he still wasn't sure where Dave was. Just then, Cliven got another call and disconnected. It was good news: Dave was free and waiting for Cliven to pick him up at a 7-Eleven, four blocks from the federal courthouse in Las Vegas. Back at the ranch, the family and supporters were mobilizing, calling reporters to let them know that Dave and Cliven would be holding an impromptu press conference in the convenience store parking lot. Cliven turned around and headed back toward Vegas.

A handful of local reporters—from media including the *Review-Journal* and KLAS-TV Channel 8—were already there when Cliven pulled up to the 7-Eleven. Dave looked exhausted, and he wore the same blue Brigham Young University T-shirt he'd been arrested in. His face was patchy with abrasions from being pushed into the gravel the day before.

Dave sat in a blue canvas folding chair in the shade of his father's white pickup and told his story to the reporters. When the BLM rangers had wrestled him to the ground, he'd yanked his hands away from them as he was falling, but only to keep his face from hitting the ground even harder. They wrenched his arms high behind his back for the cuffs, one officer grinding Dave's face into the gravel with his knee. They'd taken him to the command post in Toquop Wash, where they parked him in the back of a truck and questioned him for several hours. He ignored their questions, lectured them on constitutional law, preached to them nonstop, tried to convert them. He asked if they'd studied the Constitution, and how they felt about the First Amendment. Dave felt like the feds were proud of their prey, wanting to display him in the back of the truck like a trophy mountain ram. Two officers had cuffed his hands behind his back and drove him to a detention center in Henderson, just outside of Las Vegas. His wrists were on fire, and he told them their treatment was far from humane. He wondered how long he'd be behind bars.

"I laid on that steel bunk last night," Dave told the reporters, pausing to choke back tears. "I asked myself if I was really a criminal. You go in the cell, and they close the door behind you, and it's dark and it's cold, and they issue you a little blanket, and you have a little jumpsuit on. And I thought mostly of my family."

What scared him most was that he was in the hands of the feds. However, after several hours, they'd simply issued him a court summons on two misdemeanor charges—one for resisting arrest and the other for refusal to disperse. And that was it. He was free.

The mini press conference wrapped up when a clerk from the convenience store emerged and asked them to move along, saying that Cliven's pickup was blocking actual customers. Before they'd even left the parking lot, someone told Cliven that Dave's battered face and emotional words were already on the news. Cliven was amazed, but that was modern life, he supposed. Things were moving awfully fast.

WHILE DAVE AND CLIVEN WERE TALKING TO REPORTERS, ABOUT ONE HUNDRED people showed up at a protest site near Bundy Ranch in response to the "range war" blog post from the night before. They ate sloppy joes and Popsicles. They prayed and gave speeches.

Stetsy Cox, Cliven's youngest daughter, mingled with the crowd at the event. She wore boots with spurs, a pink cap, and a black T-shirt that bore the words: "Guts. Glory. Bundy." At one point, she relayed the good news that Dave hadn't been swallowed by the federal judicial system.

"They gave him lunch and let him out," she said.

A cheer went up.

The rally took place on a stretch of land on Riverside Road beside the Virgin River a couple miles from Cliven's house. The BLM had designated two protest areas—they called them "First Amendment Zones"— but the Bundy supporters were making a statement by leaving those spots empty. Instead, a neighbor had given the Bundys permission to stage the ongoing protest on his private land. The protest site provided a strategic view of the backcountry where the BLM was rounding up cattle. The protesters unpacked and strung up an old hand-lettered banner the Bundys had used at range-war rallies for two decades: "Has The West Been Won? Or Has The FIGHT Just Begun!" On a nearby hill, they erected two fifty-foot flagpoles bearing metal script letters that read "We The People," high enough to be read by drivers on the interstate. They flew the Nevada state flag above the Stars and Stripes to signify their belief in state supremacy over the federal government.

It was evening by the time Ammon hit the exit ramp for Bunkerville off Interstate 15. He turned right toward the Virgin Mountains, rattling over the bars of the cattle guard that kept the Bundy herd off the highway, and then drove two more miles of undulating desert road and saw the tall white flagpoles and the people gathered at the protest site. He pulled into the site and unhitched his travel trailer. He'd stay here as long as his family needed him.

ONE OF THE PEOPLE AT THE RALLY WAS A QUIET-SPOKEN MAN NAMED ADAM Sully. He spent about three hours just hanging out, listening to speeches, chatting with people. He paid attention to what they were wearing, what gear they brought, and especially what they said.

Sully was a special agent with the Bureau of Land Management. He'd worked for the BLM in Salem and Eugene, Oregon, for fifteen years, the first ten as a ranger and the last five as a special agent. Rangers resembled patrol officers, enforcing the law on BLM lands, and special agents were like police detectives, responsible for investigations. Sully had seen an email requesting assistance with a cattle seizure in Bunkerville, Nevada. The assignment looked interesting to Sully, so he'd volunteered. He'd arrived four days earlier and was placed on the investigative team, but he'd spent most of his time escorting civilian helicopter pilots and contract cowboys from Gold Butte to their hotel in Mesquite.

The night before, he'd received a new assignment. The BLM was monitoring the Bundy Ranch blog and had seen a new posting Sunday night about a Monday-morning rally, including the words: "Range War begins tomorrow at Bundy ranch."

The investigative team leader dispatched Sully and another special agent to the rally to assess the threat level. Sully wore plain clothes and had a cover story that would blend him into the crowd. At the rally, he saw lots of blue jeans, western-style shirts, cowboy hats, ball caps. The vehicle license plates were from Nevada and Utah, a few from Arizona. He didn't observe anybody carrying firearms. He took some pictures and helped put up protest signs and erect the flagpoles.

Sully and his partner headed back to the BLM command post and briefed their team leader. The rally had been pretty much what they'd expected. Locals, for the most part, fired up about a neighbor rancher, and they had the usual Dixie dislike of the federal government. No militia, no crazies, no huge crowds, no heavy-duty firepower. No reason for the BLM to change tactics.

The Bundy family, Sully reported, was not a major threat.

Chapter 2

RANGE WARS

In September 1857, twenty-four-year-old Nephi Johnson was working his farm in southern Utah when he heard about a large wagon train of strangers passing through Mormon country.

Several years earlier, Brigham Young, the president of the Church of Jesus Christ of Latter-day Saints, had sent Johnson and other settlers to cultivate the watershed of the Virgin River. Young wanted to create a vast Mormon empire, Deseret, stretching from Oregon to Mexico, and the 162-mile Virgin River was key. The settlers planted cotton. The crop never really flourished there, but the region's cotton-inspired name stuck: "Dixie."

When Johnson heard about the wagon train of non-Mormons, things were already tense in Dixie. Months earlier, the federal government had more or less declared war on the Mormons, dispatching 2,500 soldiers to the Utah territory to overthrow Brigham Young's rule. The army had not yet arrived, but Young had prophesied a seven-year siege. Fiery speeches were delivered, grain was stockpiled, and the local militias were fortified. Nephi Johnson was a second lieutenant in the Iron County Militia.

The wagon train passed through Salt Lake City and headed south on a route to California. The Fancher party, as the wagon train was known, contained about 140 travelers, mostly families from Arkansas. The Fancher party stopped to rest for several days in a spot called Mountain Meadows, not far from Nephi Johnson's farm. Some of the men traveling with the wagon train were hostile, reportedly saying they would help the US army wipe out the Mormons.

The Mormons believed the threat. Their religion was less than twenty years old, and they'd been sent running before, from New York to Illinois, down the Oregon Trail, before settling in Utah. Thirteen years earlier, in 1844, their founder, Joseph Smith, had been jailed after ordering the destruction of a local newspaper that had criticized him. A mob stormed the jail and fatally shot Smith as he tried to escape through a second-story window. Driven west, the Mormons had finally found a home—a Mormon Zion—in the middle of the Great Basin, land nobody else wanted. The Mormons had turned desert into farmland, built roads through inhospitable Paiute country, and navigated soaring canyons. The Utah Territory had become an LDS stronghold, protected by Mormon militias. They'd paid for this land with toil and blood and prayer, and they wouldn't give it up without a fight. They wouldn't move again.

A group of militiamen, allied with a group of Paiutes, attacked the wagon train, killing seven. The Fancher party encircled the wagons and fought back. Nephi Johnson, who knew the Paiute language, relayed orders from the militia to the Paiutes.

After a standoff that lasted several days, two militiamen approached the wagon train with a white flag. They told the Fancher party that they would be escorted safely to Cedar City. The travelers were suspicious. But they were exhausted and running out of food and ammunition, so they agreed to the plan. Women and children and wounded were put in wagons for the trip to Cedar City. The Fancher party men were disarmed and would make the trip on foot, some distance behind the wagons and flanked by armed militiamen.

As Nephi Johnson watched from a nearby hilltop, the convoy moved away. Then, as Johnson had directed, the Paiutes rushed out of the woods and joined the militia in slaughtering the Fancher party. First, they shot the men on foot. Then they set about killing the wounded men and the women and even the children. Within minutes, the Mormons and Paiutes killed around 120 people, sparing only seventeen of the youngest children, those considered to be too young to tell the story. Those children were eventually sent home to relatives in Arkansas. The bodies of the dead were left, mostly unburied, scattered across a rocky valley.

Nephi Johnson lived for sixty-two more years. He was the first white man to traverse Zion Canyon. He explored much of Dixie and helped found several communities, finally settling in Bunkerville, Nevada, sixty-one miles southwest of Mountain Meadows, where he served as the patriarch of the Mormon community. But the slaughter he'd been part of tormented him. In 1919, he died in a delirious state in Mesquite, screaming: "Blood, blood, blood!"

Eleven years before his death, Johnson had signed an affidavit about the infamous massacre and his role in it. He tried to explain how he and his fellow farmers and ironworkers and Mormons could have participated in such a horror. The militiamen were young, he said, and they were following orders. And the Mormons had been conditioned to fear outsiders and the federal government.

"It will be remembered that at this time there was a United States army, under Gen. Johnson on its way to Utah, with the understood intention of distroying the Mormons, which filled the people with fear," Johnson affirmed.

The Mormon practice of polygamy was one of the reasons the army had headed toward Utah. Opponents believed taking multiple wives was a sin on the level of slavery, which, of course, would soon consume the States in war. Joseph Smith had married as many as twenty-eight women, but he couldn't practice plural marriage openly. It wasn't until the Mormons reached Utah that Brigham Young had felt safe to publicly endorse polygamy, which he did in 1852. The very remoteness of their new rugged homeland gave the Mormons the confidence to proclaim their beliefs. Until the government came calling.

Nephi Johnson himself was married to three women at the same time. The third wife he took was a widow with six children, including two-year-old Johnny Jensen, whom Johnson adopted.

Johnny Jensen was Cliven Bundy's maternal grandfather.

On his paternal side, Cliven's great-grandfather was Abraham Bundy. Like Nephi Johnson, Abraham Bundy led a big life. Born to Quakers in Illinois. Converted by a pair of Mormon missionaries in Nebraska. Flooded off his farm on the Virgin River in Arizona. Run out of Mexico by the revolution of 1910. And then, in his midfifties in 1916, Abraham and his son Roy rode into a valley ten miles north of the Grand Canyon's northern rim. They rode for miles through tall stands of grass, through blooming meadows on the mountain plateaus, where white sage grew thick enough to hide herds of sheep. They figured if the land could produce grass, it could grow crops and sustain livestock.

They built a dugout and a fence for Roy's two cows and one calf. They melted snow for drinking water and built a rough road for hauling water from a mountainside spring. Eventually, they laid a long pipe to the spring. Reservoirs leaked and emptied, and water was rationed. More Bundys arrived, staking out 640-acre homesteads and running nomadic herds on broad stretches of federal land on a first-come, first-served basis. They built crude lumber shacks, dug reservoirs, and planted wheat, barley, corn, and beans. They built a one-room school-house that also served as a church, dance hall, and town meeting site. The town was named Mount Trumbull after a nearby peak, but every-body called it Bundyville.

The land was treacherous. Blizzards in the winter, 115-degree heat in the summer. Sudden storms turned dry washes into torrents. Ground crumbled into sinkholes. Quicksand swallowed livestock. In 1931, fifteen years before Cliven Bundy was born, his oldest uncle was running a herd of sheep in the Grand Canyon when he took a swim in the Colorado River and drowned in a whirlpool.

By then, many of the homesteaders had experienced poor har-vests and switched to running cattle and sheep. This land wasn't as suited for growing crops as Abraham Bundy had hoped. Grazing was its only use, and the government gave away the land and grass for free. Between 1870 and 1900, the number of beef cattle ranging the West grew from 4.1 million to 19.6 million. Nobody owned the land so nobody thought of it as an asset to protect, like a family farm. As the big cattle outfits knew, there were fortunes to be made on the range if you got there first and were tough enough to hang on to it. The range was a resource to be extracted, like coal or gold. If you didn't graze a meadow, somebody else would take it.

The people were independent in this slice of Utah, Arizona, and Nevada. The impassable Grand Canyon to the south separated them from the rest of Arizona. Most Dixie residents were Mormon, but the rough country of southern Utah cut them off from the LDS establish-ment in Salt Lake City. And the vast Mojave Desert lay between Dixie and the cities of California's coast; in 1920, Las Vegas was just a cow town of two thousand people. No major roads traversed the Arizona Strip until after World War II, so this part of the country remained the Wild West long after the rest was tamed. Cattle ran unsupervised and unfenced on public lands. Cattle rustling was common, unbranded calves stolen two or three at a time. Rustlers were hanged. Range wars broke out between cattlemen and sheepherders.

The Bundys believed God had given them a hard land for a reason. Because they were Mormons. Industrious. Relentless. They could tame it. Subdue the earth. When a census taker came to Roy Bundy's home in 1930, he and his wife had eleven children ranging in age from eight months to twenty-one years old, including David Ammon Bundy, who was eight. Roy Bundy listed his occupation as "farmer." In 1940, David was eighteen years old, with an eighth-grade education. He was living in his father's house and listed his occupation as "cattle raising."

In 1952, *Collier's* magazine published an article about Dixie that included a photo of Roy Bundy at eighty years old, identified as the "patriarch of the 247-member Bundy clan."

"The Bundys have the tenacity of the ant, the industry of the bee, the strength of the eagle," the magazine noted. "They are rooted not to pavement but to earth, and the fertility of earth flows in their veins."

But Dixie's earth was losing its fertility. Across the West, much of the range was overgrazed, eroding, and depleted. Even the lushest desert landscapes, like the valley Abraham and Roy Bundy rode into in 1916, were precisely adapted, fragile ecosystems. Thousands of cattle and sheep had thrown off the balance, and many meadows had been replaced by tumbleweeds and Russian thistle. This made the land more vulnerable to floods, and long washes and deep gullies gashed the landscape.

In response, Congress passed the Taylor Grazing Act of 1934, which split the large expanses of western federal land into grazing allotments. Ranchers who owned nearby "base properties" received permits to graze on an allotment, renewable every ten years. The government established the head count of livestock allowed on each allotment. The fees to graze on public lands were typically a fraction of what private landowners would charge, but no one was using the land.

The Grazing Act brought order to the system. But it also created a labyrinth of permits and regulations that eventually drove off nomadic sheepherders and restricted cattle ranching in Dixie. One by one, homesteads were abandoned, and by 1960, Bundyville was gone. It's impossible to say whether Bundyville would have survived if the Taylor Grazing Act hadn't been enacted. Automobiles had become affordable, which meant that ranchers moved to towns like St. George and monitored their herds long distance. Still, many ranchers blamed the federal government for killing Bundyville.

In 1946, the Bureau of Land Management was created to administer grazing on federal land. With 340 million acres under its oversight, the BLM became the nation's largest landholder. BLM lands were the true leftovers. The new agency mostly took over regions deemed not beautiful enough to be a national park, too arid to be a wilderness area, not fertile enough to be a homesteaded farm, too barren to be a national forest.

SEVENTEEN DAYS BEFORE THE BLM WAS CREATED, CLIVEN BUNDY WAS born in Las Vegas.

In 1948, when Cliven was two years old, his father, David Ammon Bundy, bought 160 acres on the banks of the Virgin River in Bunkerville, Nevada. David Bundy built a small one-story stone-and-mason house on the new property and set about trying to obtain the various permissions that would allow him to ranch on the surrounding federal lands. It helped that members of his wife's family, the descendants of

Johnny Jensen, had been watering livestock at springs in the area since 1877. With these ties and the help of a neighbor, he secured groundwater rights through the Nevada State Engineer's Office.

With his base property and state water rights, David Bundy obtained his first federal grazing permit in 1954. The BLM gave him permission to graze ninety-five head of cattle on the Bunkerville Allotment, a chunk of Gold Butte that rose from the river bottom to the mountains.

At the same time, people were moving west and finding other uses for the land that was once considered useless. During World War II, the Air Force had displaced ranchers when it claimed large sections of southern Nevada desert for aerial gunnery and bombing ranges and, eventually, nuclear testing. After the war, a growing number of Americans took to outdoor activities like camping, hiking, hunting, and fishing, which raised the profile of the extensive public lands of the West. Off-road vehicle sales exploded. Starting in 1967, a desert dirt-bike race from Barstow to Las Vegas—the "B-to-V"—drew thousands of riders and twenty thousand spectators. The "wastelands" were suddenly good for something other than ranching.

Meanwhile, environmentalists began pushing the government to regard public lands as valuable in their own right, whether linked to an industry or not. BLM advisory boards once dominated by the livestock industry were broadened to include members involved in timber, recreation, and wilderness interests. Federal lawsuits forced the BLM to reduce the number of cattle on many grazing allotments. In 1976, the Federal Land Policy and Management Act further expanded the federal government's hold on public lands. In addition to grazing, the law recognized that the land also had "scientific, scenic, historical, ecological, environmental, air and atmospheric, water resource, and archaeological" value. From now on, the federal government would not be looking to dispose of its lands but to protect them.

The job of the federal range conservationists suddenly grew more complicated. In the old days, rangers often rode alone on horseback through the mountains to visit ranchers. They'd walk down to a river to inspect the range. If the land looked depleted, the ranger might suggest that the rancher move his cows to a different pasture for awhile. A hand-shake deal.

That kind of personal, intermittent contact was increasingly replaced by blizzards of paperwork, from the agencies to ranches and back again. As the West's population grew, the BLM and Forest Service were inundated with requests related to public lands—special-use permits to install gas, power, and telephone lines, mining permits, recreational permits, timber permits. The job wasn't just about grazing anymore.

Also, the science was getting more rigorous. Researchers were revealing the desert as a complex cradle of natural splendor, and the 1980s brought an exponential increase in the understanding of those ecosystems. Land managers no longer looked at a single ranch and tried to determine how it was affecting a given river. Instead, they were calculating the effects that all human activities and natural trends were having on the well-being of entire watersheds. And their subsequent decisions affected ranchers. Herds that were once allowed to graze 95 percent of an area's vegetation might now be restricted to half that, because the previous standard was leading to eroded stream banks, water pollution, and ruined wildlife habitats. So the BLM might tell the rancher to move the herd, which cost money and manpower the ranch likely didn't have. Many ranchers couldn't understand why standards that had been in place for generations were being changed. The new scientific jargon alienated them. They wondered if the federal government was making it all up, paying off scientists to come up with complicated reasons why the land shouldn't be grazed.

Ranchers weren't the only westerners who hated that

"Washington" controlled so much of their land and resources. So much western land was federally owned that the region's growing population was straining against the limits of developable private land. Cattle and sheep ranchers increasingly competed with timber, mining, highways, hunters, anglers, and parks. Westerners blamed the federal government, the absentee landlord of the West. By the 1970s, the West was growing twice as fast as the national rate and faced a specific array of problems, from illegal immigrants to water shortages. Westerners believed they were underrepresented in the nation's capital, where eastern interests dominated the agenda. They felt more like a colony than a group of states on equal footing with the East. The more far-flung the region, the more colonial-style resentment its denizens carried.

In 1979, Nevada's governor signed an act that claimed that almost all public land within the state's borders now belonged to the state, not the federal government, a breathtakingly blunt challenge to federal supremacy. The law asserted that the majority of federal lands were unconstitutional, immoral, and illegal. Almost all of the other western states began preparing similar legislation, and the movement was tagged the "Sagebrush Rebellion." It gained momentum when federal legislation was proposed that supported the Nevada law and when US presidential candidate Ronald Reagan backed the movement in a 1980 campaign speech in Salt Lake City, saying: "Count me in as a rebel."

Reagan got elected, and the rebellion, ironically, fizzled. For one thing, under Reagan, ranchers had fewer complaints about the land agencies. Also, the ranchers began to wonder if the states could really afford to take on the costs of managing all this land, or if the transfer would result in higher fees for hunters, anglers, and ranchers. So when Reagan's administration floated a proposal to sell federal property to private citizens and companies, almost nobody liked the idea. Worried that large eastern interests would grab the land, even western ranchers and miners didn't back the initiative, and it was abandoned.

The Sagebrush Rebellion failed as a political movement, but the urban West continued to grow, with cities like Phoenix, Arizona, eating up rangeland at the rate of an acre an hour. The open spaces filled. Yosemite and Yellowstone grew overcrowded, so more people began exploring public lands beyond the national parks. In 1990, the BLM recorded seventy-two million visits to lands once used almost exclusively by cattlemen. Additionally, ranchers were being squeezed by environmental regulations like the Endangered Species Act, with its ever-growing list of protected species. The northern spotted owl in Oregon. The delta smelt in California. The Snake River salmon in Washington.

And, in Nevada, the desert tortoise.

FOR ALL OF THE UPHEAVAL SURROUNDING IT, THE MOJAVE DESERT TORTOISE is a shy and unassuming beast. Mottled tan-brown shell like an army helmet that's seen some combat. Lumbering clawed legs good for burrowing out of the sun. Adults can measure more than fourteen inches fore to aft, and they can live as long as a century. They're active only in the warm months, from March to October, and dormant in their burrows all winter.

In 1989, environmental groups in Clark County sued the US Fish and Wildlife Service on behalf of the desert tortoise. The lawsuit maintained the reptile was not being adequately protected in the face of the county's massive population growth. Construction projects were rapidly destroying tortoise habitats in the booming Las Vegas Valley. Even away from the city, desert habitats were being sliced apart by power-line corridors, highways, off-road-vehicle trails. Cattle were befouling water supplies. Ravens were feasting on young tortoises. Biologists said the future of the tortoise was grim, unless steps were taken to preserve habitats.

Fish and Wildlife put the tortoise on the endangered species list, and builders in Clark County became very quickly and uncomfortably acquainted with the power and scope of the Endangered Species Act, and how a lowly reptile, with the backing of the federal government, could slow the pace of development to a crawl. Suddenly, nobody was allowed to harass, harm, or kill a desert tortoise, even inadvertently, without special dispensation from the federal government. Violators faced up to six months in jail and a $25,000 fine. Developers faced crippling construction delays that could last as long as five years.

An inevitable trade-off was at hand: urban versus rural. Hundreds of thousands of people were flowing into the Las Vegas Valley, whose cities had to keep flinging out new webs of roads and sewers and electric grids and stucco housing developments, advancing farther and farther into the edges of the valley. Away from the neon valley lay millions of acres of silent desert occupied by a relative handful of people and a few thousand head of cattle. The choice was clear. Stop billions of dollars worth of construction and stifle a burgeoning city that was the playground of forty-two million tourists a year? Or remove some cows?

Clark County struck a deal with the federal government. In 1991, Fish and Wildlife issued a permit authorizing the county to resume building within the Las Vegas Valley, though developers would have to take great pains not to kill tortoises even as they destroyed habitat. In exchange, the county agreed to set aside four hundred thousand acres of tortoise habitat in the outback corners of Clark County, the relatively unpeopled buttes and mesas and flat desert scrub miles away from Las Vegas. Clark County agreed to buy and retire the grazing permits of ranchers who were willing to sell.

Cliven Bundy, in his midforties at this time, had no intention of selling out.

He and his neighbor ranchers—the Leavitts, the Jensens, the Nays—grumbled among themselves about tree huggers who seemed to believe that human beings had no place on public lands. It was all they talked about when they saw each other out on the range. If tortoise numbers were dropping, the ranchers didn't believe it had anything to do with cattle. This was a land grab, and the tortoise was a justification. If it wasn't the tortoise, it'd be the horny toad or the spotted owl. The feds wanted ranchers gone, and they'd find a way. Cliven believed the federal government would not stop until there wasn't a cow on the desert.

Before the desert tortoise restrictions, fifty-some families had ranched in Clark County. But month after month, one by one, families the Bundys had known for more than a century sold their grazing permits to Clark County. Some stayed on their farms but sold their cattle. Others moved, working out tax-deferred exchanges for new property.

The county didn't force anyone to quit ranching, but eventually, as the implications of the BLM's tightening restrictions became clear, even the most adamant families sold out. After all, these were not major cattle operations. These ranchers generally had other sources of income, and they ran a couple hundred cattle on the desert for extra profit and because their families had done so for generations. Many ranchers were older, and often their kids lived elsewhere and didn't want the ranches, which were becoming financial liabilities.

By the early 1990s, Cliven was one of only two ranchers still running herds on public lands in eastern Clark County. He was sad to see other families give up their birthright for $60,000 or $75,000. What had all the grinding toil of their forefathers been for? They'd lost their heritage, their foothold in the land.

Then the BLM told Cliven he would have to remove his cattle during the spring months, except in years of unusually heavy rainfall. Year to year, the BLM would decide whether the desert's forage was thick enough to support both cattle and tortoises between March and May, when the tortoises were breeding.

Cliven knew this new restriction would break Bundy Ranch. Spring was the most crucial time of the year for the herd to be out on the range because the cows were giving birth and fattening up. The BLM wanted him to interrupt this cycle by rounding them all up, a monumental task as the herd was scattered over hundreds of thousands of acres. Even if he could pull this off, the Bundys' 160-acre homestead, the land his family actually owned, wasn't large enough to stock and feed hundreds of cattle for those spring months. His only option would be to round up the entire herd each March and haul the cattle to a stockyard and sell them. Then, if he wanted to continue ranching, he'd have to buy a new herd and put it on the range in the summer. It would take time and money he didn't have.

"I'm screaming as loud as I can scream," Cliven told a reporter after a BLM advisory council meeting in 1992. "As far as I'm concerned, I'm not coming off the range."

A SIMILAR DISCONTENT WAS BREWING ALL OVER THE COUNTRY, ESPECIALLY in other rural areas like Dixie. Over the decades, various organizations and movements had worked to drastically curtail the power of the federal government, from the John Birch Society in the 1950s to the Posse Comitatus in the 1970s. In the 1990s, such groups began describing themselves as Patriots.

A series of recent events had stoked a renewed backlash against the federal government. In June 1992, President George H. W. Bush signed Agenda 21, a United Nations plan regarding sustainable development. Patriots believed it was a UN plot to deny property rights and force citizens to move to cities. Two years earlier, Bush used the words "new world order" to describe a new era of post–Cold War global cooperation. Patriots borrowed the phrase and gave it a treasonous connotation.

Two months after Agenda 21 was signed, US marshals traveled to an isolated mountaintop in Idaho to arrest an apocalyptic white separatist named Randy Weaver for failure to appear on gun charges. A shoot-out ensued that left both a US marshal and Weaver's fourteen-year-old son dead. Operating under unusually aggressive rules of engagement, an FBI sniper then shot and killed Weaver's wife. Outraged Weaver sympathizers bonded during the eleven-day siege at Ruby Ridge.

In February through April of 1993, another federal siege went horribly wrong. An illegal weapons raid sparked a gunfight near Waco, Texas, between federal agents and members of the sect known as the Branch Davidians. The shoot-out left four federal agents and six sect members dead. After a multiweek standoff, the FBI launched a tear-gas attack to force the Branch Davidians out of their ranch compound, and a massive fire broke out and swept through the buildings, killing some seventy-five people, many of them women and children. The Justice Department later affirmed that sect members started the fire, but many Patriots blamed the government.

And in November 1993, Congress passed the Brady Handgun Violence Prevention Act, known as the Brady Bill, which imposed background checks and a five-day waiting period on gun purchases. Patriots feared this was the first step toward gun confiscation and repeal of the Second Amendment.

These events galvanized the deep slice of America that already had a beef with the federal government. Public opinion researcher

Daniel Yankelovich tracked the decline of Americans' trust in government by asking, "How much of the time can you trust the government to do what's right?" In 1964, 76 percent of Americans answered "always" or "most of the time." By 1984, that figure was 44 percent. By 1994, it was 19 percent.

In early 1994, civilian paramilitary outfits began popping up, starting with the Militia of Montana and the Michigan Militia. By 1995, the Southern Poverty Law Center documented 224 militias and support groups in thirty-nine states. Most members were men. Most were Christian. Many were military veterans. They believed Americans were losing control over their own government to globalist forces. Life was changing, and not for the better. Joining a group of like-minded men and arming themselves felt like a way to regain some control, to be part of something important.

Every Patriot offshoot had its own agenda. The Posse Comitatus organization believed that county-level government was the supreme authority, more powerful than the state or federal governments. Sovereign citizens didn't recognize the United States at all and believed themselves to be free of its rule of law, nations unto themselves. Tax protesters believed that the Internal Revenue Service was unconstitutional. Militias focused on gun rights and government tyranny. A stubborn element of bigotry was embedded in some Patriot organizations, while other groups and leaders specifically renounced racism and anti-Semitism. Specific priorities varied from one Patriot group to another, but they all shared a common enemy: the federal government.

Patriot organizations took root in small towns and rural areas, especially on those fringes where expanding suburbia was swallowing land that had always been countryside. Places where new laws and restrictions were encroaching upon the habits and freedoms of long-time residents. Places like Clark County.

Western ranchers burdened by new environmental regulations

began attending meetings and protests with various branches of the Patriot movement. Ranchers learned Patriot lingo and philosophies. They monitored events like Waco and Ruby Ridge. It became hard to tell where the land-use movement ended and the Patriots began.

IN THE EARLY 1990S, AMMON BUNDY WAS FOCUSED ON HIS OWN TEENAGE life more than Cliven's struggle, but he did absorb dinnertime conversations with neighbor ranchers, discussions that increasingly revolved around the Constitution. A neighbor had given Cliven a packet of notes handwritten by the Mormon thinker W. Cleon Skousen, a Constitutional theorist and former police chief of Salt Lake City. Skousen opposed all federal regulatory agencies as a dangerous detour from the original intent of the Constitution's drafters.

Cliven and his neighbor, Keith Nay, the only other remaining rancher in eastern Clark County by this time, began studying the Constitution in earnest, finding connections to LDS scripture. Over the years, their writings turned into a 175-page manuscript. Cliven also traded information at meetings of groups called "Wise Use" and "People for the West!" He met other embattled ranchers, men like Wayne Hage and Cliff Gardner, who'd been fighting the BLM for years. Hage had written a densely researched book, *Storm Over Rangelands*, published in 1989, that detailed the tangle of conflicting laws and rights and agencies that were strangling western ranches.

Cliven learned a lot, and one piece of information stood out as a life-saving beacon: The United States government was not allowed to own the Bunkerville Allotment or Gold Butte or almost any of the public lands in Nevada. The federal government couldn't lease the land, couldn't regulate it, couldn't exploit its resources. It was all right there in the Constitution, in a passage called the Enclave Clause. It was cited at Wise Use meetings like gospel: Article 1, Section 8, Clause 17.

The Enclave Clause said Congress could purchase specific parcels "by the Consent of the Legislature of the State in which the Same shall be, for the Erection of Forts, Magazines, Arsenals, dock-Yards and other needful Buildings." Cliven saw no military structures or docks or government buildings at all on Gold Butte. The Constitution hadn't given the federal government the right to own this land. Cliven believed Washington bureaucrats had simply assumed control on their own accord.

It was so simple. The life Cliven treasured, the life he and his father had built, was slipping away, but the solution was right in front of him. The Constitution of the United States of America. How had he lived this long without knowing this? Like everybody else, Cliven had grown accustomed to doing what he was told, to believing that the federal government had absolute power, total control. He hadn't known what was right. Now he did. It was a powerful feeling.

Like others he saw at Wise Use meetings, Cliven got a small Constitution and tucked it into the breast pocket of his Western shirt, like a talisman. It would protect him.

UNBEKNOWNST TO CLIVEN, THE WISE USE CONSTITUTIONALISTS WERE wrong. They focused on the Enclave Clause, but the federal courts had repeatedly ruled that the US government's authority to own land was bestowed by a different Constitutional passage: the Property Clause, Article 4, Section 3, Clause 2. It stated, "The Congress shall have power to dispose of and make all needful Rules and Regulations respecting the Territory or other Property belonging to the United States."

Sometimes the Wise Users simply ignored the Property Clause, and sometimes they seized on the words "dispose of," arguing that the framers of the Constitution intended the Property Clause to be a temporary provision, that they had expected the federal government to give away land, not hold on to it forever. But Supreme Court rulings had interpreted the Property Clause as giving the federal government broad control over its lands, and moreover, the court has long held that Congress has the implicit power to take actions that are not explicitly stated in the Constitution so long as they are linked to a stated Congressional power.

Besides, Nevada itself had relinquished the land. Nevada gained statehood in 1864, as President Abraham Lincoln recognized that the Union needed the region's silver for the Civil War. The Nevada Constitution had very specifically renounced its citizens' rights to most of the land in the state.

> That the people inhabiting said territory do agree and declare,
> that they forever disclaim all rights and title to the unappro-
> priated public lands lying within said territory, and that the
> same shall be and remain at the sole and entire disposition of
> the United States.

That didn't mean it was good public policy for the federal government to own more than 80 percent of Nevada's landmass. It didn't mean that the federal government was a good or honest steward of the land. Intelligent people could disagree about the intent of the framers or whether the Supreme Court's decisions were well reasoned.

But it was the law of the land. For the time being, the federal government owned the vast majority of Nevada and much of the rest of the West and could do pretty much what it wanted with it.

IN JANUARY 1993, THE BLM SENT CLIVEN AN APPLICATION FORM FOR A new ten-year grazing permit that would force him to take his herd off the range during the spring months. By now, however, Cliven had heard about Wayne Hage's defiance of the government. He'd heard Posse Comitatus ideas about the supremacy of the county. He'd memorized the Enclave Clause.

Why, Cliven wondered, was he contracting with the BLM at all? The agency was supposed to be managing the land that he was permitted to graze. But the agency was managing his ranch out of business. It occurred to Cliven that if the Constitution didn't allow the federal government to own the land, then the only thing giving the feds authority over the Bunkerville Allotment was this grazing permit application. Why should he sign over control of his ranch to the BLM?

What if he just didn't return the BLM's permit application? What if he stopped paying the fees? Basically said: *Thank you for your previous management, I no longer need it, have a nice day.*

What if he fired the BLM?

ONE YEAR LATER, IN JANUARY 1994, A BLM OFFICIAL TRIED TO HAND deliver a letter to Bundy Ranch. Cliven refused the document, saying the BLM had no authority to manage Gold Butte. The BLM official placed the document on the dashboard of Cliven's truck. Cliven got out, tossed the papers on the ground, and drove off. One of Cliven's sons picked up the papers and tore them to shreds.

A year had passed since Cliven had notified the BLM that he intended to continue grazing his cattle on the Bunkerville Allotment without a federal permit. His bold action had grabbed attention and launched him into a position of authority in the Wise Use stratosphere. He didn't just attend meetings now. He was the featured speaker. People were learning about the Constitution from *him*. And Cliven didn't mind being the center of attention. He may have spent his life wrangling cattle in the desert, but he was no stereotypically taciturn rancher. He could talk for hours.

Reporters caught wind of the Nevada rancher who was defying the feds. Cliven gave fiery, no-holds-barred interviews to the *Rocky Mountain News*, the *Las Vegas Review-Journal*, even *USA Today*. In 1994, he told the *Washington Times* that "hundreds" of ranchers in southern Nevada were planning to block the government from rounding up Bundy cattle.

"I've got friends who are really worried that this is going to come down to a Waco situation," Cliven said.

Cliven developed the go-to phrase he would use for decades.

"I'm willing to do whatever's necessary to defend my land," he said.

He said it over and over. *Whatever's necessary. Whatever it takes.* The phrase sounded hostile, yet too vague to call a specific threat. It had a ring, a whiff of anti-authoritarian menace, akin to Malcolm X's "by any means necessary," which was borrowed from a Jean-Paul Sartre play.

The BLM didn't immediately move to confiscate the Bundy cattle. A lot had happened in the previous two years, namely the infamous sieges at Ruby Ridge and Waco. The BLM wanted to avoid what federal agents called "Weaver Fever," the kind of aggressive law enforcement that had led to the shootings of Randy Weaver's wife and son. The Ruby Ridge deaths had convinced an entire generation of Patriots that the government was willing to kill its own citizens, deepening resentment and extremism. So the agency counted Cliven's trespassing cows, calculated fees and fines, and continued sending Cliven flurries of legal notices and bills. And Cliven continued to ignore them. He didn't even appeal the BLM decision, because, he said, the BLM had no jurisdiction over Gold Butte. It was a moot issue.

Other federal land agencies felt the BLM was making things worse by *not* acting. Jim Nelson, supervisor of the Humboldt-Toiyabe National Forest, said delaying the seizure of the Bundy cattle set a bad precedent.

"If we don't take aggressive action to deal with lawlessness, we encourage it," Nelson told an *Audubon* magazine reporter in 1995. "We haven't stood up to the bullies yet."

ON A THURSDAY EVENING IN LATE MARCH 1995, SOMEONE SLID A PIPE bomb under a windowsill at the Forest Service office in Carson City, Nevada. The blast shattered a computer and upended a desk. The same night, on the other side of the state, another bomb exploded in an outhouse in a national park campground. Nobody was injured in either incident.

The office belonged to Guy Pence, a veteran ranger who was outspoken in his support of more rigorous standards for grazing permit holders. In just the past four years, Pence had canceled three ranchers' grazing permits and suspended others.

"The United States forests belong to the public, to all of us, to future generations," he told a reporter for the *Los Angeles Times*. "These are our lands. Someone treats them poorly, they're stealing from you and me. It's a goddamn crime, it shouldn't happen. These lands are an inheritance we can pass along. What a tremendous gift."

Pence wasn't the only target. In the mid-1990s, Forest Service and BLM employees reported more and more threats and confrontations. Most rangers lived in the small rural communities they covered. Increasingly, their families were cursed, refused service in stores, snubbed in church. They got threatening letters. A federal wolf biologist in Idaho found her dog poisoned. A federal biologist in California was shot at. Men with guns disrupted a series of national forest meetings in southern Oregon. Some rangers stopped driving their official vehicles or wearing their uniforms in public.

After the Pence office bombing, the federal land agencies issued war zone–like instruction memos to rangers:

> Travel in pairs, plan escape routes, and stay in radio contact. Let angry people vent. If feeling threatened, don't drive official vehicles or wear uniforms.

Receptionists were trained to spot letter bombs. Office security was beefed up and panic buttons installed. The National Park Service began offering a course for rangers called "Extremist Groups on Public Lands." Forest Service rangers were given pocket cards with instructions:

> If you are confronted, detained, or placed in custody by state or local authorities, do not resist . . . everything will be done to have you released as quickly as possible.

Three weeks after Pence's office was pipe bombed, Gulf War veteran Timothy McVeigh parked a Ryder truck filled with forty fifty-pound bags of ammonium nitrate fertilizer in a drop-off zone underneath a day-care center located in the Alfred P. Murrah Federal Building in downtown Oklahoma City. The 9:02 AM explosion sheared off the face of the building, killing 168 people.

McVeigh was not part of the western public lands debate, nor was he a militia member. However, he was enraged by the federal government's handling of the Ruby Ridge and Waco sieges, and he had even visited the scene of the standoff at the Branch Davidians compound. The Oklahoma City bombing focused attention on antigovernment sentiment and the newly revitalized groups affiliated under the banner of the so-called Patriot movement. The news media, politicians, and regular citizens woke up to the fact that a significant percentage of Americans believed the federal government was out of control.

McVeigh himself didn't officially belong to a Patriot organization, but law-enforcement analysts believed the movement's explosive rhetoric gave unstable McVeigh types an implied license to set their fuses. The Patriot message attracted many mainstream Americans who wouldn't hurt anybody. But the deeper an individual traveled into the movement, the more radical the ideas. The head of the Montana Human Rights Network described the Patriot movement as a funnel moving through space, collecting lots of people at the wide mouth, and radicalizing smaller and smaller numbers, until, "Finally at the narrowest end of the funnel, you've drawn in the hard core, where you get someone like Tim McVeigh popping out."

IN 1998, THE BLM TOOK CLIVEN TO FEDERAL COURT OVER THE CATTLE. HE represented himself, employing all the knowledge he'd amassed from his years of constitutional research. He claimed he was a citizen of Nevada and not the United States. He cited the Enclave Clause, international treaty laws. He quoted religious texts.

The judge said none of Cliven's arguments were relevant. She ordered him to remove his cattle by the end of the month. Any cattle remaining on federal land after that date would cost Cliven $200 per head per day. The judge said it was within the BLM's rights to just take the cows, but BLM officials said they hadn't done so because they didn't want to provoke a physical confrontation. A year earlier, the FBI had managed an eighty-one-day standoff with the antigovernment Montana Freemen that ended without bloodshed, and the new, less-aggressive protocol was now the standard. So the feds never came for the cattle, and Cliven kept grazing, ignoring the mounting fines. A year later, in 1999, Cliven sent a "Demand for Protection" to the Clark County sheriff and other state and local officials. He said he feared for his family's safety "because of what federal agents did at Ruby Ridge and Waco."

He wrote: "This fight today is no different than the civil rights days when Rosa Parks defied illegal local law and took her rightful seat in the front of the bus."

He was no "wacko extremist," his letter said. "I do not advocate violence and only want a legal and peaceful conclusion to this issue and my rights protected."

The BLM also wanted a peaceful conclusion. The agency preferred to deal with outlaw ranchers through the mail and courts, because when the agency tried to round up an unpermitted herd, it often didn't end well.

In 2000, for example, the agency clashed with a cantankerous rancher named Mary Bulloch over her wild herd of one hundred longhorns that grazed on an allotment in southern Utah. Bulloch had refused to follow drought restrictions, and the BLM ordered her to remove the cattle. Ranchers from throughout Dixie came to her aid when Bulloch wrote a fiery letter to the Kanab newspaper about her plight. The BLM had fenced off a water hole, and some of her cattle had died. Then, using a helicopter, the BLM seized about fifty head of cattle and took them to a livestock auction house. A group of fifteen ranchers from three states descended on the auction house, herded the cattle into livestock trailers, and took them back to the grazing land. The Sevier County sheriff watched, saying later he wanted to avoid a "Waco situation."

One of Bulloch's cattle died during transport. Bulloch beheaded the cow, drove to the BLM office, parked, and hung the severed head from the side of her truck. She displayed a handwritten sign that read: "Direct Result of BLM Grazing Management Plan."

For ten years after the 1998 federal court order, the BLM left Cliven Bundy pretty much alone.

Perhaps it was because his herd was so large and widely distributed. Perhaps it was because he'd vowed to oppose a seizure with "whatever it takes." At any rate, no helicopters or cattle trailers showed up in Gold Butte. Some six months after the clash with Mary Bulloch, a BLM spokeswoman told a Las Vegas newspaper that the agency was still mulling its options regarding the Bundy case.

"We do intend to take action," she said.

But more years passed, and Cliven's herd multiplied and spread beyond the original Bunkerville Allotment, breaking through deteriorating fences and ranging west and south all the way to Lake Mead's northern arm. Cattle also strayed east, invading a community garden in Mesquite, chawing off the tops of corn ears. Cliven brought the gardeners a truck full of melons as an apology.

In 2006, a Park Service ranger called Bundy Ranch because he wanted someone to remove a temporary corral that had been erected near Lake Mead. A Bundy ranch hand showed up to remove the corral. In his truck was a MAK-90, a rifle like an AK-47. The ranger cited him for carrying a loaded weapon in a national park.

The ranch hand gave up the rifle without protest. But he told the ranger that Cliven Bundy would not be so accommodating.

He said: *If you confront Cliven Bundy, you better be ready for a gun battle.*

In April 2008, Mary Jo Rugwell became the manager of the Southern Nevada District Office of the BLM, which included Clark County. Rugwell was briefed immediately on the rogue rancher named Cliven Bundy and decided the situation had lingered long enough. She told her staff to begin documenting the Bundy cattle in earnest.

BLM rangers took hundreds of photos of cattle gazing fixedly at the camera, some standing in patchy mountain snow, some in parched desert, others in the shallow trickle of the Virgin River and the sandy banks of Lake Mead. The rangers documented not only the cattle but the destruction they left behind. Corrals, water troughs, and riverbanks were ringed with dusty ground and no vegetation, innumerable hoof-prints in the dirt. Watershed restoration projects on the Virgin River were destroyed when cattle knocked down barbed-wire fencing and gnawed on hundreds of native saplings that had been planted along the river. At archaeological sites, the cattle had rubbed against ancient petroglyphs, erasing the markings. Rangers saw evidence of Bundy's work, including salt licks, temporary corrals, pipelines, and plastic "Keep Out" signs wired to fence posts on public roads.

Rugwell wanted to negotiate with Cliven, but the rancher kept ducking her. She asked a county commissioner to arrange a meeting, but the appointment was canceled at the last minute, no explanation. In 2011, she encountered Bundy at a Nevada Wildlife Commission meeting in Las Vegas, where the rancher displayed a slideshow entitled "We the People" and opined that the federal government was violating the equal-footing doctrine in Nevada. Afterward, Rugwell tried to speak to him, but he ignored her.

So Rugwell got serious. She wanted to methodically document the number and locations of Bundy's cattle before attempting to seize them. She sent ground crews and helicopter teams to track the number of livestock roaming Gold Butte. The helicopter crew zigzagged across the desert in a grid pattern and radioed GPS coordinates of cattle to five ground crews in trucks and all-terrain vehicles. The ground teams noticed that the farther the cattle had roamed from Bundy property, the less likely they were to be marked at all—they were just reproducing and spreading across the desert, searching for forage and water, closer to wild animals than domesticated livestock. The BLM counted more than 903 cattle, six times more than the Bundys had been authorized to graze in the 1970s and 1980s. Less than half had Bundy brands or earmarks. The five-day cattle inventory operation cost $124,000 but was only part of Rugwell's four years of painstaking documentation of the Bundy herd.

In 2012, Rugwell was finally ready to seize the Bundy cattle. She asked Sheriff Gillespie to make the rancher an offer. If Bundy didn't interfere with the roundup, the BLM was willing to gather the cattle and ship them to a facility of Bundy's choice. The rancher would get the proceeds from the livestock sale. Bundy refused.

The locals weren't cooperating either. After talking to Bundy, Sheriff Gillespie wanted Rugwell to postpone the roundup, and the Nevada attorney general said the state wouldn't allow the cattle to be moved and sold out of state without a federal court order specifically approving the seizure.

So the BLM canceled the roundup and went back to court. More than a year later, a federal judge granted the BLM the specific authority to seize the Bundy cattle. Planning resumed, and at long last, the roundup began on April 5, 2014, a Saturday. On Sunday, BLM officers arrested Dave Bundy on Riverside Road.

On Monday, April 7, a thirty-year-old man who lived eight hundred miles north in the green mountains of Montana read a story about Dave Bundy's arrest and believed it was the call to arms he'd been waiting for.

Chapter 3

THE TEAM
ASSEMBLES

Ryan Payne lived in a six-year-old log cabin nestled in a valley at the foot of Montana's Anaconda Range. He was the creator of a national network of citizen militias called Operation Mutual Aid. His OMA cofounder, who lived in Pennsylvania, emailed him a story about the Bundys: "Have you seen this?"

Payne had not heard of the Bundys at all. He read about Dave Bundy's arrest and became fixated. Here was the situation he'd been looking for. Someone he could help. It had been years since he'd lent anybody the specific kind of help he was trained to give.

A missive went out to the OMA membership: "We do not have a go on this yet, but I strongly suspect we might in the near future. At this time we need everyone to help us make this story go viral."

Instead of waiting for a request for help, Payne decided to be proactive. He called Cliven Bundy himself.

Payne was average height, athletically built, handsome in a nondescript way, his right arm inked with tribal tattoos, left arm unmarked. He favored baseball caps and wraparound shades and sometimes grew in his thick beard, though right now he was clean-shaven. His resting stance was a soldier's at-ease, chest out, arms crossed at his belt, right-hand fingers loosely grasping his left wrist. Except for that, he looked like a million other Southern California dudes, which is exactly what he used to be.

The early turning point in Payne's life had occurred when he was a high schooler east of Los Angeles in the 1990s: the day he rented the movie *Sniper*. The 1993 movie starred Tom Berenger as a Marine sniper in the Panamanian jungle, a grizzled and cynical veteran who nonetheless believed that his seventy-four confirmed kills were done in service of liberty and freedom.

Payne thought: *I want to do that.*

When he was age seventeen in 2001, Payne joined the army and became the next best thing to a sniper: a long-range surveillance expert working beyond enemy lines. He served in the Eighteenth Airborne Corps' Long-Range Surveillance Company and participated in combat and intelligence-gathering missions. He wanted to become a CIA agent, but one war experience soured him. As he tells it, his six-man team was chasing an intelligence target in Iraq's Sinjar Mountains in 2005 when they were attacked by twenty-six fighters, and promised air support never showed up. Payne survived the air attack, but the episode upended his worldview. He became convinced that his superiors had planned to sacrifice his team. Over time, his suspicion evolved into a broader distrust of the federal government.

After five years of active duty, three more in the reserve, and two deployments in Iraq, he was honorably discharged in 2009 at the rank of sergeant. The army had awarded him multiple commendation medals, including one that recognized his "exceptionally meritorious service" and his "outstanding initiative, professionalism, and dedication to duty." By this time, Payne had come to believe that the US government was the world's great oppressor. He told people on Facebook he liked the desert farmers he had met in Iraq and sometimes thought about returning there to help their militias.

He'd been on the wrong team all along.

In April 2009, the year Payne was discharged from reserve duty, the Department of Homeland Security released a report prepared by its domestic extremism analysts. The ten-page report noted that right-wing Patriot groups were flourishing. Reasons included the wake of the election of an African American president who favored gun control as well as rising unemployment and millions of foreclosures. Online Patriot chatter centered around fears of martial law, massive illegal immigration, racial conflict, the creation of citizen detention camps, end-times prophecies. It was the 1990s all over again, boosted by the internet.

Further, the report noted that thousands of military veterans were returning home from Iraq and Afghanistan, and many were struggling to reintegrate into civilian life. "Returning veterans possess combat skills and experience that are attractive to rightwing extremists," the report noted. "DHS is concerned that rightwing extremists will attempt to recruit and radicalize returning veterans."

The report was distributed to local law enforcement. It wasn't classified, but it was not supposed to be released to the media or general public. But within a few days, someone slipped it to a blog called the *Liberty Papers*. Conservative media and politicians from both parties were outraged. DHS secretary Janet Napolitano apologized to veterans, and the Extremism and Radicalization Branch that had created the report was quietly dismantled.

As the years passed and the Patriot ranks swelled, however, the unit's report looked more and more prescient. Only 149 Patriot groups were operational in 2008, according to the Southern Poverty Law Center, but that number skyrocketed after Barack Obama's presidential election, reaching a high of 1,360 in 2012.

Veterans were a significant part of the movement. Two weeks after the report came out, a new Patriot group called the Oath Keepers mobilized for the first time in Lexington, Massachusetts. The group was made up of former or current soldiers and police officers who vowed to continue upholding their oath to "defend the Constitution against all enemies, foreign and domestic."

Its founder, Stewart Rhodes, was a retired army paratrooper who later graduated from Yale Law School. He practiced law, dabbled in politics, but his mission changed one day in 2008 when he read a letter from a retired colonel that declared "the Constitution and our Bill of Rights are gravely endangered," and it was up to members of law enforcement and military to save them. That's when Rhodes decided to create Oath Keepers. Most of the organization's members were retired from service. Active-duty were welcome to join, too, but Rhodes suggested they remain anonymous. For one thing, he didn't want them accused of treason. Also, the organization was more powerful if nobody knew how many people were involved, because, that way, *any* soldier might be a member.

RYAN PAYNE STRUGGLED IN CIVILIAN LIFE. BACK IN CALIFORNIA, HE WENT to work for his uncle's company that built custom, high-end dune buggies.

But the economy soon faltered, and California began to regulate dune buggy emissions, squeezing smaller manufacturers out of business.

Payne became convinced that the government was deliberately undermining average Americans in order to concentrate power in the hands of a few, just as he thought his army superiors had purposefully withheld air support when his team was under fire in Iraq. He plunged further into a profusion of interlinked theories about organized and widespread treachery. He came to believe that a cabal of Jewish bankers was controlling market forces. That the Founding Fathers intended for the states to act as sovereign countries. That it was legal to kill a police officer who was making an unlawful arrest. Payne went from being an agnostic to embracing a fringe religion that called itself Messianic Judaism; he believed that Jesus was the Jewish messiah.

Uniting all of these ideas was Payne's master theory that a small group of the ultrawealthy was purposely implementing environmental regulations to make it impossible for rural Americans to make a living. Those elites wanted the land, the gold, the oil, the coal for themselves.

In 2012, he moved with a girlfriend and their baby to Montana and found work as an electrician. They had a second child. He spent lots of time on conspiracy websites. On some online forums he claimed he'd been an Army Ranger, which wasn't quite true. The denizens of this world may have hated the federal government, but there was no higher badge of honor or legitimacy for them than to have been a US soldier, particularly a highly trained one who'd seen combat. Payne exaggerated his credentials, using the term "ranger" loosely—he'd been through similar training but hadn't actually graduated from Ranger school.

Payne founded a local militia called the West Mountain Rangers Militia, and then, when he realized how fragmented the larger militia movement was, he cofounded Operation Mutual Aid, a loose national coalition of militias that could act together if someone made a request. He loved the idea of thousands of trained militiamen from different states converging on a situation, helping citizens in trouble. Bringing food and muscle and guns to people threatened by a flood, a hurricane, an enemy invasion, a terrorist attack, a downed electrical grid or communication network. Or a tyrannical, unconstitutional federal government.

The problem was, OMA was little more than a 215-person email list. No one had ever actually made a request for OMA's services, maybe because few people knew the network existed. In 2013, Payne tried to mobilize OMA to back a West Virginia boy who'd been suspended from school for wearing an NRA T-shirt, but the teen's family didn't want militia help.

Then Payne read about Dave Bundy's arrest and called Cliven. On the phone, Cliven didn't seem scared, exactly, but he seemed to understand the direness of his situation. He needed men who were willing to insert themselves between his family and the feds. Payne was impressed by the deeply religious, stalwart rancher. Payne told Cliven he could bring militia units and Patriots from all over the country.

While they were talking, the OMA cofounder in Pennsylvania was messaging back and forth with Carol over Facebook.

He wrote: "Looks very much like we will be coming."

Carol wrote: "Thank you. We do live in a wonderful country."

"Used to, time to take it back."

"Let's do it."

"That's the plan, dear."

By the time his call with Cliven ended, Payne was deeply excited. He hadn't felt this sense of purpose since soldiering in Iraq. The next day, he packed his ancient Jeep Cherokee with two sleeping bags, his army rucksack, and a Rock River Arms Operator LAR-15 semiautomatic rifle and set out for Nevada. It was a twelve-hour drive, so he'd be on the road all night. But a West Mountain Rangers buddy was coming along, and if they traded off, they could make it by morning.

Payne emailed and messaged militia members all over the country, telling them the OMA network finally had a taker for its services.

> We have made the decision to mobilize to Nevada. Units are underway as I type this . . . At this time we have approximately 150 responding, but that number is growing by the hour . . . May God grant each and every one of you safety, wisdom and foresight, and courage to accomplish the mission we have strived for so long to bring to fruition. All men are mortal, most pass simply because it is their time, a few however are blessed with the opportunity to choose their time in performance of duty.

Payne provided directions to Bundy Ranch as well as grid coordinates.

TUESDAY MORNING, APRIL 8, 2014, AS RYAN PAYNE PACKED HIS WEAPONS and messaged his network, a woman named Shawna Cox was driving to Bundy Ranch when she noticed some chemtrails streaking the blue skies.

Chemtrails—what some folks called the long-lasting white streaks left in the atmosphere by passing jets—were a topic of great debate in Patriot circles. Scientists said the trails were simple condensation, but many Patriots worried that the government might be purposely spraying chemical or biological agents to control human population levels, to manipulate the psychology of the citizenry, or to just kill people. At the very least, Cox thought it was odd that there were so many unusual formations, including a figure eight, above Bunkerville on this particular week. She pulled off the road to snap some pictures.

Cox, who lived in Kanab, Utah, had recently appointed herself the official Bundy public relations specialist, in charge of handling interview requests from the news media. She and Cliven had known each other for years, both being well-known figures in the range war circles. Cox was a people person, a networker who coached Little League and served as a scoutmaster. She'd attended early People for the West! workshops and eventually became secretary for the local chapter. It was a good job for her. She was an organizer, not a leader. Give her a task, and she'd get it done. In 1996, she helped coordinate opposition to President Clinton's designation of the Grand Staircase–Escalante National Monument in southern Utah. Four years later, she rallied the ranchers who helped Mary Bulloch take back the wild cows the BLM had rounded up from the monument's lands. Cox learned about reporters, how they were nice to your face but put a devious spin on their stories.

In the ensuing years, Cox had never tired of the conspiracy-tinged intrigue at the epicenter of the Dixie state's-rights movement. At age fifty-seven, she had a ruddy face and big, cheerful pale-blue eyes under flaxen tresses that looked like they belonged to a much younger woman. Her first husband and infant child had died in a car wreck many years earlier. Cox's second husband and many children were used to her causes. In 2012, Cox was in a Tea Party meeting when she got an email from Cliven pleading for help. Cox helped Cliven organize opposition to the Rugwell-led BLM roundup, which was later canceled. Now, Cliven was calling again. Could Cox get folks in Utah ready to come in groups of twenty-five with horses and trailers? Cliven wanted people willing to serve four-day shifts. Cox got to work.

When she reached the ranch on Tuesday, the house was filled with the sound of ringing phones, the table crowded with laptops. When reporters called, whoever picked up the phone would talk to them. Cliven was spending so much of the day talking that his high-pitched voice was growing thready with overuse.

Cox helped Carol and Cliven organize their sprawling family into a flowchart, giving each sibling a different duty. They turned their dining room and kitchen into a war room, taking down the family pictures and putting up notices and lists of contact information. Cox made sure media requests were funneled through her, and she decided whether to put on Cliven or one of the sons or daughters and gave the interviewers a time limit.

Up to now, coverage had been sporadic and mostly regional, but the news media was beginning to pay more attention to the brewing conflict. Cliven's fight had been going on so long that multiple generations of reporters at the *Review-Journal* in Las Vegas and the *Spectrum* in St. George had covered it. In the 1990s, when federal land disputes were hot, Cliven had been mentioned or quoted regularly in news stories. Then the BLM had largely left him alone for fifteen years, and the tale of the rogue cattleman seventy-five miles east of Las Vegas had receded into western range wars history. But when the BLM began threatening to finally round up his cattle, reporters rediscovered the rancher who kept saying, "Whatever it takes."

On Sunday, April 6, the day after the roundup began, the Las Vegas TV stations had aired stories, as did a couple of regional papers. An Associated Press story went out and was picked up here and there. Over the next two days, interest ticked up with news of Dave Bundy's arrest and the "range war" call to arms on the Bundy Ranch blog.

During interviews, Cliven often got tangled in his own verbosity, as when he told the Las Vegas ABC affiliate on Monday that he abided by all Nevada laws, but then added a postscript that detractors used as evidence of his extremism.

"But I don't recognize the federal government as . . . as . . . as even existing," he groped.

Nevertheless, conservative blogs like *Right Wing News* and *American Clarion* realized there was a story here and began a frenzy of back-and-forth sharing of details and outrage. Even more than Dave's arrest, the aspect of the story that seemed to provoke the most indignation was the free-speech zones. The BLM had set them up on the first day of the roundup. One was just off the interstate near Bunkerville. The other was west of Mesquite off Riverside Road. Neither was within eyesight of the seizure operation. BLM workers pounded stakes into the ground in big circles and attached orange plastic temporary fencing and black signs proclaiming "First Amendment Area."

Protesters howled. First Amendment rights couldn't be restricted to an area, they said. You carried them with you wherever you went. A Bundy family friend from Las Vegas drove to one of the BLM-designated spots and fastened a hand-lettered sign to the orange fence: "First Amendment Is Not an Area." The protesters called the zones "pigpens" and left them empty.

The Bundys scored a big win on Tuesday. After supporters flooded Cliven's office with calls, Nevada governor Brian Sandoval blasted the First Amendment areas, saying they trampled on Nevadans' constitutional rights and should be dismantled.

"No cow justifies the atmosphere of intimidation which currently exists nor the limitation of constitutional rights that are sacred to all Nevadans," Sandoval said.

Cox was thrilled. Their message was getting through.

IN A SMALL INLAND SOUTHERN CALIFORNIA TOWN CALLED HESPERIA, A motormouthed podcaster named Pete Santilli was deciding whether to do something he'd never done before: take his show on the road.

Santilli heard about Bundy Ranch from his producer, who kept nagging him about the rancher guy who was fighting the feds. Santilli wasn't interested.

He said: *I don't do ranching. I'm a New York guy. I don't know anything about cows. The American people don't care about cows.*

The producer said: *Pete, this is bigger than cows or ranching.*

Santilli also heard from a fan who messaged him about Dave Bundy's arrest: "What do you think about getting a movement down to Nevada against the FEDS? Time we stopped all this huffing and puffing and bullshit over the microphones and computers and go down and do what we got to do."

Santilli wasn't sure. In the five years he'd been hosting *The Pete Santilli Show*, he'd never covered an event in person. Mostly he ranted about whatever was in the news, riffing on stories aired on Fox News, or CNN, or right-wing blogs. When people called in, he'd talk to them. Sometimes his producer set up interviews. But Santilli did it all out of his home studio north of the San Bernardino Mountains.

Santilli was an ex-Marine in his late forties, graying goatee and toothy grin and thinning black hair slicked back over his dome. He'd begun *The Pete Santilli Show* podcast in 2009, and had recorded 674 episodes, live on YouTube most weekdays, 10 AM to 1 PM. He *loved* the show, and his gusto came through on every episode. When his chair couldn't contain his enthusiasm, he'd adjust the microphone so he could stand, often sucking on a silver vape pipe and letting out a billow of vaporized nicotine. When he got really excited, his off-kilter eyes would bulge with an emphatic, erratic gleam.

What got him revved up was the idea of being part of a moment, an event that would undermine the federal government. He believed the government was irredeemably corrupt, that al-Qaeda founder Osama bin Laden was a CIA asset, that President Obama had been born in Kenya. He didn't know much about the range wars, but he did believe that the UN's Agenda 21 was a ruse to depopulate the western states. Santilli's highest profile moment had come eleven months earlier, when during a rant about Benghazi, he said he wanted to shoot former US secretary of state Hillary Clinton "in the vagina." A minor flurry erupted on liberal blogs, and the Secret Service looked into the matter and presumably decided it was more joke than threat. Santilli replayed his own sound bite on the show, grinning. Since then, Santilli had upped his shock-jock game, winning more headlines. He interviewed New Hampshire state representative Stella Tremblay, who suggested the Boston Marathon bombing was a "black op" by the federal government. He featured an animated video on his show in which a sentient Constitution assassinated President Obama. He called himself "the most controversial talk show host in the USA," "the alternative to the alternative media."

Santilli read about Cliven Bundy and decided, cows or no cows, this was the real deal. He told his producer to book the rancher for a telephone interview. Santilli wrote:

> We're having [Cliven Bundy] on my show to cover the story & drum up support. Let's go to Nevada ... Let's fucking go you ready? Get a team of militia members.

In his forty-minute interview with Cliven, Santilli was respectful and subdued, for him. He didn't talk about "vaginas" or "fucking libtards." He asked Cliven if he was expecting another Waco or Ruby Ridge.

"Until the state steps up and says no or the county sheriff says no, this thing is going to keep escalating until the point that we're gonna have to take our land back and take our rights back," Cliven said. "Maybe that's the time we're at in life, I don't know. Somebody's gonna have to back off or we the people are gonna put our boots down and walk over these people."

"That's absolutely right," Santilli exclaimed. "I want to make something very clear to anybody who would misconstrue what I'm suggesting. I'm suggesting a constitutional defense of we the people against a tyrannical government."

"Let me tell you what they're up against," Cliven said. "They're up against a man that says, 'I will do whatever it takes.'"

By the time they disconnected, Santilli was all in. This man was different than his fans, different than the folks he usually talked to on air. Cliven Bundy was a bona fide rancher-cowboy, standing up to the federal government. This could be the moment Santilli had been waiting for. The flashpoint the federal government feared. He didn't want to miss it.

Santilli grabbed his iPad and a microphone and hit the road. Wednesday's episode of *The Pete Santilli Show* would be webcast live from Bundy Ranch.

RYAN PAYNE AND HIS WEST MOUNTAIN RANGERS BUDDY DROVE ALL NIGHT and got to Bundy Ranch at 7:30 AM on Wednesday, April 9. Cliven was glad to see them, relieved to see men with guns on their hips. From that moment on, he rarely went anywhere without militia bodyguards flanking him.

Payne and Cliven sat down to talk things over. Cliven said he wanted his cattle back. Payne had three objectives. One, keep everyone safe, including the Bundys, their supporters, and even the BLM. Two, reopen the public lands in and around Gold Butte. Three, return all cattle and water infrastructure to the Bundys.

That sounded good to Cliven. The BLM was posting cattle-seizure numbers on its website each day, and this morning the total was up to 236, a little less than half of what Cliven believed he owned, though the feds kept saying his herd was 900 head strong.

Payne got back to work mobilizing Operation Mutual Aid. His cell phone was burning up with messages and calls from groups in Texas, Florida, New Hampshire. Militia were streaming toward Nevada in pairs and small groups. He arranged for incoming militia members to camp on a stretch of mesquite-dotted land between the road to the Bundy house and the river.

OMA was operational.

CLIVEN HAD TOLD AMMON TO MANAGE THE PROTEST SITE ON RIVERSIDE Road, about two miles from Bundy Ranch. So Ammon cooked breakfasts and lunches for protesters on the two big propane grills he'd brought. The family knew how to host lots of people; hundreds of descendants of Abraham Bundy held a gigantic family reunion each year at the abandoned former site of Bundyville on the Arizona Strip. Still, providing two meals a day for the protesters was a major effort. As the week went on, the protest site grew crowded with vehicles, recreational campers, lawn chairs, tents. After the big rally on Monday, protesters had ebbed and flowed to and from the site. There'd be forty or fifty throughout the day, and then the crowd would swell in the evenings after work to a hundred or more.

Ammon wanted to get organized. The family needed to communicate with its supporters about where they should park their campers and set up their tents, about when to show up for meals and where to use the bathroom. It'd also be good to know who some of these folks were. Maybe the family needed to have a meeting. He told his father as much, and Cliven, characteristically, shrugged off the advice and issued only the broadest of instructions.

Cliven said: *Everybody's welcome. Just take care of them.*

The protest site had a sweeping view of the river valley and the long slope of desert lands rising to the base of Virgin Peak, some seven miles away as the crow flew. The BLM cowboys were gathering cattle out there in the backcountry, too far away to see. The family had heard gunshots echoing from the hills, and since the BLM and its hired cowboys were the only ones out there, they believed the feds might be killing cattle. Even a normal roundup was stressful and could lead to injuries, and when cattle went down, it was not unusual to shoot them. After a cool weekend, a heat wave had set in, and temperatures were climbing to 93 degrees, which would nearly break an April 9 record. It was far too hot for the cattle to be running. One Bundy relative reported seeing a helicopter flying low near the river, herding cows, and that some calves had been separated. They'd also spotted cows with tight bags—engorged udders—a sure sign they'd been separated from their calves. The newborns wouldn't last long without their mothers.

Shortly after noon on Wednesday, Ammon was preparing lunch at the protest site when he noticed far-off dust clouds swirling upward from the hills. He grabbed a pair of binoculars and studied the landscape. It had to be a convoy of BLM vehicles kicking up the dust because the land was closed to everybody else. The only route out of the mountains led to Riverside Road. A convoy that size—they must be doing something important.

A MAN NAMED BRAND NU THORNTON WATCHED THE MAN HOLDING THE binoculars. Never shy, Thornton sidled over and introduced himself, then asked what Ammon was looking at.

Ammon told Thornton that his family believed the BLM was killing cattle and either burying them or hauling them out of the mountains. This convoy could contain dead cattle or maybe water infrastructure.

Thornton added this information to the massive repository of religious, political, and scientific notions he carried around inside his head. Sixty-one years old, with flowing white hair and beard set off by his deep Mojave tan, Thornton wore a camouflage baseball cap and had a white rectangular Bluetooth earpiece jammed in his right ear. Among the protesters, he was a little hard to categorize. He lived in the city, in an apartment in a pleasant, tree-lined gated complex in Las Vegas, his walls filled with the mounted heads of pronghorn antelope and bighorn sheep he'd bagged. He owned a small company that installed air-conditioning systems. He belonged to the Southern Nevada Militia, which advertised itself as sort of a family-friendly militia, open to all races and religions, people who simply wanted to protect their neighbors and the Constitution.

Thornton had been following the Cliven Bundy story since the 1990s, and his mother said they were distantly related, but they'd never met until this week. Two days earlier, Thornton had read about Dave Bundy's arrest and drove to Bunkerville. A friend accompanied him, a retired Army lieutenant colonel named Roy Potter who claimed a long, mysterious background in military intelligence. Potter had built a devoted YouTube following with his rambling video explanations of arcane religious texts and cataclysmic global geopolitics. He was staying at Thornton's apartment in Vegas, and Thornton appeared in many of Potter's videos. A year earlier, a combat veterans' website had looked into Potter's background and built a pretty good case that some of Potter's military claims were bullshit.

Thornton was from a Mormon family; his great-great-grandfather was a bodyguard for Joseph Smith, he said. But Thornton's worldview was eclectic, too mazelike to fit into a single structured belief system like LDS. Thornton cursed, drank alcohol, and could even be persuaded to smoke a little weed now and again. And in other ways, he'd transcended the typical practices of modern Mormonism. He believed he was also an Israelite and practiced certain Jewish rituals.

So when they'd arrived at the protest site on Monday, Thornton and Potter had gone down to the bank of the Virgin underneath the Riverside Road bridge. They draped white prayer shawls over their heads and said prayers in Hebrew and English, asking God to intervene, to stop the federal war on the Bundys. The United States was no longer the world's bastion of freedom. America had become an evil empire, and they asked God to damn Obama.

"In the name of the great Elohim," Thornton had intoned, "we blow the trump of God that the righteous may come hither and the wicked shall be responsible for the blood upon their own hands."

Potter raised a spiraled, polished ram's horn shofar to his lips and blew a sustained note that lifted briefly at the end. Then two more.

Other protesters had watched quizzically as the two aging Mormons ritually washed their feet in the Virgin's waters, speaking in Hebrew, video recording each other with a cell phone. They were an oddity at first, but as the days passed and Thornton and Potter pitched a tent and camped out nearby, they had become part of the developing community of Bundy protesters.

Now, as the BLM convoy made its long, slow descent down rugged mountain trails toward Riverside Road, Potter videoed the scene, adding authoritative commentary.

"This whole area's being patrolled by these guys, definitely tactical-type patrolling of the roadways," Potter narrated. "They had a lot of training to do this in Fallujah. These are supposed to be BLM cops, right? Well, probably not. Just using their vehicles and uniforms."

As the convoy got closer to the road, the protesters could see that it contained more than a dozen vehicles, including a dump truck hauling a big yellow backhoe loader on a trailer. Several protesters piled into jacked-up pickups and headed for the spot where the trail emerged onto Riverside Road, about a quarter of a mile away. They wanted to get a closer look at the convoy and give the feds a piece of their minds.

PETE SANTILLI HAD ARRIVED AT BUNDY RANCH ONLY HOURS EARLIER, BUT he was in the thick of the action.

In combat boots, a Rambo-style bandanna over his shaved head, and camo fatigues, he drove his sedan to the intersection where the dirt road from the backcountry met the paved Riverside Road.

The first white federal SUV pulled onto Riverside, but Santilli maneuvered the sedan onto the dirt trail, blocking the rest of the convoy. If the dump truck contained dead cattle, Santilli believed that was evidence of a crime, and he didn't want to let the convoy escape until he could get a sheriff out there to investigate.

The ranger in the lead vehicle yelled at Santilli to move the car. Santilli hesitated for about fifteen seconds, which gave protesters on foot time to mass at the intersection. Then Santilli put the sedan in reverse and backed up to let the convoy pass.

Four dusty, white ranger SUVs pulled onto Riverside, parking crosswise bumper to bumper across the road to form a blockade between the protesters and the other federal vehicles exiting the trail. Several khaki-clad agents scrambled out of the SUVs along with two German shepherds on leashes.

On foot, the protesters surged past the row of ranger SUVs. Santilli grabbed his iPad and jumped out of his car.

AMMON HADN'T FOLLOWED RIGHT AWAY. HE'D ALREADY HAD ONE ALTER-
cation with the BLM that morning. An hour or so earlier, Dan Love
and another BLM agent had stopped by to drop off some of the possessions they'd confiscated from Dave Bundy three days earlier. Ammon
had never met Love. He had refused to shake the BLM agent's hand
and told Love to get off the Bundys' land.

Ammon had said: *We're gonna win this war, guaranteed.*

Now, Ammon figured the protesters would simply chant and
wave signs at the convoy as it pulled onto the paved road. But when he
saw the government SUVs block the road and the agents and dogs get
out, he thought he'd better get down there.

Ammon jumped aboard a four-wheeler and gunned it down the
road, circling up behind the dump truck trailing the convoy, trying to
get a look at what was in back.

At the trail exit, the crowd of protesters, a near-equal mix of men
and women, yelled at the agents on the road. Some held cell phones
aloft, recording the chaos. Pete Santilli's combat boots were planted
firmly on the yellow center line of Riverside Road, videoing the stream
of heavy-duty BLM vehicles pouring off the backcountry trail.

Cliven's sister, Margaret Houston, a deeply tanned brunette
woman of fifty-seven years, approached a federal pickup truck, her
arms outstretched, cell phone in one hand, bottle of water in the other.

A few steps away, Mike Roop, the chief BLM ranger for Washington and Oregon, eyed the brunette woman jeering at the federal pickup
truck. Roop was buzz-cut and wore a khaki uniform, sunglasses, and
black gloves. His long, hot day in the mountains was getting worse.
Along with dozens of other rangers, he'd been dispatched to southern
Nevada for the impound operation. The BLM was not only rounding
up cattle, it was dismantling Bundy's now-unpermitted water systems.
The dump truck contained pipes and other water infrastructure they'd

demolished, and Roop was helping to escort it out of the mountains, past the protesters.

Up to this moment, the most public operations Roop had been a part of were patrolling the Burning Man festival in northwest Nevada and the time Gunner, his German shepherd, had sniffed out sixty-eight pounds of marijuana in a Tacoma, Washington, attic. Gunner had died in 2008, and Roop didn't have a dog today, though two of his fellow rangers did. People tended to comply, Roop knew, when you had a big, barking police dog with you.

But this Bundy crowd wasn't like those at Burning Man. They weren't drinking and having a good time. They were sober, angry, ready to blow.

Her back to Roop, the brunette woman continued heckling, crowding the vehicle as it passed. Roop's stride lengthened, quickened, and he got to her just as she was yelling something into the driver's window. Roop spread his arms, and then he wrapped the woman up like a linebacker making a tackle. He yanked her to his left, swiveling 180 degrees, and let her go.

The woman crumpled to the ground.

A man yelled: "Hey! *Hey!*"

The protesters surged forward. And the rangers with the dogs came in.

Up the road, the shape of a man on a four-wheeler materialized through the dust, coming closer.

AMMON HADN'T BEEN ABLE TO GET A CLEAR VIEW INSIDE THE TRUCK BED, so he had accelerated cross-country to Riverside Road and approached the truck from the front. He stood up on the four-wheeler to try to get a view of the confrontation. He hadn't seen his Aunt Margaret get thrown down, but he could sense that the raucous tension had sharpened to a violent edge. This wasn't a protest anymore. It was an ejection. One side or the other would be gone soon.

None of the protesters appeared to have firearms, but one man grabbed a fist-sized stone and brandished it. A ranger grabbed his arm from behind, forcing him to drop the rock.

Ammon reached the dirt-road exit and skidded to a halt, right in front of the dump truck. He wanted to stop the truck so he could get a look in back, perhaps snap a photo. But the dump truck kept coming, and Ammon leaped off the saddle just as the truck's bumper nudged the four-wheeler.

Ammon tried to climb onto the truck to peer into the bed, but several rangers saw what he was doing and ran across the road. Ammon jumped down, faced the line of agents. Several unholstered their black-and-yellow Taser guns and aimed at him. Two gripped the leashes of straining dogs.

Over the noise of the crowd, one of the agents yelled: "Get back! Police! Get back! Get back now!"

Ammon did not retreat. He bounced back and forth on the balls of his feet like a boxer, yelling and pointing at the truck, demanding to know what was inside.

One of the K9 rangers thrust out his arm, siccing his dog on Ammon. The dog lunged forward, and Ammon kicked awkwardly at it with his left leg. The dog recoiled, and the ranger sicced him again. The dog lunged once more, and Ammon kicked back.

Another ranger pulled the trigger on his Taser.

POLICE BEGAN USING ELECTRIC CATTLE PRODS—BASICALLY TWO CHARGED prongs attached to a long barrel—to disperse civil rights activists in the 1960s. Cattle prods weren't designed to incapacitate, just to deliver a painful shock. Over the years, stun guns were developed that delivered an even-larger voltage that would overwhelm the body's nervous system.

In the 1970s, a NASA researcher took the device a step further when he developed a model that fired a pair of electrodes connected to the gun by wires. Early model Tasers used gunpowder to project the electrodes, but recent models use compressed air. Pulling the trigger breaks open a compressed gas cartridge, which launches the electrodes toward the target. The electrodes have barbs, like a straightened fishhook, designed to grab onto the target's clothing, or flesh. The advantage to this design is that the user doesn't have to get as close. The downside: You get only one shot. The electrode wires must be rewound and gas cartridges replaced.

If both electrode darts connect, one delivers 50,000 volts, 500 to 1,500 of which actually flow into the body, as long as the other probe grounds itself in the body or ground, completing the electrical circuit. The further apart the two probes, the more muscle groups seize up from the electrical flow.

Stun guns are not harmless. They regularly are used for torture around the world. They can trigger ventricular tachycardia and stop the heart. But they're less destructive than a bullet, and used judiciously, probably save lives, both law enforcement and civilian.

THE ELECTRODES FLEW ABOUT FOUR FEET AND HIT AMMON. ONE OF THE barbed darts plunged into the left side of his neck. The other went through his thin, gray-plaid short-sleeved Western shirt, through the white T-shirt underneath, and buried itself in his left upper chest. Ammon jerked away from the agents and staggered a few steps, hunched over.

Then the electrodes sparked, over and over, each individual spark its own distinct sound but so rapid that they tumbled over each other:

tk-tk-tk-tk-tk-tk-tk-tk-tk-tk-tk-tk-tk-tk-tk. Convulsions seized his upper body, the pain flowing through him, and his mind slowed down, everything slowed down. Yet his legs felt strong. He crouched lower, his hand feeling wooden but seeking the wires, finding one, ripping the prong from his chest, throwing the wire aside as he straightened and whirled back to face the row of agents, looking every bit like the running back he once was. Someone else yanked the wire attached to his neck, and the wire broke, the dart still hanging on his neck. Ammon pulled it out, threw it aside. He stalked back toward the row of agents and dogs, in a fighter's stance, arms akimbo. The protesters surged with him.

Another ranger pulled the trigger and the darts found Ammon again—*tk-tk-tk-tk-tk-tk-tk-tk-tk-tk-tk-tk-tk-tk*—but Ammon seized up only for a moment before someone else yanked them out. Again, his legs felt steady.

Thornton marveled at Ammon's courage. What strength! It was almost supernatural.

Thornton rushed forward, too, yelling and pointing at the feds. A ranger tried to push him off the dump truck's bumper, and Thornton swatted away the man's hands. Other protesters charged, too, including Ammon's sister, Stetsy.

"Back up, you're gonna get bit!" an agent yelled, hauling on his dog's leash.

"I'm pregnant, so you watch that dog!" Stetsy yelled back at him.

A ranger boarded the four-wheeler to try to move it so the dump truck could pull onto the road. Ammon jostled over to stop him, grabbing his arm, and another agent tased him, point blank. Ammon fell back, staggering into the crowd of protesters. They knew what to do by now and yanked the wires away.

Ammon turned once again to face the agents. His mind wasn't tracking normally, but he knew one thing for sure. These men didn't believe the Bundys had rights on this land, but they did understand and respect power. So Ammon would show them that he was powerful, that he was possessed of a power greater than himself. And they would respect him and respect his followers.

He called out to the agents: *Whoever is in charge here, you need to get your men out of here! If you stay, this is not going to end well!*

Ammon knew the Lord was protecting him.

After the crowd ripped the Taser wires off Ammon for a third time, the tension seemed to subside just a notch, the sharp edge dulled. The agents were out of options. They'd tased Ammon three times, and he was still standing, blood beginning to soak through his shirt. They'd thrown down Margaret Houston, and she was right beside her nephew, scratched up but even more defiant than before. Unless the agents were prepared to start shooting, the protesters had the upper hand.

The row of agents edged backward. One backed up the four-wheeler, and the dump truck moved out onto the road and pulled slowly away, dragging the backhoe. Ammon jumped onto the truck and got a look inside the bed and saw no dead cattle, only pipes and other water equipment.

Pete Santilli wandered through the chaos, recording the entire scene on his iPad. Part documentarian, part activist, he'd join in, and then stand back and record. He advised the protesters to comply with the agents' orders to back off, but then he'd get in one's face.

As the BLM retreated, a distraught young man in a bright red shirt screamed at them: "Who's the aggressor here? Who's the aggressor! Am I carrying an AR?"

Santilli interjected, speaking rapidly to the man.

"Let it go, let it go, let it go," Santilli said. "Don't give them the satisfaction of taking you in. All right? Stay with me. Get on the record. Talk to me."

The young man faced Santilli's iPad, crying behind his sunglasses. "This is the road I grew up on," he said. "I just saw federal agents throw my aunt on the ground. I saw my cousin get tased three times." The crowd began chanting: "No BLM! No BLM!"

Hoarse with rage, Brand Nu Thornton gave one departing BLM agent a vigorous, two-handed middle-finger salute: "Get outta here! Get the fuck out!"

One BLM officer with a graying handlebar mustache shrugged dismissively.

"We're done," he said.

Thornton jabbed a finger at him: "You're far from done."

Santilli swirled around the action.

"I'll stay back, I don't mean any harm," he told one agent. But then he couldn't resist adding: "I'm just recording your brutality."

As the remaining ranger vehicles departed, heading east toward the command post, the crowd exulted. Thornton scampered around, high-fiving everybody.

Santilli knew he had his trigger event. This video was everything he'd been talking about for the last five years on *The Pete Santilli Show*. The flashpoint. And he had captured it all, right here on his iPad.

"That's right, baby!" he crowed. "B-L-M. Go A-WAY! B-L-M. Go A-WAY!"

The crowd took up the chant: "B-L-M. Go A-WAY! B-L-M. Go A-WAY!"

Part II

Chapter 4

TEN THOUSAND PATRIOTS

Pete Santilli was accustomed to getting a few hundred views per YouTube episode. His interview with Cliven Bundy, for example, was watched 858 times in the first twenty-four hours, which by Santilli's standards made it a hit.

But the video of the feds tasing the cowboy detonated like a truck packed with ammonium nitrate. Santilli's producer posted the video to YouTube shortly after the incident on Wednesday, April 9, 2014, titling it "Ranch Riot!! Bundy Ranch Protestors Tasered by Federal Agents." Within hours, it hit seventy-five thousand views. By the next day, more than half a million. It crossed the one million mark early Saturday afternoon.

However, that was only a tiny percentage of the video's total viewers. It was everywhere in the Patriot news universe. Santilli's producer shipped it to Infowars and Fox News, and there it was, on repeat, the words "The Pete Santilli Show" floating over images of the group of angry Americans in jeans and T-shirts facing off against a row of khaki-uniformed federal agents brandishing Tasers and holding snarling police dogs.

Even before the Santilli video went viral, Sean Hannity, a Fox News talk show host, had picked up the Bundy story. Hours before Ammon got tased, Hannity had done a live remote interview with a squeaky-voiced Cliven. It was the Bundys' highest-profile moment yet, but not a particularly exciting segment as Hannity delivered a fairly evenhanded breakdown of the history of the range wars over shots of the desert, cows, and ranch. Hannity might have dropped the story after that, but then Santilli's gripping video emerged, and Hannity took the story under his influential wing. He dispatched correspondents to the ranch and led with a story on Friday that devoted a full twenty minutes to showing the Santilli video and aerial shots of the federal command post as well as interviews with Cliven and Ammon.

"I'm having a hard time understanding why the government would create a confrontation like this on land that they don't even want, for a turtle that doesn't apparently need protection, that the cattle are not going to hurt," Hannity said.

It was a visually stimulating broadcast, made for TV with cowboy hats, pocket Constitutions, fluttering flags, and now, Taser guns and rifles and attack dogs. And it had Cliven Bundy, who wasn't great at explaining the technicalities of his stances or situation, but who did deliver good sound bites: "I'm getting angry enough to swear." Cliven looked like everything American, or at least everything a particular slice of the populace remembered as good and right about this country, and those hearts thrilled to the notion that someone was finally standing up to the beast, and that the someone was not some blogger or politician but an honest-to-goodness rancher. Cliven Bundy *looked* like a cattleman, his head at home under a Stetson. He slouched in a saddle like Clint Eastwood or John Wayne. He was at ease in front of cameras, didn't mind the attention, in fact seemed to love it. He rode a bay mare, wore a cowboy shirt with stitching and snaps, sleeves rolled up to elbows, sometimes showing off his lasso tricks. He was an instant folk hero.

The images associated with the feds were striking, too, in a different way. Squads of silent men in khaki uniforms, black storm-trooper gloves, faces concealed by sunglasses. Blurry black silhouettes of men hunched and watching from distant ridges. Low-flying helicopters and sprawling command posts. White government SUVs, seemingly endless dark-windowed convoys of them. None of these images looked good juxtaposed against the colorful Bundy clan and their free-wheeling band of supporters. On Thursday, the BLM took down the orange-fenced "First Amendment Areas." No one was using them, and they had become a symbol of federal ham-handedness.

Everyone in the conservative media sphere wanted to interview Ammon. He was the most camera ready of the Bundys. Despite Cliven's folk-hero status, even ardent supporters tended to disconnect as the elder Bundy mixed up words and rambled, running down tangential verbal trails, and then doubling back. Unlike their father, both Ammon and Ryan knew what they wanted to say and had no trouble calling up the right words. But Ryan's lopsided face and forceful nasal bark didn't play as well on TV. Ammon looked and sounded all-American, mainstream, his rich tenor his most distinctive feature, perhaps the most formidable tool in his arsenal of personal characteristics. It was soft without being passive, moderate without being monotone, and most of all it came across as *reasonable*. Ammon could champion a cause most Americans believed to be radical, and even the staunchest Bundy opponent might find it difficult to reconcile the maverick message with the sensible-seeming man.

Even better, Ammon was, apparently, one tough hombre. Alex Jones, the voice behind Infowars, which was the Patriots' favorite information source, could barely contain his enthusiasm about Ammon's gritty encounter with the feds. Jones's eyes widened as he described the Santilli video.

"Then they tasered him over and over, and he just pulls them out," Jones said, making a yanking motion. "That's a real cowboy family."

His correspondent at the ranch interviewed Ammon, with Jones cutting in to offer commentary. The federal government, Jones said, *wanted* the Bundys to get violent. If federal agents died in a conflict with Patriots, the government would have an excuse to declare martial law.

"The feds want to get a physical confrontation going on," Jones said. "But then they are going to bring in the UN troops. I'm not kidding."

Infowars commenters went wild for Ammon.

CHIEFCLICKCLACK: Ammon Bundy is very well spoken . . . hell, he speaks better than Obama . . . lol.

THE_MAN_FROM_EPSILON_CRUCIS: [A]nd he doesn't need a teleprompter!

MANDALORIAN PATRIOT: "Id vote for him!"

Fox News host Greta Van Susteren weighed in too.

"Right now, go to gretawire.com and answer this," Van Susteren instructed her viewers. "Are you Team Cliven Bundy or Team Federal Government?"

Thousands of Fox News viewers voted. Ninety-seven percent said they were Team Cliven Bundy.

A Dixie rancher named LaVoy Finicum watched the Santilli video and decided to go to Bundy Ranch. Finicum wanted to look Cliven Bundy in the eye and determine for himself whether the rancher's crusade was righteous.

Finicum, age fifty-three, ran a part-time cattle operation about two hours from Bundy Ranch, which by Dixie rancher standards made them neighbors. Like Cliven, Finicum was the head of a big, complicated Mormon family: he and his second wife, Jeanette, had a total of eleven children between them. He'd always wanted to be a rancher. When he was eight years old, he designed his LV cattle brand. He had a picture of himself in full cowboy regalia at the age of four and another with a coyote he'd shot at age thirteen. He was a survivalist and had strong misgivings about the federal government. But Finicum had never met Cliven. The only news media he allowed in his house was TheBlaze, and the conservative outlet's founder, Glenn Beck, was dubious about the Bundys. And despite Finicum's mistrust of the feds, he'd had a good relationship with the BLM.

The Finicum ranch was a break-even operation, a passion, not a vocation. LaVoy and Jeanette made their living taking care of foster children, teenage boys who had been abused. They dealt with boys so traumatized and violent that one had killed the family chickens. Over eighteen years, the Finicums fostered more than sixty boys, sometimes for weeks, sometimes years.

In 2010, the Finicums moved to Cane Beds, Arizona, where LaVoy's grandparents and parents had ranched for decades. The sparsely populated community was a couple miles south of Colorado City, Arizona, a town best known as the headquarters for fundamentalist Mormon sects that practice polygamy. The key event in the town's history took place just before dawn one summer day in 1953, when more than 100 national guardsmen and police moved into the town of 400 and took everyone into custody, removing some 263 children. Some parents never regained guardianship, and the traumatic event was woven into the town's culture. The Fundamentalist Church of Jesus Christ of Latter-day Saints is based there, and polygamy and, reportedly, underage marriages, are still common. In this area, mistrust of government came with the territory.

When the Finicums moved to Cane Beds, they purchased twenty head of cattle and began grazing on a seventeen-thousand-acre allotment of federal land previously used by LaVoy's father. LaVoy's interest in self-reliance grew into a passion for survivalism. If catastrophe struck, he wanted to be prepared to protect his family. He taught his sons and daughters how to ride a horse, to change a truck's oil, to shoot a semiautomatic rifle. The family and their foster boys worked the ranch, herding the cattle from summer to winter ranges and back in traditional horseback cattle drives, with Jeanette operating as the chuck wagon in her SUV. The kids learned how to brand calves, clip ears, castrate young bulls. They learned how to build sheds and can their own food.

In 2013, Finicum began writing a novel about a fictional ranching family in the American Southwest and their struggle to survive in the wake of an apocalypse. He finished the manuscript on Jeanette's birthday in June, printed it out, and asked her to read it. *Only By Blood and Suffering* tells how China and Russia had detonated nuclear weapons over America, melting down the country's electronic infrastructure with a violent electromagnetic pulse. The Bonham family makes their way back to the ranch, using survivalist skills. The story is filled with Tom Clancy–like exploits, complete with technical footnotes about the workings of both the Federal Reserve and the Sig Sauer .45 pistol. Characters give speeches in the style of objectivist Ayn Rand. "Generations ago, people in this country took care of one another without the government in the middle," the family patriarch tells a crooked politician just before roping her with his lariat and stringing her up on a barn rafter. The saga ends with a face-off in a sandy desert wash between the patriarch and three Department of Homeland Security agents who are working to implement the New World Order in the aftermath of the calamity. The rancher shoots all three federal agents with his rosewood-grip six-shooter. Jeanette loved the story, and they had big hopes for the book.

Finicum had recently taken to "vision-boarding": putting up pictures that represented his various goals. He was a meticulous and methodical man who shaved his head and the ruddy angles of his jaw every day, kept himself lean and fit, and planned ahead for most contingencies. Vision-boarding suited him. He stuck the photos on a wall with painter's tape. The Finicums knew their lives were about to change—their youngest children would soon be out of the house—and they had many goals. They wanted to retire from foster parenting within a few years. They wanted to spend more time on their soaring grazing allotment, a dozen miles from the Grand Canyon's Toroweap Outlook. And Finicum wanted to publish the book and sell a million copies. He'd driven all the way to Irving, Texas, with a copy of the manuscript in hopes of talking his way into Glenn Beck's studio. He didn't get past the guard booth, where he left the manuscript. He didn't know whether Beck got it.

In April 2014, Finicum went to a vision-boarding conference in Salt Lake City, hoping to hone his goals. But he was distracted. The Bundy conflict had been heating up all week, and now there'd been a face-off with federal agents. Finicum saw the Santilli video, in which Cliven Bundy's sister was thrown down and his son was tased, and he knew he shouldn't be spending the weekend learning about vision boards. He called Jeanette, who was at home.

He said: *I'm not staying for the conference. I need to go down and talk to Mr. Bundy. I need to meet him and understand why he's doing what he's doing.*

Jeanette knew almost nothing about Cliven Bundy, but she gave her blessing.

Finicum drove five hours to Bunkerville and went straight to Bundy Ranch, where Cliven and Carol welcomed him into their home. Finicum asked Cliven all about the conflict, and Cliven invited him to come to a big rally the next day: Saturday, April 12. His curiosity satisfied, Finicum drove the two hours home to Cane Beds.

Finicum said: *Jeanette, I'm going to go back tomorrow morning and stand with the Bundys.*

This scared Jeanette. By now, she had done some reading about the conflict at Bundy Ranch. Glenn Beck thought it was dangerous, and so did Jeanette. She didn't want her strong-willed husband facing off against armed federal agents in a sandy desert wash. This was real life, not an apocalyptic thriller.

She said: *What?*

LIKE LAVOY FINICUM, PEOPLE ALL OVER THE COUNTRY WERE WATCHING the Santilli video and feeling the same pull toward Bundy Ranch.

In Los Osos, California, above a spectacular stretch of coastline halfway between Los Angeles and San Francisco, a sun-browned former hippie named Neil Wampler woke up, poured himself a cup of coffee, lit a Pall Mall menthol. Then he fired up his computer and went on his daily hunt for what he called "liberty-minded news." His life had been a series of monomanias, the pursuit of one very different obsession after another: golf, alcohol, woodworking, and now, investigating the overreach of the federal government.

Wampler, age sixty-six, had bushy salt-and-pepper eyebrows, a hawkish nose, and dark-brown eyes that could lose their grandfatherly warmth in a flash and go to a rageful glare. Which is what happened when he came across the Santilli video. He'd never heard of the Bundys and knew little about the range wars. Within hours, he knew a good deal about both and was in his battered 1963 Plymouth Valiant, wending his way across the Sierra Nevada mountains toward Bundy Ranch, a nearly eight-hour journey. Wampler's wife and son weren't home when he took off, so he left a note.

Wampler brought little with him, didn't pack a firearm. In fact, due to a dark event in his long-ago past, Wampler was not allowed by law to possess a gun.

IN HAILEY, IDAHO, A THIRTY-YEAR-OLD ELECTRICIAN NAMED ERIC PARKER had been following the Bundy story on social media, but when he saw the Santilli video he knew he had to go. He was particularly angered when he saw the young man in the red shirt crying about his aunt being thrown down by the federal agent. Parker wasn't a militia member and never served in the military, but he wanted to prevent the BLM from making unlawful arrests or pepper spraying protesters. He wanted people to know he was heading to Bunkerville, so as he often did, he wrote about it on Facebook.

"The citizens of the United States fought the toughest, biggest Army in the world in 1776," he posted. "Do not think we can't do it again."

Parker grabbed his Saiga .223 semiautomatic rifle because it was good for desert shooting; a little sand wouldn't jam it. He also packed two extra thirty-round magazines, a gas mask, body armor, camping supplies, and a Motorola two-way radio he'd picked up at Walmart. He told his wife and two children goodbye, and he and a couple of buddies drove twelve hours to Bunkerville in Parker's truck. They kept an eye on social media, because rumors were flying that Homeland Security was setting up checkpoints on the routes to Bunkerville.

They arrived unmolested at the protest site around 1 AM on Saturday. Despite the late hour, one of the Bundy sons was still there greeting people, and he showed the newcomers where incoming militia were camping. At the camp entrance, a guard asked them if they could take the rest of his watch duty so he could get some shut-eye. The guys who were supposed to relieve the guard had gotten drunk.

IN THE DIRT-ROAD MOUNTAINS EAST OF SAN DIEGO, A WOMAN NAMED TERRI Linnell had noticed some Facebook chatter about the Bundy family, but she didn't pay much attention until she saw the Santilli video. That's when she decided to throw her considerable Patriot influence behind their cause.

Linnell, age forty-eight, had twinkling dark eyes and a big mane of gray-streaked brunette hair. She was outgoing and conversational, though her speech was often punctuated by prolonged pauses as she seemed to search for a thought gone astray. She and her husband lived in a dome-shaped house perched on a mountainside, surrounded by their menagerie of dogs, horses, and chickens. After the financial crisis of 2008, Linnell's husband had spent two and a half years unable to find work in construction, and Linnell had evolved from stay-at-home mom to Patriot maven. She'd gone to early Tea Party meetings and even to leftist Occupy movement rallies in San Diego, any cause that seemed to share her mistrust of the powerful forces running the country. She ran for US Congress in 2012 and garnered 3 percent of the vote in her district. She moderated an Oath Keepers message board and her iron-fisted approach earned her the nickname "Momma Bear," which she loved. In the fall of 2013, she had helped organize a Patriot protest in Washington, DC. One night, US Capitol Police raided her campground in Maryland, supposedly looking for a protester who had posted inflammatory remarks on Facebook, and they handcuffed Linnell before letting her go. The incident gave Linnell the heebie-jeebies. Back at home, she noticed helicopters flying over her dome house and became convinced the government was spying on her because she was a Patriot organizer.

Now, Linnell played the Santilli video on her cell phone for her husband and posted an announcement on Facebook that Momma Bear was heading to Bunkerville. "Get your asses to NV now," she typed to her followers.

Just then, she heard a helicopter above the house again and marveled that the government was spending so much tax money to watch her from above. She smiled wryly at her husband, who rolled his eyes.

He said: *I guess they know you're going to Nevada.*

IN ARIZONA, BRIAN CAVALIER AND BLAINE COOPER HAD BEEN PLANNING to go to Bundy Ranch, and the Santilli video only strengthened their resolve. This was too good to miss.

Cavalier and Cooper made quite a pair. Both men had long arrest records, Cavalier mainly for driving under the influence, and Cooper for felonies such as aggravated assault. Gap-toothed and buzz-cut, Cavalier, age forty-two, was a tattoo artist with tattoos on his eyelids and a gigantic naked Buddha inked onto his enormous belly—they shared a navel. Cavalier sometimes called himself "Booda" and sometimes "The Raging Unicorn." He liked to boast about his days in the Marine Corps. Another tattoo on his neck read *"veni, vidi, vici"*—Latin for "I came, I saw, I conquered."

Cooper, age thirty-four, was tall and muscle-bound and had been born Stanley Blaine Hicks. He'd changed his name to Blaine Cooper in 2006, mimicking the handle of Jesse Ventura's character in the 1987 Arnold Schwarzenegger movie, *Predator*. Cooper was a member of the Arizona Border Recon, a self-appointed border patrol militia. The feds had investigated him in 2013 after he posted this message on Facebook: "Having a badge seems to be a free ride to be above the law but soon don't worry I am going to shoot a shit load of federal agents and cops in the war for freedom, so get ready."

Despite that investigation, Cooper had taken to Facebook again this week, posting about the Bundy situation: "I say we go their armed together and help him fight if there was ever a time to make a stand against the feds now is the time. Good so let's go there 100 strong loaded to the teeth and shoot all of them that try to take this man's cows and land."

Late in the week, Cavalier and Cooper made good on the call to arms, setting out together for Bunkerville.

In Las Vegas, a young married couple, Jerad and Amanda Miller, were already looking for a revolution when they saw the Santilli video.

Two years earlier, Jerad had published a series of posts on the website Planet Infowars, an offshoot of Alex Jones's conspiracy news empire. Jerad, then age twenty-nine, wrote that he was on probation for selling marijuana and couldn't find a job. He had a rotting wisdom tooth and couldn't afford dental care. Because of his criminal record, his fiancée, Amanda, nine years younger than Jerad, wasn't allowed to have a gun in their house. His anger had become focused on the police, the justice system. He believed the country was veering into fascism. "I feel that I have been violated and tread upon," he wrote. "That the so called justice system has done me harm. I do not wish to kill police. I understand that most of them believe they are doing the right thing. Yet, I will not go to jail, because I have not committed a crime!"

In early 2014, Jerad and Amanda moved from Indiana to Nevada, and they had tried to volunteer for a conservative Clark County sheriff candidate but were turned away when the candidate discovered Jerad's criminal record, which included assault and driving under the influence. For money, Amanda worked at Hobby Lobby, and Jerad dressed up like comic book characters to pose with tourists on the Vegas Strip for tips. He posted a video of himself in garish makeup and green hair like the Joker, giving a political rant about Obama and the New World Order. He bulged his eyes at the ceiling, spread his fingers dramatically, rasping: "[Obama has] also voted for this UN gun treaty that will take away all your guns. Like, what better way to terrorize people when they don't have weapons?"

Hours after the Taser incident at Riverside Road, Jerad interviewed Margaret Houston on video at the protest site, asking Cliven's sister to show him the scratches on her knee and hand. He also interviewed Ryan Bundy. Their four-minute exchange was ordinary enough, but something about the sunken-eyed newcomer made Ryan uncomfortable. Even among the ardent and angry gathering in Bunkerville, there was something odd about the Millers. They seemed too eager, like they were *hoping* the confrontation would blow up.

LaVoy Finicum. Neil Wampler. Eric Parker. Terri "Momma Bear" Linnell. Blaine Cooper and Booda Cavalier. Jerad and Amanda Miller. They were just a handful among the hundreds, then thousands, who arrived at Bundy Ranch for Saturday's big rally.

Few knew each other before April 2014. Some, like Eric Parker and LaVoy Finicum, stayed for a few hours. Others, like Booda Cavalier, remained for days, weeks, months. Some carried secrets that they didn't want their new compatriots to discover, and some told lies. They'd all lived their lives mostly outside the spotlight, mostly on the margins of society. Before long, one by one, they would all become renowned or notorious members of the movement. Before long, several would be locked up, and three would be dead.

A FEW OF THE PEOPLE HEADING TO BUNDY RANCH WERE ALREADY well-known, at least in Patriot circles. Oath Keepers founder Stewart Rhodes flew to Nevada the day after the Santilli video emerged. Rhodes briefly visited Bunkerville but left soon thereafter, and some militiamen got the impression that he wasn't happy to find Ryan Payne running things. After all, Payne wasn't a Patriot big shot. Yes, he'd founded Operation Mutual Aid, but the militia network had never actually launched a successful mobilization, and the Oath Keepers had been doing this kind of thing for years.

The Oath Keepers issued a press release, calling for Patriots to gather at Bunkerville, and specifically citing the Santilli video: "The courage and resolve displayed by Ammon Bundy and his relatives is inspiring, and may well go down in history as a watershed moment—a turning of the tide."

But Rhodes and the Oath Keepers had recognized the import of the Bundy crisis a little too late. It was Ryan Payne who'd been the first militiaman to call Cliven and offer his help. It was Payne who'd driven all the way from Montana and was one of the very first to put boots on the ground in Bunkerville. And even before the Santilli video emerged, it was the fledgling Operation Mutual Aid, not the better-known Oath Keepers, that had mobilized many of the militias that were now streaming toward Bunkerville. Consciously or not, Payne had done what Stewart Rhodes and the Oath Keepers had been trying to do for the last five years—find a trigger event, a flashpoint, an example of federal overreach that had produced outrage, and then harness and mobilize the energy of the moment.

So because he got there first, nobody gained more status than Ryan Payne. With the Bundys' blessing, Payne assumed the all-important role of liaison between the Bundys and the militia, and he went about the job with grim-faced seriousness.

Payne stood out, young and clean-cut compared to most of the militia, who tended to be grizzled, weathered men in their forties to sixties. Payne wore a sidearm but did without the tactical duty belts full of clanking gear that many militia members favored. He wore athletic clothes and baseball caps instead of fatigues. Some of the Patriots were garrulous with each other, rambling into flights of patriotic passion and cloak-and-dagger intrigue. Payne liked to talk, too, but his statements were well constructed, precisely enunciated, and grandiloquent, almost like he'd memorized them from a war movie. He signed letters: "Eternally, your most faithful and humble servant."

Payne set up the militia camp and organized the arriving militia into units. Bundy neighbors who owned the stretch of property between Gold Butte Road and the Virgin River allowed the militia to camp there. A handwritten sign read: "MILITIA SIGHN IN." Non-militia Bundy supporters camped around the protest site. As the weekend approached, more and more tents and campers populated the hills.

Mel Bundy took Payne on tours of the area so the ex-soldier could do surveillance and figure out a strategy. Later Payne said he learned where the high ground was, decided where he'd dispatch snipers, what areas had concrete barriers to set up behind, where the lines of fire were. He said he wanted overwhelming tactical superiority, and he referred often to the Army Ranger handbook he considered his bible.

When Booda Cavalier and Blaine Cooper arrived, Payne detailed Cavalier to Cliven and Carol Bundy's personal security. By his own account, Cavalier was not only a combat vet but a trained bodyguard. One of his first missions as Cliven's security guard occurred Friday morning, when Sean Hannity's correspondent asked the rancher to take his crew on a guided aerial tour. Cavalier volunteered to go along, just in case any feds tried to threaten or intimidate Cliven. They climbed into the helicopter together, and the ride turned out to be a great opportunity for reconnaissance. As the chopper soared low around Bunkerville, Hannity's cameras shot sweeping video of the Virgin River. Then they headed to the BLM command post in Toquop Wash. From the air, it looked even more imposing than from the ground: rows of dozens of vehicles, mobile offices, portable toilets, and, jammed into a series of geometric temporary corrals, hundreds of head of milling cattle. Except for the livestock, the site looked like a stopgap military post in Afghanistan.

During the flight, Cavalier wore shorts and a faded black New Orleans Saints jersey with Drew Brees's number 9 on the front, a holstered sidearm on his hip. If Cliven had any qualms about associating with the hard-drinking man with the eyelid tattoos, the devout and abstinent Mormon didn't show it. In fact, the two men appeared to hit it off, laughing at each other's jokes. As far as Cliven was concerned, if people came to Bundy Ranch and offered their help, the family should welcome the support, no matter who they were.

As usual, Ammon didn't think it was quite that simple.

The last few days in Bunkerville had wrenched him out of his busy but comfortable existence in Phoenix and had upended his beliefs. For all his libertarian leanings, Ammon had worked within the system throughout his entire adult life, and the system had rewarded him. In 2010, for instance, he had wanted to grow Valet Fleet Service and had taken out a $530,000 loan from the Small Business Administration loan program, a federal initiative designed to aid businesses that couldn't obtain financing from private banks. It was profoundly difficult for him to accept the notion that the government was, in fact, his family's enemy.

But then he got tased by government agents, and the shocks jolted him into a revelation. The government was not going to protect his family. The feds had occupied the ranch, and the county law enforcement was too weak to stand up to the invasion. It was up to the *people* to protect themselves from the *government*.

And after the Santilli video, the people came, in vast numbers and from great distances. The incoming flood of supporters ebbed and flowed and spread out over the landscape, so getting an accurate head count was difficult. Ammon believed it was in the thousands. Mel Bundy took charge of telling new arrivals where to camp. Dave hauled a flatbed trailer to the protest site and turned it into a makeshift stage. Ryan rigged up a water truck so people could take showers. Ammon handled food. The family slaughtered a couple of cattle, butchering them in a shed they'd installed for that purpose. Donations flowed in, trucks arriving with food and water. Mismatched cartons of bottled water were stacked in a pile the size of a pickup truck. Some donations were made anonymously, some came with supportive notes. A delivery vehicle from a Mesquite restaurant pulled up, and the driver had sixty pizzas. A supporter all the way from Finland had ordered them for the protesters.

The furor made Ammon both grateful and anxious. He wondered why these people cared about the Bundys. And what did his family really know about the new arrivals? Most were strangers, and some of the militia were clearly hard-living characters, drinkers, smokers. It was disorienting to see his quiet boyhood home invaded by men who cursed and bore tattoos. On the other hand, the militia seemed organized and professional to Ammon. They might not have known much about the range wars, but they appeared sincere in their concern for the Bundys' constitutional rights. One militiaman with a rifle stationed himself outside the travel trailer where Ammon slept all week, and this greatly impressed Ammon, the fact that this man was willing to risk everything to protect a stranger.

BACK IN PHOENIX, LISA HAD DECIDED TO HEAD TO BUNDY RANCH TOO.

On Wednesday, she'd been sitting in her car outside her children's school, waiting to pick them up, when she checked Facebook on her phone. She came across a post from Ammon's cousin asking for prayers, and she suddenly felt certain that something had happened to Ammon. She called Carol, who told her Ammon was okay, but he'd been tased.

She brought the kids home and finally connected with Ammon, who assured her he was okay. The kids were too young for phones, so they hadn't seen any news from Bunkerville. They knew their grandfather was fighting the government over the ranch, but Lisa wasn't sure how to explain to them what had happened to their father without terrifying them. She did her best.

Lisa's first instinct was to stay at home with her children. She avoided the Santilli video. But when she finally watched it and saw how her husband remained upright during the tasings, she knew she had to go to him. Ammon's cousin, who lived nearby, took the children for the weekend, and Lisa flew to Las Vegas on Friday. A sister-in-law picked her up and drove her to the protest site, where hundreds of people were gathered. Flags flew high on the two poles. Flanked by men with guns, Ammon and Cliven were giving a joint interview to Fox News.

When she saw this, Lisa knew that her world would never be the same, that her blissful family life in Phoenix was already part of the past.

Each morning, the Bundys gathered at the ranch for food and prayer. Cliven liked a big breakfast most days—meat, potatoes, and Tabasco sauce. Despite this ritual of family unity, nerves would wear thin as the day wore on. While Cliven had occasionally made headlines over the years, the Bundy family wasn't accustomed to being at the epicenter of a major developing news story. Some of the Bundy siblings wanted to stay out of the spotlight, but a number of them took part in the news coverage, which led to miscues, yelling, and slammed phones. Still, the Bundys had surprising media skills for a family from the remote desert. The third-youngest sibling, Bailey, age twenty-two, had taken over the Bundy Ranch blog, adding a donations button and a linked Facebook account. By Friday, a few days after Bailey launched it, the Bundy Ranch Facebook page had fifteen thousand followers, and more than $2,000 in donations had trickled in.

At the Bundy house, the phones rang constantly. On Monday, Cliven's impromptu press conference in the Las Vegas 7-Eleven parking lot had attracted only a handful of local reporters. Now, just a few days later, Shawna Cox could barely keep up with interview requests from all over the world. To relieve the pressure of having to speak to every reporter individually, the family eventually decided to hold a single 1 PM press conference each day at the protest site. But there were also talk show hosts and journalists from websites and radio stations and publications all over the country who wanted to speak to Cliven over the phone. Cliven didn't want to give up any opportunity to tell his story, so he spent most of the week in his bedroom, doing one phone interview after another. Midweek, several hundred locals turned out at a town meeting in nearby Moapa to hear him speak, and almost all of them blamed the feds for the dispute, many complaining that the Gold Butte shutdown was killing Lake Mead tourism. When one man ventured that he paid his grazing fees and perhaps Cliven Bundy should, too, the crowd audibly growled.

While the Bundys appeared to be winning the war of images and words, that damaging phrase kept coming up: grazing fees. Specifically that Cliven Bundy owed more than $1.1 million of them to the BLM. Which wasn't really true. The feds charged about sixteen dollars to graze a cow-calf pair for a year. So even if Cliven had been grazing one thousand head since 1993, which is a vast overestimation of his herd throughout that time, he'd have owed about $340,000. The truth was, most of that $1.1 million was in fines and administrative costs the feds had assessed in their various cattle counts. But most news stories simply reported that number as the amount Cliven hadn't paid. Which in turn led many commentators to use descriptors like "deadbeat rancher" and "welfare cowboy."

Despite their efforts, the family found it impossible to control the message, because reporters went to the protest site and talked to anybody who was willing. A reporter from the CBS affiliate in Las Vegas interviewed Jim Lardy, a big-bearded West Mountain Rangers militiaman who rode to Bunkerville from Montana with Ryan Payne. The news camera lingered on Lardy's big green AR-15 assault rifle with its twenty-round magazine.

"Why the gun?" Lardy said, and then gestured at the sweep of backcountry where the feds were gathering cattle. "Well, they have guns. We need guns to protect ourselves from a tyrannical government."

That wasn't exactly the image Ammon wanted to portray. He preferred the protesters to look like cowboys, not heavily armed anarchists. He wanted to educate the public about the fact that the federal government controlled around 80 percent of the landmass of Nevada, which was something that few of the incoming supporters knew much about.

But Ammon also believed the Bundys needed hard men like Lardy and Payne. He knew he was toeing a line when he asked people to be careful what weapons they brought to the big upcoming rally on Saturday. He admired and appreciated the militiaman guarding his trailer with a rifle, but he wanted the cameras to capture horses and flags, not assault rifles.

"We don't mind that you carry sidearms in camp, but we ask that you don't carry rifles," he told the militia.

UNLIKE AMMON, WHO HAD DELIBERATELY CHOSEN TO BE UNARMED, MOST of the week Ryan Bundy wore a wooden-grip revolver in a leather belt holster, a real cowboy's gun. Like their father, Ryan was less inclined than Ammon to worry over the details. Besides, he'd had an experience earlier in the week that had fortified his faith that everything was going to work out in the Bundys' favor.

The insight had come during a fast. When Ryan was looking for divine guidance, he sometimes would stop eating and drinking for a few days. Fasting on the first Sunday of each month is a Mormon tradition, but Ryan took the practice further, going on multiday fasts since he was young. One of his early fasts had become a family legend. It had happened when he was a student at Virgin Valley Elementary School in Mesquite. Cliven was still married to Jane, who had signed up the kids for a free school-lunch program. The family was financially strapped at the time. Cliven opposed the free lunches, and he quarreled with Jane. He didn't want the children to think that government handouts were okay. Ryan absorbed his father's message and one day just refused to eat lunch. The cafeteria staff tried to coax him into eating, but Ryan wouldn't. He didn't eat that night either. Or the next day.

Three days later, as family lore had it, Jane went back to packing lunch for all five kids.

When the roundup began, Ryan wanted spiritual direction, so he stopped eating and drinking. The first day was the hardest, as his stomach was shrinking. The second day was painful as well. Sometimes he took a sip of water, but he didn't want to fill his stomach and trigger hunger pains. But on the third day, as his body began to feed on its own fat stores, Ryan felt a return of energy. And on the fourth day, Tuesday night, as he was driving north on Interstate 15, Ryan suddenly knew what would happen.

It wasn't a vision, like looking at a movie screen. He didn't "see" anything. It was simply an understanding, a foreknowledge, of the events that were going to take place on Saturday in Bunkerville. He knew his father would triumph, and he knew it would happen Saturday.

He'd had moments like this before, during his LDS mission and, most powerfully, on the night in Orderville in 1994 when he watched his father lecture at the Wise Use meeting about the proper form of government, and the Lord had told him that Cliven had been right to fire the BLM. But Ryan had never before known the future, and this understanding was accompanied by an amazing feeling of enlightenment. Driving north on the interstate, Ryan had felt close to God, and it was wonderful, wonderful. Saturday, Ryan believed, would be a mighty victory for the Bundys.

For the first five days of the roundup, the BLM's hired cowboys brought in cattle at a good clip, averaging about seventy head a day. But then things slowed down. On Thursday, the day after the Santilli video exploded onto the internet, the cowboys captured only twenty-five animals, for a total of 377. BLM officials knew it would probably take weeks to get the remaining five hundred. The cattle they'd collected so far were mostly the ones that grazed and watered closer to the Virgin River and were more accustomed to the sight of humans. The back-country herds were wild and wily, with bulls that would gore a cow-boy's horse if the rider wasn't careful.

Complicating matters further, Ryan Bundy had been organizing protests at the livestock auction house in Utah, and the auction house had backed out of the contract. This meant the cattle already gathered would remain packed into the corrals at the BLM command post until they could find another alternative. They found one in Arizona, but that fell through. Then they found a stockyard in Ontario, California. The Bundy supporters somehow learned about it and posted the auc-tion house's contact information on Facebook.

All the way back in Washington, DC, the agency's second-in-command, Acting Deputy Director Steve Ellis, a BLM lifer since 1979, had seen the Santilli video and was thinking about flying to Nevada. Federal intelligence analysts were monitoring social media accounts connected to the Bundys and known militia groups. As soon as the Santilli video went viral, the analysts began getting more and more hits: militia members all over the country were talking about the Bundys and many seemed to be traveling to Bunkerville.

On Friday, Adam Sully was instructed to go undercover again. This time, the BLM special agent wouldn't just dip in and out. The analysts were concerned the roundup could turn violent, and the BLM needed Sully to monitor the situation from the inside. Sully and his partner went to a thrift store and bought some used Western clothing. They also rented two cars in Las Vegas and booked a hotel room in St. George. They were being careful because the Bundys seemed to have eyes everywhere. Sully didn't want to be seen driving a government car or turning off the highway onto the BLM command post. The agents couldn't afford to blow their cover. Sully studied photos of several individuals, including Ryan Payne and the Bundy brothers, and was advised to pay special attention to anything they did or said.

PETE SANTILLI WAS AN EVER-PRESENT IRRITATION FOR THE BLM. IMMEDIately after arriving in Bunkerville on Wednesday morning, even before the tasing incident, Santilli had gone to the command post in Toquop Wash to ask about getting media credentials. Dan Love, the BLM commander, met him. Love was furious that individuals like Pete Santilli were steering the public's understanding of the roundup, furious that the BLM wasn't more aggressively countering the Bundy family's propaganda campaign. Love believed the BLM's passive approach to public relations was adding to his own headaches by triggering the Patriot flood to Bunkerville. He'd raged about this to his superiors all week, to no avail.

Now, as interstate traffic roared past nearby, Santilli introduced himself to Love as a radio talk show host who was there to both report on the incident and act as a liaison between the Bundy followers and the BLM. Santilli said he didn't want anyone to get hurt. "What are you going to do if ten thousand people show up?" he demanded. "Are you prepared for this?"

Santilli was obsessed with that number—a crowd of ten thousand. On Thursday, he estimated that about fifty militia had shown up, but Santilli could see in his mind the splendid image of several brigades worth of armed Patriots marching toward the command post, demanding that the cows be returned, that the land be opened. There'd be no way to arrest that many people, no way for the government to reasonably respond, except to back down, which was the most thrilling scenario Santilli could imagine. He repeated that number as he did Skype interviews with various Patriot commentators around the country. "We need ten thousand people to come here," he said. The head count in Bunkerville gradually grew into the thousands, but it never reached Santilli's magic number. .

Over the next few days, the shock jock seemed to be everywhere. Santilli confronted BLM rangers who were providing security for the contract cowboys gathering cattle. At night, he drove through the parking lot of the Holiday Inn Express where the BLM personnel were staying, shining a flashlight on federal vehicles, and then going inside to ask the receptionist how many BLM employees were there. Early Friday morning, Santilli returned to the command post to talk to Dan Love again. Both Santilli and Love had alpha-dog personalities and intractable opposing views, and both men were voluble.

Santilli said thousands of people were coming, and they were going to demand the return of the cattle.

"It's going to be nonnegotiable," Santilli said. "I want to make sure that any individual with the BLM is given the opportunity to stand down."

Love had heard enough and interrupted: "That's not gonna happen. So here's the deal . . ."

Santilli tried to continue, but Love kept going.

"I understand that you think what you're doing is right," Love said. "But that Constitution you speak of—we actually have two federal court orders issued by two federal judges. If you impede or interfere, you will be arrested. You will be taken into custody."

"If you choose to go face-to-face and people get hurt, we're going to hold you personally accountable," Santilli said.

"And I'm going to hold you legally accountable," Love said. "And I guarantee you, the Constitution is on my side."

Santilli said that if the BLM agents didn't abide by the Constitution, they would be arrested. Love was incredulous.

"I don't know how you plan on arresting me, but good luck with that," the BLM agent said.

"Well, there's going to be some law-enforcement officers going to jail after this is done," Santilli said.

"I've seen your numbers right now, and you better hope ten thousand show up, because if you show up with those numbers, we got plenty of people here to take all those people to jail," Love said.

Santilli said the feds had incited the problem.

"We're lawfully here," Love said patiently. "You see all these signs? You're in a closed area on federal land. You don't have to like it, but it's the law."

"It is not federal land," Santilli said.

"It is federal land," Love said.

"You think so?"

"I'm positive."

"I bet you lunch," Santilli said.

"Mr. Santilli, if you were right, I wouldn't have a job," Love said. "So you know what? Be right, get it changed, and then I'm happy not to wear this little gold shield I have on my hip."

"You're managing this land," Santilli explained. "You're not the owner of the land."

"If that's your theory, do it the legal way: Go get the sheriff and come on down here and make it happen."

Santilli uttered a spontaneous grunt of frustration. Both men ran out of words for a moment, at an impasse, each man positive he was right. And that was the moment they found something they could agree on.

"I'm very concerned at this point," Santilli said.

"I'm very concerned too," Love said.

Three hours later, Adam Sully got to the protest site. It was around 10:30 AM, and the agent was struck by the difference in atmosphere since his first visit on Monday. It wasn't just the Bundys and their neighbors any longer. He saw license plates from California, Idaho, Montana. The crowd was much larger and included many men in fatigues and camouflage. Sully counted about twenty people with firearms, including several assault rifles.

Sully had a memorable exchange with a camo-swathed man who said he had brought better firepower than the BLM. The man disparaged the growing ranks of Bundy supporters who didn't belong to a militia.

The man said: *They're just a bunch of drum-beating hippies.*

Cliven Bundy showed up to the rally around 1 PM, and this time, he was accompanied by five armed men. They escorted him to a makeshift stage and faced the audience. One of the bodyguards had an earpiece, and another a radio. On the hillside across the road, Sully counted four men with rifles providing security from the high ground.

Sully left the rally around 3:30 PM and drove to his hotel in St. George. He and his partner briefed their team leader on the change in atmosphere at the protest site, and how in the span of five days, Cliven Bundy had transformed from an angry but isolated rancher into some sort of local warlord. Sully said he didn't think the BLM should continue the roundup. The cattle weren't worth risking lives.

Sully said: *It's too dangerous.*

Around the time Sully was leaving the rally, an employee at the Holiday Inn Express in Mesquite told a BLM special agent that the front desk had received a half-dozen threatening calls. One caller told an employee to eject the BLM personnel staying there or the hotel wouldn't be standing in the morning.

121

One caller said: *If you don't kick those pigs out of the hotel, you'll be dragged out into the parking lot and shot dead.*

Three hours later, at 6 PM, Dan Love and his boss and the other key operation officials gathered in the command trailer for a conference call. On the other end of the line was top brass in the Department of the Interior as well as an FBI deputy assistant director who did most of the talking. What he said was chilling.

The FBI believed what was happening at Bundy Ranch was historic. In the twenty years since the Militia of Montana had been formed, effectively launching the modern militia movement, the FBI had never witnessed a Patriot event of this size and scope. If the BLM continued to gather cattle, the deputy assistant director said, it could be a flashpoint. If the BLM attempted to transport the cattle, it could be a flashpoint. If the BLM fled the area en masse, it could be a flashpoint. Any of those triggering events could end in a bloodbath. He recommended that the BLM end the operation immediately and try to negotiate a peaceful exit.

Even the brash Love was daunted. After the conference call ended, Love met with his boss, and they decided to conclude the roundup.

But that didn't mean the job was over. They still had to dismantle the command post and find a way to get everything and everyone out of there safely. It had taken ten days to get the roundup operation up and running. Taking it down would take at least a day or two. There were trailers, lights, corrals, vehicles, heavy equipment.

And 377 head of cattle. Cattle that had taken millions of dollars and thousands of man-hours to gather. Historic threat or not, Dan Love would be damned if he'd let those cattle go.

Chapter 5

STANDOFF AT TOQUOP WASH

L aVoy Finicum was the first cowboy to arrive at the protest site on Saturday morning.

Only one day had passed since he'd decided to drive from the vision-boarding conference in Salt Lake City to visit the Bundys for the first time. Then he'd driven home that night and broken the news to Jeanette that he was heading back to Bunkerville in the morning to stand with the Bundys at the big rally. He got up before dawn, loaded his roan mare, Esperanza, into a trailer and drove to Bunkerville. He was unarmed, having taken his rifle out of its scabbard and the scabbard off the saddle, leaving both at home. This was unusual for Finicum—he typically carried wherever he went.

Minus the gun, he wore full cowboy regalia—a cream Stetson

over his bald head, fringed leather chaps, leather gloves, and a rag kerchief loosely knotted around his neck.

At the protest site, he saddled up Esperanza and waited, watching people trickle in. Several were from the Cane Beds area. Finicum greeted them, surprised. He didn't know they were coming.

AT THE BUNDY HOUSE, SHAWNA COX WAS ALREADY UP AND WORKING around 7 AM, reviewing the day's schedule. The Bundys' self-appointed spokeswoman and general assistant had turned the eating area into her war room, the kitchen table into her desk. The rally at the protest site was supposed to start at 9 AM. There would be speeches accompanied by a lot of cowboy pageantry and Patriot spectacle for the TV cameras.

Various groups of Bundy relatives bustled through the house. Carol Bundy stopped by Shawna's makeshift desk.

Carol said: *Have you received a priesthood blessing, Shawna?*

Cox said she had not, but she would love one.

Cox followed Carol into the master bedroom. Cliven and a son-in-law were inside. The men rested their hands on her head, anointing her with sacred oil. They recited a blessing of peace and strength. Cox's eyes filled with tears.

One by one, Cox and the Bundys dispersed, heading to their various assignments. But Cliven didn't budge from the brown leather couch in the living room, even as the rally start time came and went. Sheriff Gillespie had agreed to come to the Bunkerville protest site this morning to speak to Cliven about the situation. But Cliven refused to head to the protest site until he got word that the sheriff had arrived there.

As the week had gone on and the furor had intensified, Cliven had embraced the magnitude of the role that was being thrust upon him. The fight was bigger than Cliven Bundy, yet "Cliven Bundy" had become the fight. His name was on everybody's lips. His face was on millions of TV screens. Which is perhaps why Cliven had taken to referring to himself in the third person.

He'd woken up around 3 AM, knowing what to do. The Constitution was hanging by a thread, just as Joseph Smith had prophesied, and it seemed to Cliven that this showdown in Bunkerville was the crucial moment, and that he, Cliven Bundy, had been chosen as the citizen who would deliver the message that would save the United States of America from destruction. Through Cliven, God was revealing His will to the entire country, and only Cliven knew what His message was.

The sheriff was the highest elected law-enforcement official in the land, but on this day the sheriff would have to wait for Cliven Bundy.

AFTER HIS LONG DRIVE FROM IDAHO AND IMPROMPTU GUARD-DUTY STINT, Eric Parker woke up around 7 AM in a cluster of tents at the militia camp near the river. He pulled his ballistic vest over a flannel shirt, put on a black baseball cap, and made his way to the militia headquarters, an open-air milking barn, for instructions.

The militiamen running the show briefed him. They were doing background checks because there were a good number of weirdos flowing into the camp, including one guy who carried an English broadsword everywhere he went—he'd been asked to leave, along with some others. Unstable folks could inflame the situation, Parker was told.

The leaders wanted Parker and his buddies to handle crowd control at the protest site. So he went there around 9 AM and found it was getting hard to nab a parking spot. Hundreds of vehicles, campers, tents were jammed into the stretch of Riverside Road on the north side of the bridge over the Virgin River. Militia members in fatigues, cowboys in Western gear, and everyday people in shorts and T-shirts roamed around, spilling onto the road. The stage was bedecked in American flags and colorful bunting, including a big yellow-and-brown Oath Keepers banner. Microphones awaited Cliven's arrival.

CLOSE TO 9:30 AM, A BLACK-AND-WHITE PICKUP TRUCK WITH RED AND BLUE lights and "POLICE" on the side pulled up, a silver sedan behind. Sheriff Gillespie and three khaki-uniformed deputies got out of the sedan, to the astonishment of some in the crowd who didn't believe the sheriff had the nerve to show.

Sheriff Gillespie's plan was to meet with Cliven in private to figure out how to resolve the conflict without bloodshed. He and the deputies walked up the road toward the stage and then bowed their heads with the rest of the crowd for a group prayer. The deputies eyed the rifles and sidearms around them, wondering whether these men knew how to handle a firearm safely. This wasn't what they'd expected.

Dave Bundy escorted the sheriff's officials to Ammon's travel trailer adjacent to the rally stage. Ryan Bundy was inside. Ryan called his father at the ranch house, and Cliven said he didn't want the sheriff to come to the house. He'd meet the sheriff in front of the people.

AMMON BUNDY TOOK THE STAGE AND TOLD THE CROWD THAT HIS FAMILY was amazed by the country's fevered reaction to their story.

"How many of us were in kind of our own little world before this?" Ammon said. "Thinking that we have these thoughts and these beliefs, but thinking there weren't very many people out there with those same thoughts and same beliefs. Thinking that we have these problems and these challenges, but we might be the only ones having them. Today, we know that it's not like that."

Ammon's words captured Neil Wampler's feelings. The ex-hippie from California had been in heaven ever since he'd arrived in

Bunkerville a couple days earlier. He'd been to some small demonstrations before, but this felt different. The fellowship and energy were stronger and more spontaneous. It was like an impromptu and chaotic national convention for liberty-minded folks. He'd slept in his ancient Plymouth and spent the days just tripping on the scene, trading theories about gun rights and federal civil-asset forfeiture with anyone who would listen. He was excited to see the real-live cowboys, local guys, mostly, who kept to themselves, taciturn and not that interested in getting to know all these yammering Patriots from other places. When the pizzas ordered by the supporter in Finland were delivered, Wampler had torn off a box top and had people sign their names and hometowns on the cardboard as a memento.

TWENTY MINUTES AFTER THE SHERIFF ARRIVED, AS A DIFFERENT SPEAKER was holding forth, heavy-duty engines rumbled. Heads turned to see a convoy arriving. A silver pickup truck with a half-dozen fatigues-clad militiamen in back was followed by a broad-beamed black Humvee and another pickup behind it. Men got out of the Humvee and opened the rear doors, and Cliven and Carol stepped out. A squad of militia members escorted them to the stage, and the crowd parted as if the Bundys were royalty. On Cliven's right flank, his bodyguard, Booda Cavalier, stood out among the security in his casual shorts and black T-shirt. One of the Bundy boys started to tell Cliven that Sheriff Gillespie was ready to speak to him, but the old rancher just brushed by, saying he'd meet the sheriff on the stage.

Cliven and the sheriff boarded the stage, and a row of eight or nine stone-faced Arizona State Militia members formed a human wall between them and the crowd, arms crossed behind their backs, chests out. Ammon asked the crowd to be respectful and handed the microphone to Gillespie, who looked a little nonplussed to be addressing a thousand riled-up Patriots. Cliven just stared at him, arms folded tightly above his belly, hands in the armpits of his starched white Western shirt.

"Um, Cliven, my purpose this morning is to continue to keep a very emotional issue safe," the sheriff said. "That being said, I believe a press release has already been put forth that the BLM is going to cease this operation."

The crowd exploded, whooping, hollering. The sheriff grinned. Unsurprised by the revelation, Cliven stood stock-still and stared hard at the sheriff. When the hoopla died down, Gillespie continued.

"The Gold Butte allotment will be reopened to the public."

More cheers.

Watching from his crowd-control position at the rear of the throng, Eric Parker thought: *I guess we came a long way for nothing. Looks like we're heading back to Idaho. It's over.*

"What I would hope is to sit down with you and talk about how that is facilitated in a safe way," Gillespie said.

A man watching from the hillside across the road said to his buddy: "Yeah, they get the fuck out. They pack up and leave. That's it."

"You and I have had the ability to sit down and talk before on a number of occasions," Gillespie continued. "We may not have always agreed, but we have been respectful of each other's opinions and of the process."

Cliven just gazed at Gillespie, arms folded, giving him nothing.

"But the next steps is something you and I should talk about," the sheriff said.

A man yelled from the crowd: "Where's the cows?"

Gillespie wrapped up his brief statement and didn't clarify what was going to happen to the cattle. Cliven stepped to the bunting-wrapped podium, put on his reading glasses, took the microphone. Gillespie backed off a couple steps and watched the rancher turn to the crowd.

"Good morning, citizens of Clark County, Nevada!" Cliven said, grandly. "Good morning, America! Good morning, world! It really is a beautiful day in Bunkerville."

Cliven meandered for a few moments, basking in the crowd's enthusiasm. Eric Parker was not impressed with his first glimpse of the man at the center of the fray. He could barely follow what Cliven Bundy was talking about. Cliven eventually got to the point, turning to address Gillespie face-to-face. It was time to deliver the divine commandment he'd received this morning.

"Sheriff, this is what we the people are asking this morning."

He paused.

"Disarm the Park Service at Lake Mead . . ."

The crowd bellowed at the audacious suggestion. The sheriff squinted at Cliven, thumb hooked in his gun belt.

". . . and Red Rock park and all the other parks the federal government claims they have jurisdiction over. Take your county bulldozers and loaders and tear down the entrance places where they ticket us. You take the equipment out there and tear down those things this morning."

"Immediately!" one man bellowed.

A few in the crowd glanced at each other quizzically.

Growing more vehement, Cliven repeated that he wanted the sheriff to take away federal rangers' guns.

"We want those arms delivered right here under these flags in one hour," Cliven said, thrusting his notes at the sheriff.

Sheriff Gillespie ran a hand over his head, looking bemused. He was supposed to take away the federal government's guns? In one hour?

"One hour!" Cliven said. "We're gonna stand here one hour!"

Cliven cradled the microphone, turned away from Gillespie. The sheriff tried to catch Cliven's eye, and then turned to Ammon.

Ammon said: *I'm not the negotiator here, Sheriff.*

Gillespie glanced back once at Cliven, who had plunked himself down on a table and folded his arms again. And then the sheriff left, threading his way through the crowd and back to his vehicle, moving briskly. Some men on the hillside jeered.

"Get a pair, Gillespie, get a pair! Grow some nuts!"

Eric Parker was simply bewildered. Disarm the Park Service? What the fuck had he gotten himself into here?

SHERIFF GILLESPIE AND HIS OFFICERS DID NOT ATTEMPT TO DISARM THE Park Service or the BLM, but they did drive to the BLM command post to relay Cliven's demands.

The command post was on high alert. Security forces had been doubled. A team of lookouts was stationed on Flat Top Mesa, a mile northeast. Dan Love hadn't gotten much sleep the night before, and neither had most of his agents.

Sheriff Gillespie told Love that Cliven Bundy meant business. He'd never let the BLM truck all of the cattle away, not without putting up a fight. And he had a lot of angry armed people backing him now.

Gillespie said: *I think you should just release the cattle.*

The BLM commander flatly denied the sheriff's request. The cattle had been illegally grazing on federal land for decades. Love hadn't gotten all of Cliven's herd, but he certainly wouldn't give the captured ones back. Cliven Bundy may have forced the BLM to demobilize the roundup, but they'd be taking the cattle with them when they left.

He said: *Those cattle are federal property now, and what happens to them is my decision.*

Sheriff Gillespie didn't force the issue. When the meeting was over, he headed to Las Vegas to meet with the governor about the crisis, leaving behind his assistant sheriff, Joe Lombardo.

LIKE A WEDDING PLANNER, SHAWNA COX MOVED AROUND THE CROWD AT the protest site, her reading glasses on a string around her neck, checking her phone. She was pleased with the event she'd helped orchestrate. While the crowd waited for the sheriff to return, they passed the time watching some cowboy pageantry. About forty men and women on horseback lined a ridge across the road, and Arden, Cliven's sixteen-year-old son, planted an American flag atop. The crowd marveled at a formation of geese that repeatedly circled over the general airspace of the command post. A spontaneous cheer broke out: "USA! USA!"

Cox traded text messages with a congressman in Utah, who told her that he'd confirmed the BLM was backing down. The congressman messaged: *Don't do anything crazy.*

Cox headed for the stage to show Cliven the text, confirmation that the BLM was indeed giving up. Before Cox could reach Cliven, the rancher picked up the microphone. It was around 11:15 AM, and more than an hour had passed since Cliven had given the sheriff his deadline.

"His time is up," Cliven said. "Now we're gonna go and take our land back and declare freedom and liberty here in this land. Is God gonna be with us?"

Whoops from the crowd.

"Cliven Bundy's gonna turn the cattle out on his farm," Cliven said. "They're gonna go out on the open range where they belong."

More applause, and Cliven got specific about the plan.

"We need a little bit of safety here," Cliven said. "We're gonna go up the freeway. We're gonna block the freeway. When we get to Toquop Wash, we're gonna get out of our cars and go open the corrals. The horse people are gonna ride up to Powerline Road and gonna meet us at the Toquop bridge. Get 'er going, cowboys! Let's get 'er done!"

The cowboys spurred their horses down the hill and onto a dirt road that led toward Toquop Wash. LaVoy Finicum noticed that a handful in the posse had rifles in their scabbards or sidearms on their hips, but most, like himself, were unarmed.

Lisa Bundy had been delivering water to the riders on the hill. She ran down and found Ammon.

Lisa said: *Are we really doing this?*

Ammon said: *Yes, we are.*

They got in his truck to head for Toquop Wash. A Fox News reporter ran up and asked for a ride. Ammon said sure, and the man jumped in.

AT HOME IN ARIZONA, JEANETTE FINICUM COULD NOT REACH LAVOY.

She had no cable TV, so she looked for stories on Infowars, whose top headlines were all about Bundy. "Federal Thieves Forcefully Strip Rancher of Property." "SPLC Labels Cliven Bundy Domestic Terrorist." "Report Claims Cell Towers in Bundy Ranch Area Shut Down." Was that why she couldn't reach LaVoy?

The top headline was most distressing: "The Cliven Bundy Standoff: Wounded Knee Revisited?" The story was accompanied by a grainy black-and-white photo of dead Lakota warriors, killed by the US government, on the snowy 1890 battlefield.

Jeanette called a friend she knew was in Clark County and got through. Her friend said everybody was heading toward the federal compound in Toquop Wash, including LaVoy on Esperanza.

TOQUOP WASH IS A RAVINE DOTTED WITH MESQUITE AND SAGEBRUSH, ITS steep sandy banks flanking a wide, flat wash bottom. It's typically dry, but during storms the wash fills with waters that flow down into the

Virgin River. High above the wash bottom, two bridges arc overhead—the divided northbound and southbound highways of Interstate 15.

Underneath the southbound bridge, the BLM had erected a makeshift cattle fence to prevent unauthorized people from reaching the command post area a half-mile away. Two federal officers guarded an entrance gate beneath the bridge.

The officers heard on the radio that Bundy supporters were headed their way. Then they saw a group of them gathering underneath the northbound bridge, about the length of a football field from the BLM entrance gate. The officers called for backup.

At the command post, Dan Love burst out of his office trailer and pointed at his subordinate.

Love said: *They're coming. Get everyone to the gate.*

ERIC PARKER WAS STILL CONFUSED. WHEN THE SHERIFF SAID THE BLM was ceasing operations, he assumed the cows were coming home. Now it sounded like the Bundy supporters were going to get the cows. He also didn't know what or where this Toquop Wash was. Nevertheless, the crowd was moving, and Parker went along. He and his two buddies from Idaho piled into a truck that belonged to one of their militia camp neighbors, and they sped to Interstate 15.

Despite his uncertainty, Parker fired off a cocksure Facebook post: "Bundy gave the sheriff one hour to disarm the BLM. He did not reply. We are now going to free the cattle by any means. The sheriff claimed that the BLM is standing down, but offered no proof. This is when Mr. Bundy gave him the do-it-or-else. We will not be lied to."

The protesters cruised toward Toquop Wash, militiamen crowded into pickup truck beds, flags rippling in the breeze. Several people carried yellow Gadsden flags—like the ones used during the American Revolution—with the crude coiled serpent and the words "Don't Tread

On Me." Before they reached the northbound bridge over the wash, everybody pulled off the interstate to the right, turning an expanse of desert into a massive impromptu parking lot. Traffic slowed to a standstill on the interstate, so Parker hopped out of the truck, leaving his rifle inside, and walked to the new protest site. Local and state police weren't hassling anyone. In fact, a row of Las Vegas Metro Police patrol cars escorted the lead pack of protesters down the highway, and then deputies began directing traffic, waving arriving protesters into the parking area. Parker chatted with other Bundy supporters, trying to get his bearings, figure out where the BLM command post was, where the cows were.

A plane did low, lazy circle eights in the sky, and two helicopters buzzed around. A woman holding a collapsible telescope told Parker there were snipers atop a nearby mesa, about a mile to the northeast. He peered through the telescope and saw several figures. The sun glinted off one, and Parker believed the flash might be a reflection from a rifle scope. Unnerved, Parker went to the truck and retrieved his Saiga .223.

Another woman hurried up the slope.

She said: *The feds are pointing weapons at the people in the wash!*

Everyone began moving toward the dusty ravine.

AMMON AND LISA HAD PARKED AND THEN MADE THEIR WAY TO THE BOTTOM of the wash underneath the northbound bridge. Protesters were climbing down the banks into the wash, following them. Ammon held out his hands, signaling everyone to stop. He didn't want the group to enter the wash until they had superior numbers.

Lisa looked up the ravine toward the southbound bridge. On the other side of the BLM entrance gate, white ranger pickups were pulling up, and federal agents were massing, carrying rifles.

Shawna Cox led the group of several dozen protesters as they knelt on the rocky slope and bowed their heads in prayer. Then, at Ammon's instruction, the group formed a line and swung out across the wash, facing the BLM troops like an old-fashioned infantry line, except that few of them were armed and most wore T-shirts and jeans.

Over a bullhorn, a BLM officer near the other bridge ordered them to leave. A couple of protesters began to comply, but Ammon urged them to stay.

He said: *We must stand together. Whatever it takes. If it takes two days, we will stay here. We'll bring in food and water.*

Other protesters seemed to be in a fever, pacing, cursing, threatening to just charge toward the southbound bridge. Decades of wrath bubbled up inside them. This was the moment they'd waited for all these years, a rebellion, a mass rejection of federal authority, and they didn't want to wait. Lisa didn't like the cursing and was about to speak up, but Ammon spoke first.

He said: *We don't need any of that. We're not here to act that way.*

His words seemed to calm the agitated people.

Ammon wanted to wait until the cowboys arrived before confronting the feds. Lisa held Ammon's hand and looked at the federal agents assembling under the other bridge. About eight figures crouched behind the doors of their white BLM ranger pickups. They wore olive-drab fatigues and helmets, and they carried a tear-gas launcher and rifles. Another group wore plain clothes but had body armor and rifles. They looked like a small army. Lisa tried to stay calm for Ammon, but she couldn't fathom what was happening. This was over cows?

She said to Ammon: *We have five children at home who need a mom and a dad. Are you sure this is the right thing to do?*

THE COWBOYS KICKED UP A CLOUD OF DUST AS THEY RODE DOWN THE SLOPE into Toquop Wash and broke through the line of protesters underneath the northbound bridge. They slowed their horses to a walk as they moved toward the feds, and then paused about halfway between the bridges to form a ragged line. LaVoy Finicum raised a jaunty hand and waved at the people on foot already there, then urged Esperanza to a position on the east side of the wash.

During the ride, a Bundy son-in-law had given the posse hard-bitten instructions. Provoke no one. Speak to no one. Form a line and advance toward the feds. Stand your ground. Show no fear.

The protesters on foot followed, hands raised toward the sky. They were mostly men, but a good number of women, and even a couple of kids. By now, more than four hundred Bundy supporters were spread around the area, and more than half were in the wash, including about forty on horseback. They faced some thirty federal officers on the other side of the gate.

Word trickled through the line of protesters: Let the unarmed people go first. Terri "Momma Bear" Linnell was carrying a pink pistol in a holster, so she let the others pass her, and she took pictures of the flag-wavers in front of her, of the horses' rear ends, of a surveillance plane in the sky. She looked off to the side of the wash and was surprised to see a group of young children playing on the bank, out of the line of fire, as if nothing was happening.

"You're going to have to arrest us all or shoot us all!" one protester yelled.

Linnell didn't believe the federal agents would shoot into the crowd. Previous protests had taught Momma Bear that there was strength in numbers, and the protesters vastly outnumbered the feds. On the other hand, her parents had been students at Kent State University in 1970, when members of the Ohio National Guard had shot and killed four students during a mass protest. So Linnell knew it could happen. At least this time, Linnell thought, the protesters could shoot back.

The line began advancing toward the feds under the southbound bridge. It was high noon.

ERIC PARKER MOVED IN THE DIRECTION HE THOUGHT WOULD TAKE HIM TO the wash, and he ended up on top of the northbound bridge instead of underneath it with Ammon's group of protesters. Traffic was almost completely blocked, backing up for miles, as Bundy supporters wandered freely on the highway.

Parker looked through binoculars at the feds gathering underneath the southbound bridge. He heard the droning voice from a bullhorn below the other bridge say something about being authorized to take lethal force. Or maybe it was nonlethal force. It was hard to hear with the shouting, the traffic passing slowly behind him, the swirling winds.

Parker crouched behind the bridge's concrete barrier. There was a two-inch engineered vertical crevice in the concrete. Kind of like a gun slit in a military fort. Parker lay down on the sun-warmed asphalt and slid his Saiga .223 into the crack. The opening was narrow, and his rifle had only iron sights, no scope. Through the crack, Parker could see about two-thirds of the width of the wash, including the fatigues-clad men around the white vehicles.

Still lying "proned out," the most accurate position for a sniper, Parker sighted down the rifle barrel. Bystanders gaped at him. Two state troopers were directing traffic on the bridge, moving the vehicles into a single lane so they wouldn't hit all the pedestrians clogging it. One trooper came over, but he just asked Parker to move his legs so they'd be a little farther away from the passing traffic. He didn't want Parker to get injured.

Several other riflemen were spread out on the bridge, including

Parker's two Idaho buddies, and they yelled back and forth to each other.

"I've got a clear shot at four of them," one said.

"I'm ready to pull the trigger if fired upon," another said.

Despite his cocky Facebook persona, Parker had no idea what he was doing. He'd never been in the military or worked in any type of security role. He'd certainly never been in a situation anything like this. He could barely move his gun from side to side because it was wedged tightly in the crack. His trigger finger bore a green shamrock tattoo, and he kept it extended along the barrel, making sure to not put it on the trigger itself.

People were watching him, taking pictures, even asking him questions, and they probably thought he knew what he was doing. Parker lay there, sighting down the barrel of his rifle, playing the part of a militia sniper.

RYAN BUNDY WAS ON THE BRIDGE TOO. A SHERIFF'S DEPUTY PULLED UP IN his patrol car. Ryan knew him, a local guy. Ryan leaned in his window to talk.

Ryan said: *I want you to know, we're not the aggressors here. No harm has been done.*

The deputy said: *Oh, yes, there has.*

Ryan said: *Not by us.*

The deputy said: *Not by you. By them.*

He meant the feds. The deputy drove off.

Ryan wanted to go down into the wash and join the line of horses and protesters. But that wasn't what he'd been instructed to do when he'd had his fast-induced moment of understanding on Tuesday night. He knew he was supposed to go talk to the sheriff.

BRAND NU THORNTON PERCHED ON THE SLOPE UNDERNEATH THE NORTH-bound bridge. He wore a green camo shirt and cap and his ever-present Bluetooth earpiece. He had a general's sweeping view of the field of conflict. What he saw both thrilled and horrified him.

Below him, in the wash, the ragged line of horses and people moved haltingly toward the gate underneath the feds' bridge. A few had rifles slung over their shoulders, but most were unarmed. More people were joining the line, skidding down the slope of the wash, even one guy on crutches.

The protesters looked relatively helpless, but Thornton could see they were backed by clusters of heavily armed militia. Not only were there riflemen atop the bridge, but Thornton also counted many dozens of rifles scattered around and underneath, behind the concrete pilings, in dark caves where the upslope of the wash met the bridge. Most of the militia seemed to be carrying .308 semiautomatics, but he spotted a .338 sniper rifle and, holy shit, a Barrett .50-caliber sniper rifle on a two-legged stand.[*]

Thornton believed the federal agents in the wash were sitting ducks. The militia's big guns were well concealed under the bridge and had the high ground. The wash was a kill zone. If the shooting started, some of the protesters and militia members would doubtless be taken out, Thornton thought, but all of the federal agents in the wash would be dead in thirty seconds.

---

[*] This description of militia firepower comes from the author's interviews with Brand Nu Thornton and a YouTube video that Thornton and Roy Potter posted the day after the standoff. Thornton said the big rifles were difficult to spot from most vantage points, which may explain why they did not show up in photos of the standoff. A photo of a .50-caliber rifle, allegedly at the militia camp near Bundy Ranch, did circulate on social media.

THE KNOT OF FEDERAL AGENTS ON THE FRONT LINE UNDER THE SOUTH-
bound bridge didn't say it to each other, but inside they were pretty
much in agreement with Thornton's assessment. If a gunfight broke
out, they were fucked. And they didn't even see the combat Barrett
.50-caliber.

The agents clustered around the three white ranger pickups, posi-
tioning themselves in rows alongside the vehicles, crouched behind the
open doors. The front agent held a shield. Some had rifles in a ready
position, pointed at the ground a few feet in front of them. Another
had a tear-gas launcher. Another scanned the approaching crowd
through binoculars. When he saw weapons, he called out locations
and identifiers of the people carrying them.

"Fat dude, right behind the tree, he's got a long gun," the spotter
said.

The horses began filing into the wash.

"Here they come," one agent said.

One minute later, Dan Love gave the frontline agents permission
to launch pepper spray into the crowd. The agents discussed this. None
of them liked the idea much. Launching gas into this crowd could
trigger a gunfight. All it would take was one nutjob pulling a trigger.
And how were the agents supposed to respond? They couldn't just fire
indiscriminately into the crowd.

Tight with anxiety, the agents traded wry remarks and chuckles
as the crowd got closer.

"Are these fucking people stupid or what?"

"Pretty much a shoot-first, ask-questions-later situation."

"No gun. He's just holding his back, standing like a sissy."

Fifty yards behind the front line, a dozen federal vehicles had
pulled up. Adam Sully, the BLM special agent who'd worked undercover at the rallies, was among the agents clustered there.

Sully had spent the night guarding the Mesquite hotel that had been the target of the bomb threat, and then he'd been helping take down the command post when he got word that Bundy supporters were flowing toward Toquop Wash. He'd spent the week at their rallies, listening to them rant about the evil federal government. He'd heard Pete Santilli threaten BLM law enforcement with arrest. He'd seen some of the militia Facebook posts about shooting federal agents. Now they were here, rifles facing rifles, and anything could set this off.

Sully had been a law officer for eighteen years, and he'd never felt this level of fear, not only for himself and his fellow officers, but also for the advancing Bundy protesters.

"We gotta have some fucking fire discipline here," a nearby agent said.

Sully couldn't agree more.

TWO AND A HALF MILES AWAY AT THE PROTEST SITE ON RIVERSIDE ROAD, Cliven and Carol watched an aircraft circling over the BLM command post. Cliven studied the river valley, expecting to see cows streaming his way. But an hour passed, and nothing had happened.

Cliven couldn't understand what was taking so long. Getting the cattle back shouldn't have been a difficult task. He decided he'd get the job done himself.

Booda Cavalier drove him to the river, where Cliven had stashed his big yellow Caterpillar D7 bulldozer. He figured he'd drive the bulldozer up to Toquop Wash and force his way through the gate. He fired up the machine and rumbled across the river. But then the brakes and steering seized up, becoming difficult to control.

Later, Cliven told people that he got off the bulldozer and knelt in the mud beside the Virgin River and prayed for instructions, barely able to think over the roar of the diesel engine. He said God answered him: *This is not your job.*

Cliven went back to the vehicle where Booda and Carol waited.

Cliven said: *This is not my job. It's their job.*

They headed back to Riverside Road to wait.

ABOVE THE WASH NEAR THE INTERSTATE, RYAN BUNDY PLEADED WITH sheriff's officials to release the cattle and end the standoff. He was emotional, tearful. He found the assistant sheriff, Joe Lombardo, who was in charge in Sheriff Gillespie's absence.

Ryan said: *If the BLM fires on the people, people are going to die. We need some intervention right now.*

Lombardo agreed. Ever since the protesters flooded into the wash, Lombardo had been zigzagging between the Bundy brothers and Dan Love, trying to negotiate a peaceful end to the crisis. The guns on both sides of the wash had made the hair on the back of his neck stand up. He'd tracked down Dave Bundy and draped a friendly arm around his shoulder, smiling and using all of his stress-training techniques to stay calm as he asked Dave to make sure the militia gunmen did the same. Dave told him Cliven wanted the BLM gone and the cattle released within an hour. Dan Love told Lombardo he was keeping the cattle and needed much more time to demobilize the operation.

Lombardo had initially believed the sheriff's office's role was to provide security and prevent a gun battle from breaking out. Now it seemed to him that releasing the cattle was the only way to accomplish those goals. He talked to Sheriff Gillespie on the phone and told his boss that he'd made the decision to release the cattle, no matter what the BLM wanted. They could take his job, but he needed to end this.

Ryan Bundy, Lombardo, and Dan Love huddled near the highway. Lombardo told Love that he had made the decision to release the cattle.

To Ryan, it was a confirmation. Events were playing out as he'd come to understand during his Tuesday night revelation. The people had stood up, forcing local law to assert its constitutional supremacy over the feds. Sitting in a deputy sheriff's patrol car, Ryan called his father to report the news. Lombardo leaned close to Ryan's cell phone and listened in on the call.

A QUARTER AFTER NOON, DAN LOVE, WEARING A BACKWARD-TURNED BASE-ball cap and sunglasses and a flak jacket with the word "POLICE" across his chest, strode the twenty meters between the front line of federal vehicles and the gate. He exuded a professional calm, draping his arm across the metal bar of the gate, but he'd lost the swagger of his exchanges with Santilli earlier in the week. Half a mile behind Love, the BLM was packing up the command post. The roundup was over, and Love had lost.

BLM acting deputy director Steve Ellis had flown from DC to Las Vegas that morning. As soon as his plane touched down, Ellis had called the command post. Around the same time Assistant Sheriff Lombardo told Love that the cattle were to be released, Ellis had delivered a similar message. When he found out that the Bundy supporters had stormed the wash, Ellis said the BLM should pull out. Immediately. Don't worry about an orderly demobilization, and don't worry about the cattle.

Ellis had said: *Get everybody out of there. Let them have the cattle.*

Still, Love's voice had a dogmatic, authoritarian edge as he asked the protesters to keep calm.

A protester shot back: "It's pretty hard to deescalate when you got guys with helmets and M16s aimed at us."

"I understand," Love said. "Get me Ammon."

The protesters only seemed to grow angrier. A stone flew through the air and bounced on the ground near Love's feet. The protesters demanded that the agents lower their rifles, and Dan Love turned to the men behind him and yelled: "No gun pointing! No guns!"

Ammon approached, and the two men faced off through the fence, as horns honked above and protesters gathered around Ammon, hollering.

"I'm currently in negotiations with your family to find a peaceful resolution to this," Love said. "Don't escalate it down here. Allow me time to talk upstairs, with Metro, up above. Push your people back off this gate. We're gonna work to release these cattle. Listen to me."

"No, no, no," Ammon said. "I understand what you're doing, and you will get that time. But we're not playing here."

"I get that," Love said. "Push them back up off the gate and let me work with you and you." He gestured at Ammon and Dave Bundy. "I'll allow you two to come in here with me."

Dave Bundy, who still had scuff marks on his cheek from his arrest six days earlier, just squinted at Love.

"We're not going in there," Ammon said. "We're staying right here."

"You're not getting arrested," Love said. "You've got my word that nobody's taking you into custody."

"I don't care. We're not going in there."

The men were at an impasse, staring at each other through the gate, until Tom Roberts, the deputy chief of the sheriff's office patrol division, came down into the wash and met Ammon at the fence. From that moment on, Ammon ignored Dan Love, giving his full attention to the deputy sheriff.

Roberts said he'd negotiated with the BLM to pack up and leave the command post within thirty minutes, but he wanted Ammon to move the protesters back so the BLM agents at the gate would feel safe enough to retreat. When the BLM was gone, deputy sheriffs would escort the cowboys to the corrals, where they would release the cattle and drive them down Toquop Wash to the Virgin River.

Roberts had a light touch, smiling and chuckling, and Ammon relaxed too. Ammon's voice was grateful, respectful. He agreed to back the protesters up. Finally, Ammon thought, the sheriff's office was accepting its constitutional authority as the supreme law-enforcement agency in Clark County. The county's sovereignty had been restored.

Ammon pulled out a pocketknife and slashed the "Closed Area" sign off the gate, thrusting it in the air, to the delight of the crowd.

The agents in olive-drab fatigues tramped backward in a crouched defensive cluster, rifles at the ready. The white ranger trucks pulled away. The crowd cheered. Ryan Bundy climbed atop a portable light-tower base and thrust his Stetson in the air, answering the question posed by the hand-painted banner that Cliven had strung up at events and protests for decades.

"The West has now been won!" he hollered.

In the milling crowd of protesters, Neil Wampler bared his teeth in a fierce grin that creased his sun-leathered face even more, and his black eyes flashed. He raised both fists and pumped them in the air.

ERIC PARKER PULLED HIS RIFLE OUT OF THE CONCRETE SLIT AND STOOD UP on the bridge, relieved but still buzzing with adrenaline. A reporter from St. George came along the bridge and stuck a video camera in Parker's face and asked where he was from.

"We saw some younger people down there, looked like they might have been children," the reporter said. "Do you think that was wise to have them down there? Do you think that was dangerous?"

Parker cocked his head back, slightly irritated at the questioner.

"It might have been the only thing that kept us from getting gassed," he said.

"Do you think it was good to have the kids down there?" the reporter pressed.

"Absolutely," Parker said, thrusting out his jaw.

Parker wanted to watch the cowboys drive the cattle through the wash, so he stuck around. At about 1:40 PM, Las Vegas Metro police blocked off the highway again, and a convoy of some one hundred vehicles from the federal command post began pulling onto the interstate and heading north as protesters yelled and flipped them off.

Parker's aunt in North Carolina called him.

She said: *Do you have a shamrock tattoo on your finger?*

Parker said he did.

She said: *You're on the front page of FoxNews.com.*

He said: *No, I'm not.*

His aunt disconnected, and a moment later he received a text attachment from her, a screenshot of the news webpage. There he was, in a photo right under the banner headline: "Feds pull back in Nev. ranch standoff." In the photo, he was crouched on the bridge, scoping out the wash over the concrete barrier, the Saiga .223 pointed at the asphalt, his tattooed trigger finger extended along the barrel.

THE FIRST TWO COWBOYS GALLOPED INTO VIEW UNDER THE BRIDGE, FOLlowed by one black cow, then four more. Then a long streaming flood, all colors and sizes, racing full-tilt toward the river.

Hundreds of people lined the wash slopes and the interstate bridges, watching and murmuring and holding up cell phones to record the return of the Bundy herd to the open range. Ryan Bundy had instructed them not to spook the cattle, so they stayed quieter than they had all day, no cheers or claps. The stream of cattle moved slower and slower, the stragglers just ambling along, trailed by several dozen cowboys. Now the onlookers broke into applause, like rodeo fans cheering a wrangler who broke seven seconds in a calf-roping contest.

Riding down the wash between the bridges, LaVoy Finicum doffed his Stetson at the onlookers, his bald head gleaming in the afternoon sun.

The posse of cowboys herded the cattle to the river and rode back the way they'd come. The other cowboys rode toward the protest site. Everybody was gathering there again to celebrate. But Finicum turned off early, heading for the spot where he'd parked his truck and Esperanza's trailer early that morning. He was a friendly man but reserved. He didn't especially like big social gatherings. And he knew Jeanette was terrified back in Cane Beds. She would not rest easy until he got home.

Finicum loaded his horse into the trailer. He was happy that the Bundys had gotten their cows back, and happier that he'd taken part in their struggle. But he was sure the experience was just the beginning of a new journey. After what he'd witnessed here, he couldn't just resume his old life. He would find a way to continue making a stand.

Chapter 6

BUNDYSTAN

A pink desert twilight fell at the protest site on Riverside Road as the sun set behind the hill where the cowboys had planted an American flag that morning.

Hundreds of supporters had gathered there after the standoff, basking in the triumph, feeling a tremendous mass exultation. The feds had thrown everything they had at the people, short of gunning them down en masse, and the people had won. The people felt awake now. Thousands had converged on this lonely slice of desert and realized they weren't alone. They were part of something larger. A movement. They believed things would never be the same.

Like the FBI, the Patriots believed they had experienced a historic event. An opportunity. Together, they could be a force to be reckoned with. That was the concept behind the Oath Keepers, and behind Operation Mutual Aid, a powerful idea that the disparate branches of the Patriot movement had never quite pulled off until now, when

149

they'd spontaneously rallied behind an obscure cattle rancher. But taking back the cattle was just a start. The next time the Constitution was in jeopardy, the Patriots would be ready to mobilize.

Ammon took the stage. He told the crowd the story of his confrontation with Dan Love at the gate. The federal agent had tried to exert control, but the people had given their allegiance to the sheriff, and that made all the difference, Ammon said.

"The sheriff's office took over, and the BLM rolled out. The feds rolled out, right?" Ammon said.

The crowd whooped. Ammon's voice gathered fury as he claimed the cattle had been mistreated, and it broke as he described taking down the corral fences at the BLM command post. He said the Bundy followers must hold the federal government accountable for pointing rifles at the protesters.

"This is a war of agency," he said. "If we look into society and peek into history, we see that man is not happy without agency. He becomes a subject of misery if he does not have his freedom. We also find that there are men and forces out there that are striving always to take away the agency of man, always. The third thing we see is that if man does not fight for his freedom and his agency, they will be taken away. Today, my friends, we fought for our free agency and we still have it!"

The abandoned command post looked like a ghost town, albeit one that had been deserted only moments earlier. In the rush to demobilize the operation, the BLM had left behind lots of equipment. Cattle prods and ropes lay discarded on the ground. Trucks and trailers sat idle. A gasoline-powered generator was left behind, still running. The corrals were empty save for one dead heifer, blood soaking the dirt near her muzzle.

The federal convoy had rushed to their hotel in Mesquite.

As a Las Vegas Metro SWAT team stood guard outside, the officers went to their rooms and hurriedly packed their belongings. Then they headed for the safety of the city—Las Vegas. After four hours of back-ups, traffic was moving smoothly again on Interstate 15, as if nothing had happened.

The officers checked into a new hotel, and BLM acting deputy director Steve Ellis huddled with the leaders of the operation. He told them they'd done the right thing by not pulling triggers. Everybody had gone home alive, and that's what mattered right now. He told them not to worry about "losing" to the militia. Let the Patriots gloat.

Ellis said: *This isn't over.*

The federal officers involved in the Bundy roundup had a variety of law-enforcement and military backgrounds. Some were combat veterans who had survived hostile fire. Some had been local police before going federal. Some had worked border patrol. At least one had guarded the president of the United States.

But none of them had ever experienced anything like this in law enforcement. As a cop, use-of-force situations typically arose when police were on the offensive, serving an arrest warrant, for example, or during a traffic stop. That's when the bad guys tended to take a shot at police: when they felt cornered. So police could predict it, be braced for it, ready.

But this had been different. The officers had been at the command post, preparing to pack up and leave, and an enemy force had come their way, on the offensive, guns ready. This hadn't felt like law enforcement. This had felt like combat. Like war.

BRAND NU THORNTON AND ROY POTTER DROVE BACK TO LAS VEGAS ON Sunday, bone tired. All week in Bunkerville, they'd been sleeping on hard desert, participating in security patrols and militia meetings, suffering bugs at night and blazing sun during the day, eating whatever was provided at the protest area. Their eyes drooped and their faces were sunburned. On the way home, they discussed what they'd seen, their exhausted minds aflame with dark thoughts.

They wanted to savor the victory. But they couldn't. They rehashed every detail, confirming each other's growing suspicions. Despite Thornton's loathing of the BLM, he'd been horrified when he saw the agents clustered in the kill zone. These were young men. They could have been his sons.

Those federal officers were sacrificial lambs, Thornton and Potter had come to believe. They had been pitted against the militia, both sides manipulated by shadowy forces on high, moved around like pawns on a chessboard until they found themselves in the face-off in Toquop Wash.

Eventually, Thornton and Potter had to acknowledge the suspicion that was staring them in the face: the federal government *wanted* a bloodletting.

If the militia slaughtered the federal officers, Thornton and Potter reasoned, then the government would have an excuse to declare martial law, send in the military. They would seize power, suspend the Bill of Rights, curtail freedom. It was a power grab by the scriptural serpent, the most subtle beast in the forest.

Thornton wanted to revel in the Bundys' victory, but he couldn't. His heart was breaking.

PATRIOT MEDIA AND RIGHT-WING NEWS SITES ALSO BUZZED WITH HUNCHES about why the government had initiated the roundup.

Many believed the Bundys were being muscled off their land for reasons that had nothing to do with tortoises or the environment. That land wasn't worthless desert, they concluded. Some speculated it was brimming with underground water. Others said it was the future home of a natural gas pipeline. Or it was wanted for a big real estate development deal. Or it contained weapons-grade uranium.

Certain Bundy supporters were constantly on the lookout for overseas interests involved in the roundup, more evidence of Agenda 21 at work. They insisted that some of the supposed federal agents "looked Middle Eastern." Or that they were speaking to each other in foreign tongues. But the most durable theory originated with an Infowars story alleging that Nevada senator Harry Reid, the Senate majority leader, was using the BLM to bully the Bundys to make way for solar energy projects.

The story had some scraps of truth to it. Reid was a long-time advocate of turning public lands in sun-drenched Nevada into solar farms. In 2011, he helped recruit the Chinese energy giant, ENN Energy, to build a $5 billion solar farm on the southern tip of Clark County. In 2012, a Reuters story had revealed that the law firm where Reid's son practiced was representing ENN, a possible conflict of interest. But as it turned out, none of this had anything to do with the BLM roundup, because the ENN deal had fallen apart in 2013.

However, there were links between other Reid-backed solar projects and the Bundy Ranch crisis. Only a month before the roundup, the BLM had recommended bolstering conservation efforts in Gold Butte to offset the environmental damage of a different Clark County solar project. The solar farm would destroy tortoise habitat, but the BLM would compensate by improving habitat in Gold Butte. One specific recommendation called for the BLM to beef up ranger patrols in Gold Butte to prevent illegal activities such as off-road vehicle use, dumping, and cattle grazing.

Therefore, one didn't have to be a conspiracy theorist to wonder

if Reid had pressured the BLM to resolve the never-ending Bundy trespass cattle situation. Especially because the new BLM director, Neil
Kornze, was a former Reid aide.

These connections inflamed the Patriot networks, where snippets
of fact and supposition and outright bullshit were tossed into a bub-
bling conspiracy stew that went something like this: Harry Reid was
stripping Cliven Bundy of his land to sell it to Communist-backed Chinese interests.

"We found out from Alex Jones that this entire area actually
belongs to the Chinese now," former Lt. Col. Roy Potter said on a You-
Tube video, panning his camera across Gold Butte's hills. "That's why
they're clearing this out. They're taking it away from the American
people and giving to the Chinese so the American government can
continue its use of debt money to enslave the rest of us and try to get
hegemony over the world. This is nothing about management of the
land by the BLM. This is a takeover by a foreign power, using the
United States government."

And then Harry Reid himself fueled the fire when he vili-
fied Bundy supporters a few days after the Toquop Wash standoff
during a public event in Las Vegas.

"These people who hold themselves out to be patriots are not,"
Reid told the audience. "They're nothing more than domestic terrorists."

AS THE DAYS PASSED, A HOST OF POLITICIANS JOINED TEAM CLIVEN.

The day after Reid's remark, Nevada's other senator, Dean Heller,
said: "What Senator Reid may call domestic terrorists, I call patriots."

Senator Rand Paul of Kentucky asked everybody to calm down
and stop throwing labels around. But the self-described constitutional
conservative made it clear which way he leaned. "This is a real, I think,
intellectual and constitutional and legal debate, but it shouldn't be about

violence of arms, and I hope that the government will not be there in full arms and provoke a showdown and something terrible will happen."

Senator Ted Cruz of Texas used the Bundy Ranch episode as an opportunity to bash the Obama administration. "Liberty is under assault," Cruz said, from a federal government "hell-bent on expanding its authority over every aspect of our lives." The Bundy standoff "is the unfortunate and tragic culmination of the path that President Obama has set the federal government on."

Real estate developer and reality television star Donald Trump went on Sean Hannity's show and hedged. On the one hand, Trump said, people should pay their fees. On the other hand, he kind of enjoyed the cantankerous rancher.

"I like his spirit, his spunk," he said, "and I like the people that—you know, they're so loyal . . ."

"I do too," Hannity said.

"I do like him," Trump continued. "I respect him. He ought to go cut a good deal right now."

Hannity continued to milk the story he'd helped launch into the national stratosphere, interviewing the Bundy family night after night.

"What's your response to Harry Reid?" Hannity asked.

"I don't have a response for Harry Reid," Cliven said. "But I have a response for every sheriff across the United States: Disarm the federal bureaucrats. Take the federal United States bureaucrats' guns away."

To many of those who'd followed the story through the lens of *Hannity*, the Bundy standoff provided a release, an anarchic excitement, proof that tyranny could be overwhelmed, defeated by sheer numbers.

But elsewhere in America, widespread disbelief reigned. To many who followed mainstream and liberal news sources, the story was baffling, partly because most of those outlets had ignored the story until it blew up. So this audience's introduction to the entire saga was the photo of the "Bundy Sniper"—a lariat-thin white man in a heavy beard, baseball cap, and flak jacket, lying belly flat on the asphalt, his semiautomatic rifle wedged between two concrete barriers, sighting down on a group of federal agents.

The photos were stark and somehow disorienting, like wartime images from a Third World hot zone, not a blocked-off interstate highway overpass one hour from Las Vegas. Questions abounded. The Bundy Sniper pointed a deadly weapon at federal agents and just got to go back home to Idaho? The Bundys incited an armed mob but got their cattle back? No one had been arrested? What would law enforcement have done if the Bundys and their followers weren't white? What if a crowd of armed American Muslims, for example, had confronted the feds? To many, the bulwarks of peaceful, reasonable society suddenly felt a little less substantial. This doesn't happen. Not in the United States.

To those unaware of the long history of the western range wars—in other words, most of the East Coast—the Bundy Sniper photo was perhaps the first major clue that something new was afoot. Something was simmering in the nation's vast, unlit backcountry. A domestic discontent. A brewing insurrection.

THE BUNDY SNIPER HIMSELF, ERIC PARKER, HAD HEADED HOME A FEW hours after the standoff. Before leaving, Parker was standing in the militia camp with his buddies from Idaho, and they were speculating about the historic nature of what they'd just experienced. Had anything like this ever happened before?

Someone pulled out an iPhone and spoke into it: *Hey, Siri, when's the last time the federal government backed down?*

The phone thought about it, and up popped the photo of Parker with the Saiga .223 on the bridge, snapped a couple hours earlier.

The Bundy Sniper photos had a life of their own. They flew back and forth on news sites, on social media. People added words to the images, creating memes. The photos made their way onto T-shirts, some with the word "Resist" baked into Parker's prone silhouette.

Hours after the standoff, one Bundy supporter posted a photo of Parker on a public Facebook thread, and a Las Vegas Metro SWAT team member was so irritated by the hero worship that he typed out a heat-of-the-moment response.

"I just wish you could see how big that guy prone with the rifle's head was in the scope of the [police] Snipers .308," wrote the officer, who actually had not been in Bunkerville during the standoff. "Don't worry, he wouldn't have felt a thing!"

Metro booted the officer off SWAT and back to the patrol division. SWAT officers had to keep their cool in crisis situations. Metro might face off against militia again. What if a SWAT officer had to squeeze the trigger next time?

Eric Parker wasn't the only one whose likeness went viral.

Michael Roop, the BLM ranger who had thrown down Margaret Houston earlier in the week, became a target. Someone pulled a screen grab of his face from the incident—sunglasses and buzz-cut, Riverside Road behind him—and people added words and spread it around the internet.

A representative example went like this:

NAME: Michael Roop
LOCATION: Portland, Oregon
OCCUPATION: BLM Thug
AGE: Old enough to know better

He likes football, long walks on the beach, and form tackling 57-year-old women with cancer from behind.

Other memes and messages traded about Roop contained his contact information. Profanity-laced messages and outright threats poured into Roop's voice mail and email, like the fury of an entire nation was directed at him. He got more than five hundred messages, and most of them couldn't be traced to a specific individual. A drunken twenty-four-year-old Pennsylvania man called Roop after seeing the Santilli video, and he minced no words.

He said: "We're going to kill you, you fucking BLM thug."

TWO DAYS AFTER THE STANDOFF, CLIVEN'S PHONE RANG AT 2:30 AM. IT WAS a state trooper. Two of the Bundy cows had wandered onto Interstate 15, he said, and one had been struck and killed. The other was in the median. Could Cliven come help?

This had happened periodically over the years, part of ranching on the open range. Cliven stumbled out of bed and went outside to his truck. But then a pair of headlights blinded him, a vehicle pulling into the dark yard, past the armed checkpoint at the mouth of the driveway. It held a couple of newly arriving militiamen from Arizona. They greeted Cliven, said they were there to help.

The headlights brought Cliven fully awake, reminding him that his life had changed. Militia were guarding him now, not the Nevada Highway Patrol. The militia had vowed to remain at Bundy Ranch, rotating in and out until the family was safe from federal harassment. They were following Cliven everywhere, bringing him bottles of water, even accompanying him to church the previous morning in Bunkerville, which had startled several congregants.

158

Now Cliven wondered if he was stumbling into a trap. Was the highway patrolman trying to arrest him?

He went back to bed. If a cow had been hit, the trooper would have to deal with it.*

AFTER THE STANDOFF, THE BUNDYS FOUND A HALF-BURIED CARCASS OF A cow in the desert. They hauled a backhoe to the spot and dug up the cow and five others, all casualties of the roundup. Elsewhere, they found two dead bulls aboveground, shot in the head. The BLM later said the bulls had posed a safety hazard. The agency didn't address the cows but said a veterinarian had ensured that humane practices were employed during the roundup.

Many of the surviving cattle had lost weight. Their hooves were sore from being run hard, and they were stiff from being corralled in tight quarters for several days. The Bundys counted twenty-seven calves that seemed to have been separated from their mothers, probably due to the helicopter herding, and a couple of the mothers even returned up the wash to the abandoned command post, looking for their young ones. The Bundy cowboys worked to reunite the separated calves with their mothers, but this was no easy task as the released cattle spread out over the range. They bottle-fed some calves, including one who'd been born at the BLM command post. They named her Liberty.

Bundy supporters wanted to know how the herd was faring, so the Bundys kept them updated via blog posts that included pictures and video of the dead animals and the motherless calves. Then, almost a week after the standoff, the family threw an all-day party for their supporters at the protest site on Riverside Road. Militia patrolled

---

* In fact, a motorist on Interstate 15 did hit one of Cliven's cows that night. Two people were injured in the crash.

the bridge over the Virgin River as hundreds of people splashed below, ate hamburgers, and listened to local country acts. Many partygoers wore name tags that read "Domestic Terrorist." Cliven posed for photos and signed autographs.

Carol wasn't as comfortable in the spotlight. She was a grandma and a rancher's wife in a tiny town nobody knew about, and now her family was famous. Two weeks after Bailey had created the Bundy Ranch Facebook page, it had more than 89,000 followers. Gold Butte Road was swarming with strangers, men with guns who seemed to regard the Bundys as the First Family of the Patriot movement. Carol put on big sunglasses that hid her appraising eyes. In large groups she tended to insulate herself within a cordon of her daughters in a way that discouraged overtures.

THE MILITIA SETTLED IN TO PROTECT THE BUNDYS FOR THE LONG HAUL. The cluster of tents and vehicles near the river was dubbed Camp Liberty. Two flags—the Stars and Stripes and the yellow Gadsden—fluttered on a hillside overlooking the camp. A field kitchen served three meals a day to the one hundred or so Bundy supporters, mostly men but a handful of women too. Militia members came and went, depending on the demands of their families and jobs. Some had traveled from as far away as Alaska, New Hampshire, and West Virginia. Dedicated militia members bivouacked together closer to Bundy Ranch. Assorted Bundy supporters who didn't belong to an actual militia set up their own encampment a little farther away. The hardcore militia members nicknamed them the "Fruits and Nuts Brigade."

Volunteers from both factions pulled guard duty, spending long shifts on "overwatch" details on the hills and patrolling the main byways that led to Bundy Ranch. The militia created a shooting range, and Booda Cavalier led firearms training sessions. Some locals found the presence of so many armed strangers unnerving. One man told police that Ryan Payne and Ryan Bundy had pulled him over as he was hauling a livestock trailer through Mesquite and demanded to see proof that he owned the cattle inside.

The camp's total numbers swelled in the first few days as people flowed in, attracted by the global headlines about the BLM's defeat. The "Battle of Bunkerville," as Bundy supporters had begun calling it, had turned out to be the biggest militia event in modern US history, a Woodstock or Selma for Patriots. And like Woodstock, everyone in the movement wanted to be part of it. It was a badge of honor, especially if you'd gotten there early, like Ryan Payne.

By contrast, perhaps the most influential Patriot heavyweight of all, Oath Keepers founder Stewart Rhodes, had pretty much missed the whole thing. Rhodes had briefly visited Bunkerville earlier in the week, then waited until the morning of the standoff before returning and had gotten stuck in the traffic jam on the interstate. He'd jumped in a fellow Oath Keeper's truck and took a dirt road to Toquop Wash, where he seemed chagrined to find the standoff was over.

"Long as it got done," he said.

Rhodes was initially respectful to Ryan Payne, offering a rotation of fresh Oath Keepers to pull tours of duty at Bundy Ranch. He also said his organization had raised money for the cause, and the Oath Keepers wrote the Bundys a check for $12,000 to cover operational costs. The Oath Keepers also distributed gear to the militia, including more than a dozen dual-band radio handsets, expensive infrared night-vision goggles, and hundreds of magazines of assault-rifle ammunition.

Despite the Oath Keepers' largesse, Payne wondered if Rhodes was just there to lend positive publicity to his organization. Among confidantes, Payne sniped about how the Oath Keepers had booked rooms at the Virgin River Hotel and Casino in Mesquite while the militia slept in the dirt at Camp Liberty.

Rhodes was equally unimpressed with Payne's operation. The communication systems were crap. More importantly, some of the troops seemed to be hotheads or nutjobs. Militias always attracted some of those, and they had to be screened out. Some thought Payne himself seemed a little too gung-ho, edgy, like he wanted to throw down with the cops. One militiaman said Payne told him to resist if the sheriff's office came for Cliven, which some thought was kind of missing the entire point. The militia wasn't a private army. Cliven himself said the sheriff was the highest law-enforcement authority.

Jerad and Amanda Miller, the strange young couple who had moved from Indiana to Las Vegas a few months earlier, had taken up residence in the Fruits and Nuts camp. They carried a shotgun and a sidearm and said they'd sold their possessions and quit their jobs to come protect the Bundys. The longer the disheveled pair hung around, the more dubious people grew. Their suspicions were not alleviated by an on-camera interview Jerad gave to the Reno NBC affiliate the day after the standoff. Jerad acted like a Camp Liberty insider, saying he knew a "couple people" who wanted to join the cause, but the militia was afraid "they might get a little trigger-happy."

"So they were advised to stay at home," Jerad said. "We only need cool-headed people here that aren't going to antagonize and make it look like we fired the first shot."

But then Jerad got a little radical himself.

"I feel sorry for any federal agents that want to come in here and push us around," he said. "I really don't want violence toward them, but if they're going to come bring violence to us, well, if that's the language they want to speak, we'll learn it."

"That sounds like a menacing statement, I have to tell you," the reporter said.

Jerad shrugged.

Off camera, he was even more volatile, asking when the shooting was going to start, saying he was going to go find the BLM, like he was looking for an opportunity to be a hero or be famous. The militia leaders grilled the Millers, and Jerad acknowledged he was a convicted felon.

The militia leaders came to the conclusion that the Millers were either working for the feds to disrupt or double-cross the Bundys and their supporters, or they were actually violent crazies. Either way, it was decided, they had to leave Camp Liberty. Jerad cried, saying Amanda had lost her job at Hobby Lobby because she'd missed work to help out in Bunkerville. One of the militia leaders gave them a couple hundred bucks and asked if they wanted to stay at a hotel in Mesquite and be the "eyes and ears" of the militia. The Millers took the money but headed back to Las Vegas.

A few days later, Jerad posted a message on YouTube: "How dare you ask for help and shun us dedicated patriots!"

THE DAY AFTER THE STANDOFF, A TEAM OF FBI AGENTS BEGAN INVESTIGATing the Bundys and their followers.

In this case, the common investigative technique of talking to witnesses or targets was tricky. After all, there were heavily armed men guarding the Bundy Ranch area, and the Patriots went on high alert every time a car they didn't recognize pulled onto Riverside or Gold Butte roads. The BLM couldn't even get Cliven Bundy to open the four certified letters they sent to the ranch immediately after the standoff. The rancher left them sealed and forwarded them to his attorney. There was no way to arrest or even talk to Cliven or his supporters in Bunkerville without risking bloodshed. For months, the law stayed away from Bundy Ranch and Gold Butte.

Still, evidence was abundant. In fact, the Bundy investigation generated far more electronic data than any other case in the history of the Nevada US Attorney's Office, with more than 2,000 videos, 1,600 audio recordings, and 82,000 emails. There were statements from the more than one hundred law-enforcement officers at the scene. There was aerial photography and video from the FBI surveillance plane. Audio and video from numerous law-enforcement body cams and dashboard cams. Many among the crowd of hundreds in Toquop Wash had been recording video or snapping photos. The news media had done the same. The internet was awash with Bunkerville imagery. And potential targets continued to chatter about the standoff on Facebook and blogs, bragging about their participation as they shared photos and videos. Some posted long recaps of their experiences. Voluntary confessions abounded, there for the taking. It was a Facebook case.

Each FBI special agent had a different task. Some pored over the Facebook accounts of certain investigative targets. Others googled keywords like "Bundy" or "militia" and began cataloging the voluminous news reports, photos, and videos. Some had special training in open-source search techniques. A firearms instructor from the FBI Academy in Virginia was assigned to build a master list of all the people and weapons in the wash. Several agents spent hundreds of hours sorting through these documents, painstakingly piecing together a person-by-person, moment-by-moment, gun-by-gun accounting of the standoff. A couple of agents spent more than a thousand hours on it. One examined half a million pages of Facebook documents.

As they pulled photo after photo, video after video, the agents became intimately familiar with the appearance of each of the hundreds of individuals in Toquop Wash on April 12, 2014. The rifleman on the bridge who wore sunglasses, black beard, and black baseball cap. The woman with the pink pistol. The cowboy on the roan mare who was bald under his cream Stetson.

Some of the pages and exchanges were public and easily harvested. But email accounts and private Facebook posts required search warrants, so the FBI agents got busy writing affidavits, obtaining judges' signatures, and delivering dozens of warrants to Silicon Valley's social media giants. Then they set about sorting through the voluminous data sets they received, more than 1.5 terabytes of information, trying to piece together connections, figure out who was in charge, who was culpable.

The feds already were familiar with some of the Bundy supporters. The FBI had been keeping an eye on Ryan Payne since he'd founded Operation Mutual Aid a year earlier. But OMA hadn't really done anything, so Payne had been just another dot on the FBI's Patriot radar screen. Until Bunkerville.

The agent tallying the guns in the wash freeze-framed still images from the videos and examined them through a jeweler's magnifying loupe. When he came across higher-quality images, he had hard copies enlarged for closer scrutiny. Each person in the wash became distinctive to him through their jackets, buttons, patches, and hats, which made them identifiable even in the grainier shots. He counted 410 protesters on one side of the BLM gate, compared to twenty-nine federal agents on the other. In the wash itself were 267 protesters, and the rest were on the bridge. Forty-two on horseback. Forty-one of the protesters bore a firearm that he could make out. However, the only bits of visual evidence that appeared to show a protester actually pointing a gun at the federal agents were the Bundy Sniper photos.

Digital information about the standoff at Toquop Wash was plentiful. Still, the FBI investigators wanted to talk to the people who were there. A couple of them hit on a strategy—an undercover operation designed to persuade the targets to open up even more than they already had.

THE BLM WAS CONDUCTING ITS OWN PARALLEL INVESTIGATION AND assigned a special agent named Larry Wooten as their lead investigator. Wooten was new to the BLM, and he took the agency's value statement seriously: To serve with honesty, integrity, accountability, respect, courage, and commitment to make a difference.

Wooten was told the Bundy case was the largest and most important investigation the Department of the Interior had ever undertaken. Toquop Wash had nearly become a great American tragedy. Just as the feds had studied the Ruby Ridge and Waco cases two decades earlier and changed their policies in reaction, Wooten wanted to learn exactly how and why the conflict in Bunkerville had occurred.

As he dug into the events of March and April, he began to believe that Dan Love had engineered a roundup operation that flew in the face of the BLM's value statement. Wooten, who didn't know Love before this investigation, concluded that the roundup operation had been conducted in the image of its leader: unduly macho and militaristic.*

For instance, the day the roundup began, Love's calm, deliberate second-in-command had been briefing the BLM law-enforcement team when Love reportedly jumped in and began yelling like a high school football coach giving a half-time speech. The official roundup plan instructed personnel to avoid confrontations with the Bundys, but Love seemed to feel it was more important to not take any shit from them. Don't cower or cater to the Bundys, Love said. Don't avoid them or only work at night or in the backcountry.

Love reportedly said: *We're gonna go right into the belly of the beast. We're gonna gather these cattle in the wide open, not in secret.*

Wooten was told that Love did everything but say they were going to kick Cliven Bundy in the teeth. Some BLM staffers who witnessed Love's speech thought the performance was bizarre.

Then, the next day, Dave Bundy had been arrested, and some of the officers at the scene seemed to have adopted their commander's

---

* The information in this section comes from a seventeen-page memo Wooten wrote in November 2017 to the US Department of Justice about the case.

Top: In 2014, Americans were riveted when hundreds of Cliven Bundy supporters, many armed, forced federal agents to abandon a court-ordered roundup of the Nevada rancher's cattle. The standoff near Bundy Ranch, located about seventy-five miles northeast of Las Vegas, was the largest uprising of so-called Patriot organizations in modern American history.

Bottom: A devout Mormon, Cliven Bundy raised his brood of thirteen children in this 1,200-square-foot home. The house stands in the watershed of the Virgin River, which is home to more than eighty imperiled species.

The Virgin Mountains tower over Bundy Ranch as evening approaches. Approximately 80 percent of Nevada land is federally managed, and many rural residents loathe the federal government and especially its land agencies within the Department of the Interior.

Cliven drinks from a spring in the Virgin Mountains range. When environmental regulations led to the demise of most ranching operations in Clark County, Nevada, in the early 1990s, Cliven stopped paying fees to the federal Bureau of Land Management but continued to graze his herd.

At right: Before the 2014 standoff, Ammon Bundy, Cliven's fourth child, was a successful business owner in Phoenix. The standoff transformed Ammon's views, and he emerged as a Patriot leader, ultimately rallying supporters to take over the Malheur National Wildlife Refuge in Harney County, Oregon, in 2016.

Carol is Cliven's second wife. They married in the early 1990s. Even the Bundy children from Cliven's first marriage call her "Mom." Before the 2014 standoff, she told a reporter: "I've got a shotgun. It's loaded, and I know how to use it."

Ryan Bundy (left) is the eldest son of Cliven. An avid believer in state supremacy and opponent of western federal land ownership, Ryan was at the forefront of both armed confrontations between Patriot militia members and the US government.

Top: LaVoy Finicum, a rancher from Cane Beds, Arizona, rode his horse, Esperanza, at the Bunkerville standoff. Afterward, Finicum followed Cliven Bundy's lead, "firing" the BLM and claiming the federal government had no right to own public land. *(Photo by Blaine Cooper, licensed under CC 3.0)*

Bottom: Jeanette Finicum stands in front of a drawing of LaVoy in her Arizona home. Initially fearful of her husband's involvement with the Bundys, Jeanette eventually took up LaVoy's cause, giving speeches across the country to Patriot audiences.

Terri Linnell sits outside of her home in the mountains east of San Diego. Nicknamed "Momma Bear," Linnell is a longtime Patriot, but her actions during the Oregon occupation caused many to question her loyalty to the movement.

Shawna Cox hails from Kanab, Utah. She was the Bundys' self-appointed publicist during the Bunkerville standoff and the Oregon occupation.

At right: Brand Nu Thornton of Las Vegas blows a ram's horn—a *shofar*—at a 2017 rally for the Bundys in front of the Lloyd D. George US Courthouse.

Until the Bunkerville standoff, Pete Santilli, host of an inflammatory Patriot podcast, had never ventured out of his home studio in Hesperia, California, to cover a live event. His video of federal agents tasing Ammon Bundy inspired a flood of Patriots to travel to Bundy Ranch. *(Courtesy of Multnomah County Sheriff's Office)*

Ryan Payne was an Army long-range surveillance expert who assisted sniper teams in the Iraq War. After an honorable discharge, he moved to Montana and plunged into a profusion of antigovernment beliefs centered around the idea that ultrawealthy globalists were establishing environmental regulations to take land from rural Americans. He was the first militiaman to contact the Bundys and offer his help. *(Courtesy of Multnomah County Sheriff's Office)*

Brian "Booda" Cavalier, an Arizona tattoo artist with a long arrest record, was appointed Cliven Bundy's personal bodyguard and wound up living on the ranch for more than a year. *(Courtesy of Multnomah County Sheriff's Office)*

David Fry, a troubled Ohio man who worked in his parents' dental office, became enamored of LaVoy Finicum's YouTube videos and struck up an unlikely internet friendship with the Arizona rancher. Later, Fry traveled cross-country to join the Oregon occupation. *(Courtesy of Multnomah County Sheriff's Office)*

From January 2 to February 11, 2016, Patriots occupied the Malheur National Wildlife Refuge in Harney County, Oregon. Many came to protest the reincarceration of two local ranchers convicted of arson on federal land. This refuge building typically houses US Fish and Wildlife Service agents and other federal land agency employees.

At right: The Oregon occupiers posted sentries in this guard tower to stand watch over the Malheur refuge.

Dave Ward, sheriff of Harney County, Oregon, was tasked with maintaining law and order during the occupation. As the crisis dragged on, Ward's family members were followed and harassed.

At left: LaVoy Finicum designed the LV cattle brand when he was eight years old. The brand has become a ubiquitous symbol of the Patriot movement and is shown here nailed to a tree in the Malheur National Forest in Oregon.

Three years after the Bunkerville standoff, a band of Bundy supporters gathered at Toquop Wash to mark the anniversary. The upside-down American flag designates a "nation in distress."

Photos by John Temple unless otherwise credited.

Jacket image: From the Interstate 15 North bridge near Bunkerville, Nevada, Eric Parker points his rifle down at federal agents gathered in Toquop Wash during the April 2014 standoff. After a Reuters photographer captured this photo and spread it around the world, Parker became known as the "Bundy Sniper." *(Reuters/Newscom)* aggressive attitude. They demanded that Dave Bundy stop taking pictures or video with his iPad from the side of the road, and when he didn't, they made the first move, throwing him to the ground. Afterward, Wooten was told, some of the officers bragged about roughing up the Bundy son, laughing about how he had little bits of gravel stuck to his face after they'd knelt on him. And the tension heightened from there. Two days later, Mike Roop had thrown down Margaret Houston and several officers had tased Ammon Bundy, which triggered the incoming flood of militia and led to the disastrous failure of the entire multimillion-dollar operation. And it could have led to much, much worse.

Part of the problem, Wooten believed, was rooted in what he saw as a debauched atmosphere in Dan Love's sector of the BLM. The occasional inappropriate remark was one thing. But nothing seemed out-of-bounds when it came to Dan Love's crew. Sex was a major topic around the office. The officers talked and messaged each other incessantly about blow jobs, masturbation in the office closet, porn addiction. Physical appearance was another theme. The officers made jokes about one person's "disgusting butt crack" and another's "leather face." Wooten believed this culture flowed from the leadership of Dan Love, who reportedly sent a photo of his girlfriend's vagina to a coworker and talked about how much "pussy" he got.

The Bundy case brought out an even richer vein of off-color commentary. The team called various targets rednecks, retards, fat, douchebags, tractor faces, and inbreds. They made fun of their Mormon faith. They traded a photoshopped picture of Ryan Bundy holding a gigantic penis.

Wooten worried that the atmosphere might damage the investigation and the potential criminal case. He was also offended. So he reported some incidents. Nothing seemed to change. People said Dan Love was protected, that the administration of the BLM's law-enforcement branch liked him.

To Wooten, the BLM's probe of the Bundys didn't feel like a federal law-enforcement investigation. It felt like middle school.

ONE WEEK AFTER THE STANDOFF, A *NEW YORK TIMES* REPORTER AND PHO-tographer were the only journalists among the fifty or so supporters at the protest site. The newspaper was attempting to catch up on a story that it had almost entirely ignored.

Up to this point, the only article written for the *Times* that mentioned the name Cliven Bundy had appeared a full four days after the standoff, and it was an opinion piece by Timothy Egan entitled "Deadbeat on the Range." Egan's by-the-numbers piece of snark broke no new ground. It simply trotted out the most inflammatory quotes, including Cliven's "I don't recognize the federal government as even existing." *New York Times* readers who wanted to know what was going on in Nevada were reading wire stories like everybody else.

However, when the newspaper did finally send a reporter to Bunkerville a full week after the standoff, the timing proved to be exquisite. Other reporters had left town by then, and Cliven's 1 PM press conferences had evolved into daily speeches to whatever audience showed up. At least one supporter was recording the speech, but if the *Times* reporter hadn't come, it is unlikely Cliven's words would have reached the larger public.

Cliven stood in the shade of a mesquite tree and spoke about what was troubling him on this day, which was the fact that very few black people had come to his riverside party the day before. Cliven believed his fight was as much theirs as it was his.

He began to expound on his views about the black community, notions that seemed to have been shaped by driving past minority

168

communities in Los Angeles and Las Vegas at different times in his life. Cliven had little experience with black people. Fewer than 1 percent of of the population in Mesquite and Bunkerville were African American. But Cliven said he'd been in Los Angeles during the riots of 1965, and the mayhem in Watts reminded him of the Battle of Bunkerville.

"People were not happy," he said. "People were thinking they don't have their freedoms."

Cliven had more to say about "colored people":

I want to tell you one more thing I know about the Negro. When I went to go to Las Vegas and North Las Vegas, and I would see these little government houses, and in front of that government house, the door was usually open and the older people and the kids—and there is always at least a half a dozen people sitting on the porch—they didn't have nothing to do. They didn't have nothing for their kids to do. They didn't have nothing for their young girls to do.

And because they were basically on government subsidy, so now what do they do? They abort their young children, they put their young men in jail, because they never learned how to pick cotton. And I've often wondered, now are they better off as slaves, picking cotton, having a family life and doing things, or are they better off under government subsidy? They didn't get no more freedom. They got less freedom.

Ammon was standing next to Cliven, and he cringed inwardly, hoping his father's words would pass unnoticed. He never considered interrupting, and later, in private, he offered Cliven only a mild correction of one aspect of the speech.

Ammon said: *Dad, you can't use the term "Negro."*

Cliven seemed genuinely perplexed.

Cliven said: *What should I call them? That's what they prefer to be called.*

Ammon believed his father, that he truly didn't realize that Negro was an outdated term.

FOUR DAYS LATER, THE *NEW YORK TIMES* RAN A FEATURE STORY THAT CONtained Cliven's musings. Other newspapers grabbed the inflammatory quote, publishing stories like the one that appeared in the *Los Angeles Times* on April 24, 2014, headlined "Cliven Bundy's 'better off as slaves' remarks about blacks draws fire."

Cliven's media and political supporters backed away en masse. Nevada Senator Dean Heller said the remarks were "appalling and racist." Kentucky Senator Rand Paul said Cliven's "remarks on race are offensive and I wholeheartedly disagree with him." And Sean Hannity, the media figure who more than any other helped launch Cliven into the national spotlight, made the most abrupt about-face: The remarks, he said, "are beyond despicable to me. They are beyond ignorant to me." His producers stopped calling Bundy Ranch.

The Bundys were horrified. Ammon tried to explain that Cliven employed a "rancher's vocabulary." Ryan believed his father had sincerely wanted to reach out to minorities but didn't know what words were acceptable.

One talking head who didn't abandon Cliven was Alex Jones, who hosted him on Infowars. As Cliven tried to explain his thinking in more depth, Jones squirmed in his seat, squinting at the camera.

"I said, 'I'm wondering if you're better off,'" Cliven explained. "Your young women are having abortions and your young men are being thrown in jail. And your older women are sitting out on the sidewalk with your children and grandchildren, and they don't seem to be happy. And what I'm wondering is, are you better off in this type of slavery than you were when you was home with your family unit, with your gardens, with your chickens, with your men working, and your family life? Are you better off now, or were you better off then? I'm wondering these things."

Jones interjected, shoving the conversation into safer territory: "What do you think of the *New York Times* trying to take this out of context and spin it?"

Cliven ignored the cue and stuck to his guns, Bundy style, doubling down on his original point: "I'm wondering, are they better off under their old system of slavery or are they better off under the welfare slavery that they're under now? I'm not saying one way or the other, but I am wondering. It seems to me like maybe they *were* happier, they maybe did have better families and their family structure was better."

Jones broke in to note that he, himself, did not endorse slavery.

The Bundy family posted an announcement about an upcoming second Bundy Ranch party, including: "A special invatation to the Hispanic and black community."

AFTER HIS ATTEMPTS TO EXPLAIN HIS SLAVERY COMMENTS ONLY FANNED THE flames, Cliven retreated from the news media limelight. He largely stopped giving his freewheeling interviews. Ammon and Ryan continued to speak for the Bundy family. At the second party, two weeks after the standoff, it was Ryan who gave an hour-long speech/press conference to an assemblage of reporters and supporters. He said Cliven was a loving person who wanted the Latino and black communities to succeed.

"He may have fumbled over his words, but I know his intent and his heart is trying to share this with those people and to bring them here so we can bring them greater liberty," Ryan said. "There may be an element of ignorance on his side."

Ammon tried to steer the conversation back to the main topic. Three weeks after the standoff, Cliven was nowhere to be seen as

Ammon and another twenty relatives and supporters gathered at the Clark County Sheriff's Office to file criminal reports against the federal agents who had conducted the BLM roundup. Before a semicircle of cameras, Ammon haltingly read a nine-minute written statement from printouts. He didn't want to make a verbal misstep.

"A few weeks ago, our community was in a state of innocence," he read. "We felt safe and mostly kept to ourselves. We thought the world's problems would only affect us through television and could be shut off with the push of a button. Our innocence has left us now."

The next evening, on the other side of the country in Washington, DC, President Obama delivered the traditionally comic keynote speech at the White House Correspondents' Dinner, and one of his biggest laughs was at Cliven's expense. Obama praised the recent Winter Olympics athletes, including a snowboarder.

"I haven't seen anybody pull a one-eighty that fast since Rand Paul disinvited that Nevada rancher to this dinner," he said, and then paused as laughter filled the ballroom. "As a general rule, things don't end well if the sentence starts: 'Let me tell you something I know about the Negro.'" The black-tie crowd roared, and Obama's mouth twitched as he held back a smirk. "You don't really need to hear the rest of it."

THE DAYS AND NIGHTS DRAGGED ON, AND MORALE DETERIORATED AT CAMP Liberty. The numbers dwindled to a few dozen. Patriots had work and families, and eventually each had to decide how much time could be spent guarding the Bundys. Several told Ryan Payne their tour of duty at Bundy Ranch had cost them their jobs.

A rift developed between Stewart Rhodes's Oath Keepers and Ryan Payne's militia. All Oath Keepers were verified former military and law-enforcement members, and they had numbers and structure and resources, so they tended to look down on militia members as ragtag wannabe GI Joes. They generally thought Payne was not just twitchy but full of shit.

After the standoff, Payne repeatedly touted his own tactical brilliance. He gave a long interview to a writer from the Southern Poverty Law Center, an organization expressly pitted against the Patriot movement, and he said he and Cliven had toured the Bunkerville area before the standoff, scouting defensive positions. He suggested that Eric Parker and the other riflemen on the interstate bridge had found themselves there not by accident but by design. The bridge was chosen, he said, because it was high ground with "great lines of fire," fortified with concrete barriers.[*]

"We locked them down," he told the *Missoula Independent.* "We had counter-sniper positions on their sniper positions. We had at least one guy—sometimes two guys—per BLM agent in there. So, it was a complete tactical superiority . . . If they made one wrong move, every single BLM agent in that camp would've died."

Some locals complained about the armed men patrolling their highways and setting up security perimeters around churches and schools, but Payne continued to enjoy the backing of the Bundys. So the Oath Keepers were forced to find a way to get along with him, although Rhodes wanted to pull the Oath Keepers out of Camp Liberty and form a separate but connected scout detachment.

When criticized, Payne tended to go on the offensive. He'd claim his detractor was a federal operative conducting psychological operations designed to disrupt the militia from within. Psy-ops were a major topic of discussion in Camp Liberty. So was electronic warfare, meaning the government jamming their handsets and

---

[*] Later, facing criminal prosecution, Ryan Payne retracted many of these statements and said he was lying when he told journalists that the standoff in Toquop Wash was orchestrated.

phones. The troops had a lot of time on their hands in the desert and spent much of it gaming out endless defensive scenarios in case of a government attack.

Ammon was receiving an education in Patriot culture. He learned about agent provocateurs—individuals who were paid by the feds to infiltrate Patriot groups for the purpose of sowing discord and encouraging lawbreaking. Then there were confidential informants, who maintained a lower profile and simply relayed information to the feds. These weren't figments of paranoia. As far back as the 1960s, the feds had used informants to bring down constitutionalist and racist groups, and the practice was so successful that many such organizations were riddled with moles. In the 1980s, for example, more than half the participants at some Aryan Nations' gatherings in northern Idaho were reporting to one law-enforcement agency or another. Fear of infiltration—and hatred of infiltrators—had become a bedrock of Patriot culture.

Rumors constantly flew, and it was hard to tell whether they'd been generated by the feds or by the Patriots' obsession with the feds. Ammon participated in some Patriot meetings and witnessed the never-ending incoming flow of so-called intelligence. He dismissed the wildest rumors, but he was struck by how genuine the Patriots' fear seemed to be. What had these men witnessed, as civilians and in the military, that made them capable of believing the feds were prepared to wipe them out? Ammon was beginning to understand their mindset. After recent experiences, he was primed to think the worst of the federal government.

Unsurprisingly, the various militia groups that came to Bunkerville never really learned to trust each other. Major Patriot organizations like the Michigan Militia had been laid low by federal infiltration, so it was hard enough to trust compatriots in your own organization. Trusting strangers from other groups was nearly impossible. So it was a constant frustration, because the opportunity made possible by the Battle of Bunkerville—a united Patriot front—seemed closer than ever but so far away.

Two weeks after the standoff, the tension boiled over when the Oath Keepers reported they'd received intelligence about an imminent government attack. The source said US attorney general Eric Holder had authorized a drone strike on Bundy Ranch. The intel reportedly came from a source in Texas, an individual the Oath Keepers believed was trustworthy and connected within the Department of Defense. The Oath Keepers were trying to confirm the information through a second source.

Stewart Rhodes relayed the rumor to Payne, who didn't believe it. Rhodes was skeptical too. Would the feds really kill American civilians in such an overt way? On the other hand, the senate majority leader had called them domestic terrorists, which perhaps opened the door to a suspension of due process. At this fervid moment, among this collection of Patriot diehards at Camp Liberty, the notion of a governmental drone strike did not seem completely batshit.

Rhodes called everybody back to Camp Liberty and briefed them on what he'd heard, and Payne was furious. Payne was in charge, and he believed Rhodes had violated the chain of command. For his part, Rhodes believed it was his duty to let the militia and Oath Keepers know about the rumored strike so they could decide whether they wanted to stay.

Camp Liberty erupted. Rival factions clashed, and at least twice, gunfights nearly broke out. Once, according to Rhodes, two militiamen were arguing with an Oath Keeper, and one ran to his vehicle and grabbed an assault rifle. The Oath Keeper drew his sidearm. In another incident on the same day, a militiaman reportedly knocked down an elderly veteran in the camp, and when the Oath Keepers reacted, another militiaman reached for a firearm.

According to Rhodes, he told an Oath Keeper: *I dare you to draw, motherfucker.*

The episode ended with the Oath Keepers pulling out of Camp Liberty and checking into a nearby hotel.

The two dozen or so remaining militia members gathered, including Payne and Booda Cavalier.

"You do not ever leave a man behind on the battlefield," Payne told the remaining troops. "You do not ever turn tail and run in the face of danger. You do not ever leave a fallen comrade to fall into the hands of the enemy. This is desertion that was done. This is dereliction of duty."

He took a vote and everyone agreed that the Oath Keepers were traitors and shouldn't be allowed back in Camp Liberty or Bundy Ranch.

"You don't fucking walk in and say 'I'm sorry,' and you're back in, brother," Payne said. "You walk in and say you're sorry, and you're lucky that you're not getting shot in the back. Because that's what happens to deserters on the battlefield."

Payne believed the Oath Keepers had come to Bunkerville simply to build membership. Or maybe they were agent provocateurs. Oath Keepers lobbed the same insult back at Payne and Cavalier—they had to be working for the feds, purposely trying to disrupt Camp Liberty. Others speculated that Payne's combat experiences had traumatized him, affecting his decision-making and behavior. Maybe he was looking for a way out, something akin to suicide by cop: suicide by feds.

The remaining militia members endlessly dissected the qualifications and characteristics of Camp Liberty's past and present inhabitants. What had so-and-so done at Toquop Wash? Had he even been there? Was he clinically insane? They debated whether their compatriots' military service was real or concocted, whether they'd actually been in combat or had received the specialized training they claimed.

But Topic Number One, as always, was: Who was working for the feds? Who in their midst was an agent provocateur? Who was an informant? Who was an out-and-out undercover FBI agent? Almost any characteristic could be a tip-off. Some people were too boisterous, some too aggressive. Some too secretive or nervous. If someone proposed breaking the law, others speculated that the action could have been suggested by an FBI handler as a way to entrap the Patriots. A classic agent provocateur move was to claim that somebody else was working for the feds, so simply lodging an accusation sometimes landed the accuser under the microscope. Generally being obnoxious was regarded with suspicion, but so was being overly buddy-buddy. Having money to spend was cause for misgivings, or having ambiguous sources of income, or springing for a hotel room when everybody else was living communally. The Patriots investigated each others' criminal records, wondering if an individual was working off a charge by spying for the feds. Patriots who had a predisposition for mysticism, like Brand Nu Thornton, claimed they could tell whether someone was a fed by just spending time with them, soaking in their aura. Turncoats had a dark cloud around them.

One of the camp's most discussed individuals was Robert "Little Dog" Crooks, who had driven his camper to Bunkerville, arriving right after the standoff, and who came off to many as a ticking time bomb. Little Dog was well-known among Patriots. He ran a tiny border-patrol outfit called the Mountain Minutemen, operating out of his aging camper on the US-Mexico border to safeguard the United States from illegal immigrants. In 2007, Little Dog had attracted the attention of the law when he posted a grainy video on YouTube that looked like it was shot through a rifle scope with night vision. Two fevered voices talk as the scope scans a hillside and then spots a shadowy figure climbing it.

"All right, where's he at, what's your twenty?" someone says over a radio.

"He's up there on the smuggler's trail," says the gunman, whose voice sounds like Little Dog's gravelly pitch. "You know what, I'm gonna take a fucking shot."

Two gunshots sound, and the figure drops.

"Oh fuck, I got him, dude," the gunman says, excitement in his voice. "I fucking got him!"

The video ends with a shot of a stone-covered grave, and the gunman saying: "Adios, asshole."

The San Diego County Sheriff's Office investigated and determined that the video was likely staged. Little Dog initially said he had nothing to do with it, and then later admitted he'd faked it.

"Who in their right mind is going to shoot a smuggler, videotape it, then post it to YouTube?" Little Dog said.

Many observers at Camp Liberty weren't sure Little Dog *was* in his right mind, or at the very least, they figured he was an agent provocateur. Controversy and trouble followed him. At the camp, he was accused of mistreating women, of stealing guns. But the militia leaders allowed Little Dog to stay for months, and many grew frustrated with this decision.

THE YOUNG COUPLE WHO *HAD* BEEN KICKED OUT OF CAMP LIBERTY, JERAD and Amanda Miller, were mostly forgotten.

They moved back to Las Vegas, where they stayed in a friend's apartment. On June 7, 2014, almost two months after the Bunkerville standoff, Jerad posted on Facebook: "The dawn of a new day. May all of our coming sacrifices be worth it."

The next morning, in a shopping plaza northeast of the Vegas Strip, Jerad walked into a Cicis pizza restaurant and glanced around. Two Las Vegas Metro officers were in a booth, on lunch break. Jerad ducked back outside, and then returned, joined by Amanda. The pair walked past the officers. Jerad pulled out a handgun and shot Officer Igor Soldo, age thirty-one, in the head. Soldo slumped over and didn't move again.

The other officer, Alyn Beck, age forty-one, yanked out his service weapon, but Jerad shot him in the throat. And then Amanda pulled out her own Smith & Wesson 9-millimeter handgun, and both she and Jerad fired several shots into Beck.

Jerad and Amanda pulled the officers' bodies out of the booth and onto the floor and took their service weapons and ammunition. They draped a yellow Gadsden flag on Beck's body. Then they used a swastika pin to fasten a note onto Soldo's body: "The revolution is beginning."

They walked out of the restaurant, grabbed their backpacks, and crossed a busy street to a Walmart, both holding their handguns by their sides. A few steps ahead of Amanda, Jerad entered the store, yelling about a revolution, and fired a warning shot into the ceiling. Shoppers jumped, scrambling toward the exit. A thirty-one-year-old man named Joseph Wilcox went against the crowd, following Jerad and grabbing for his own gun, which was stuffed in the back of his pants.

Jerad headed for the sporting-goods section, Amanda pushing a shopping cart about twenty feet behind him. Wilcox passed Amanda, apparently not realizing she was with Jerad, and ducked into an aisle. Amanda extended her arm with the gun and shot Wilcox in the ribs. He collapsed.

Jerad grabbed a baseball bat, walked behind the firearms counter, and smashed the glass on the ammunition cabinets. He tossed ammunition boxes until he found the one he wanted.

One five-officer Metro team entered the rear of the store, and another entered the front. One officer commandeered the security room, radioing information to the other officers about the Millers' locations. An officer spotted Amanda, and they exchanged shots. Jerad dropped his bag and joined in.

Amanda was hit. Blood soaking through her tank top, she lay sprawled on the floor in the auto-parts corner of the store, a pile of toppled motor-oil cartons around her. Jerad grabbed his backpack and slipped on a puddle of motor oil. He regained his footing, pulled out a bottle of water, and tossed it to Amanda.

An officer took a shot, and Jerad went down to the floor. Amanda pointed her gun at Jerad, then back at herself, then back at her husband. Lying on his belly, Jerad's head was up, and he seemed to be watching his wife, but then his head slowly drooped, like he was finally exhausted with the war he'd waged against the authorities for so long, mostly on the internet and then briefly at Bunkerville, but now for real in this shitty shopping center. Jerad's revolution was over. He lay his head down on the floor and didn't move again.

Amanda put the barrel of her gun to her own temple and pulled the trigger.

SOLDO, BECK, WILCOX, AND THE MILLERS ALL DIED THAT MORNING. The symbology of the Gadsden flag and the swastika placed on the police officers' bodies confused some observers at first. Did the Millers belong to the Patriot movement, as the "Don't Tread on Me" flag suggested? Or were they neo-Nazi fascists? Or were they just confused? The two ideologies occupied very different limbs of the radical taxonomy.

A quick peek into the Millers' extensive online history cleared up the puzzle. Jerad had been especially prolific in his online postings about hating cops and the federal government, a hatred that clearly stemmed from his criminal history. He posted regularly on Facebook, on YouTube, on Planet Infowars. The Millers were hardcore Patriots. Even Jerad's icon on Planet Infowars was a Gadsden flag. Based on Jerad's social media, investigators concluded the swastika was supposed to indicate that the *cops* were the Nazis.

Police and reporters quickly connected the Millers to the Bundy standoff. The interview Jerad had done at the Bunkerville protest site surfaced, the one in which he sounded eager to bring violence to the feds. Mark Potok, a senior fellow at the Southern Poverty Law Center, implied there was a direct cause and effect from the Bundy standoff to the shootings.

"I think that Jerad Miller's presence at the Bundy standoff is extremely important to trying to understand what happened in Las Vegas," Potok said. "I think it is very possible that Jerad Miller saw it as the opening battle in a revolutionary war against the government, which he intended to continue."

Confronted with numerous Facebook posts that demonstrated Jerad Miller was a devout Infowars fan, Alex Jones claimed the government was behind the shooting spree. The feds had staged it, he theorized, to eviscerate the Bundy movement. He'd made similar claims after September 11 and numerous other tragedies, calling these operations "false flags."

"We are in the middle of a globalist revolution against this country right now, and my gut tells me that the cold-blooded, degenerate, evil killing of two police officers and a citizen in Las Vegas yesterday is absolutely staged," he said.

The Bundys and their followers acknowledged the Millers had been in Bunkerville, which the video evidence made undeniable. The couple had interviewed Ryan Bundy and Margaret Houston on April 9, and Jerad was interviewed by a TV station on April 13, one day after the standoff. But Ammon downplayed the connection between the standoff and the shooting spree.

"They were very radical, you know, and did not align themselves with the reason that the protesters were here," Ammon said. "Not very many people were asked to leave. I think they may have been the only ones."

181

On a June 2014 evening, about a week after the Millers' shooting spree, the phone rang at Bundy Ranch. On the line was a man named Charles Johnson. He asked for Cliven, but Ammon took the call. Ammon had been shuttling back and forth between Bunkerville and Phoenix, trying to support his parents, as well as his own family.

With a smooth Southern twang, Johnson said he was a documentary filmmaker from a Nashville outfit called Longbow Productions. Oddly, he didn't seem familiar with Ammon. Odd because Ammon was one of the stars of the entire saga—he had been shot with Tasers, had commanded the front line of protesters in Toquop Wash, and had largely taken over the family spokesman duties from Cliven. He was the second most famous Bundy by now. But Johnson asked how Ammon spelled his name, and said he wanted to interview Cliven.

"I've kind of been watching this situation unfold, kind of from a distance, and just to be real honest with you, I'm amazed at the support and the actual momentum that your dad has been able to gather," Johnson drawled. "It's truly impressive to me."

A number of documentary filmmakers had made similar pitches to the family. Perhaps the most legitimate so far was a team called Free State Films that had spent time at the ranch a few weeks earlier and had produced a four-minute trailer for a proposed film they called *The Last Rancher*. The Free State Films crew appeared to be serious about understanding the range wars, and the trailer was professionally produced with honey-toned shots of the desert over the sounds of Western guitar strings.

The Bundys welcomed the attention. Since the standoff, the family had suffered one piece of bad publicity after another—the Negro speech fiasco, the militia/Oath Keepers beef, the Millers' shooting spree. The Bundys needed sympathetic storytellers.

But as far as Ammon could tell, the man from Longbow

Productions hadn't done his homework. So Ammon looked up Longbow. The company had a simple website that touted itself as a "full service production company" with more than fifteen employees. Longbow did a little bit of everything, it seemed, from commercials and documentaries to casting. "You're in luck: we're small," the website said. "We take pride in each and every project." But Ammon couldn't find actual examples of work produced by Longbow, so he was skeptical. The family was busy and couldn't afford to lend time to projects that weren't going anywhere.

"We want to reach a lot of people," Ammon told Johnson. "But we also can't do one hundred different documentaries."

Johnson said he'd like to buy the rights to the family's story. Ammon said he wasn't interested in the money, but the offer at least demonstrated that Johnson had some sort of backing. The Free State Films crew had offered no money, and in fact had launched a crowd-funding campaign to raise $15,000 to cover their preproduction and location filming costs, raising only a small fraction of their goal so far.

"I'd be willing to meet and talk with you, but I think you need to get more familiar with the story first and then really see if you want to take on this thing," Ammon said.

The team from Longbow Productions proved they were serious, showing up unannounced at the ranch less than two weeks later. Charles Johnson was a middle-aged man sporting a goatee and slicked-back hair. Booda Cavalier met the crew and immediately established his authority, saying their visit had not been approved. Since the standoff, Cavalier often acted too busy, too important to speak to people who weren't high on the Patriot food chain. Still, he gave the documentary crew a tour of the property, bragging about exploits in Iraq and Afghanistan as a Marine. The Longbow producer, a tall blonde named Anna, egged him on.

"Did you ever kill anybody?" she said.

"Yeah," Cavalier said. "I was a United States Marine Corps Scout Sniper."

The Longbow team didn't catch Cliven or Ammon that day, but they did interview Cavalier and Carol and shot B-roll of the ranch. Unlike the Free State Films crew, they weren't looking for a serious discussion of the range wars. They were after more sensational content. For the Longbow team, the problem was that the Bundys had already thrown open their lives to so many people, given so many interviews, posted so many videos themselves. They'd explained their motives, documented their actions. It was all out there in the open. It would cost a lot of money to mount this project. Was it worth it if they didn't come away with any new details?

During the trip to Bundy Ranch, Johnson worried about this.

"Do you think there's any more stuff to be gotten out here?" he asked another member of the Longbow crew, out of earshot of the Bundys. "The problem is, we're the last ones to the dance."

WEEKS AND MONTHS PASSED, AND THE ATMOSPHERE AT BUNDY RANCH lightened. The feds didn't invade Gold Butte. No drone strikes obliterated Camp Liberty. No sniper on a distant ridge took out Cliven. The sheriff didn't even drop by.

Supporters still showed up to pull tours of duty, but Camp Liberty's numbers further dwindled. Ryan Payne and Ryan Bundy had gone to Recapture Canyon in Utah in May 2014 to ride with other protesters on a four-wheeler trail the BLM had closed seven years earlier. Then Payne had gone back home to Montana, pretty sure he would be leaving again soon, either for another Operation Mutual Aid mission or maybe in handcuffs. By and by, even Little Dog drove off in his camper.

184

Eventually, only Booda Cavalier remained. He liked Carol's cooking and didn't seem to have anywhere else he needed to be. He lived in a trailer near the Bundy house and followed Cliven around. He called himself the family's head of security, but Cliven thought of him as more of a butler, dealing with visitors and generally deterring problems. Though the militia was gone, Cavalier boasted that reinforcements were close. He said he could tap a quick alert on social media and muster dozens of "heavy operators" from St. George and Las Vegas within an hour or two.

Environmental groups grew frustrated as the BLM seemed to ignore the cattle that continued to graze on Gold Butte.

"The BLM has a sacred duty to manage our public lands in the public interest, to treat all users equally and fairly," said Rob Mrowka, senior scientist with the influential Center for Biological Diversity. "Instead it is allowing a freeloading rancher and armed thugs to seize hundreds of thousands of acres of the people's land as their own fiefdom."

The BLM didn't respond publicly and in fact pretty much stopped talking about the Bundy situation altogether. Reporters called for reaction to the unfolding events and almost always got a "no comment." Many observers criticized the BLM's weak efforts at public relations. The First Amendment zones had been a disaster, and the BLM's lack of messaging allowed grazing fees to dominate the discussion, making it look like the massive and expensive operation was all an effort to collect the ranching equivalent of late library fines. Instead, posited some observers, the BLM should have done more to highlight the damage the Bundy herd was doing to public land, reinforcing that the roundup was being conducted to protect the environment of Gold Butte. But the Bundy family largely controlled the news coverage and portrayed Cliven as a folk hero, a lone cowboy standing up to an overreaching government. This, combined with Dan Love's huge, militarized roundup operation, had proved to be a recipe for disaster for the BLM.

After the standoff, BLM rangers were rarely, if ever, seen in Gold Butte, though the Bundys did occasionally cross paths with BLM civilian employees. When the Bundys spotted a government license plate, they kept an eye on it until it left the area. Most of these incidents involved Ryan Bundy, who tailed a two-person BLM fire crew for ten miles on Gold Butte Road and grilled a Las Vegas Metro cop who was escorting BLM employees about what they were doing there. The police officer said the BLM was conducting an annual plant survey.

Ryan said: *Do they know those plants belong to us, not them?*

One summer day in 2015, more than a year after the standoff, three BLM employees went to Gold Butte for an overnight assignment that involved surveying cattle damage. That evening, Cliven and his youngest son pulled up in a truck, blocking them in. Cliven joked that he'd been chasing BLM all day.

The exchange seemed harmless enough, so the employees prepared to camp for the night. However, an hour after sunset, they heard a vehicle come up the road and stop about five hundred meters away. Three gunshots echoed over the hills. The vehicle drove away. The BLM employees remained. An hour later, the vehicle returned. More gunshots. The vehicle left again. Unnerved, the BLM employees broke camp and headed for Las Vegas.

After that, the BLM disappeared altogether from the public lands around Bundy Ranch. A group called Friends of Gold Butte complained that the area had become lawless. Signs were torn down. Trash was dumped. Off-roaders tore up the desert. A pioneer gravesite was dug up, and an ancient petroglyph was riddled with bullet holes.

Gold Butte was free of governmental interference, practically its

186

own sovereign state. Cliven told people Bundy Ranch was the freest place on Earth.

Locals started calling Gold Butte "Bundystan."

STILL, CLIVEN WASN'T SATISFIED. OVER THE YEARS, THE LIBERATION OF Bundy Ranch had become secondary to his pet concern of county supremacy. That was the topic he'd received divine instruction about, and it had not been seriously taken up by the news media or law enforcement. Many sheriffs claimed to be constitutional, but none disarmed the federal agents within their jurisdictions. The Bundy standoff did shove the range wars into the national news as they had never been before, but more sensational elements of the story dominated the coverage: assault rifles, militias, the Miller murders, and Cliven's speech about "the Negro."

So there was work to be done. Cliven continued to avoid speaking to mainstream media these days, leaving that to Ammon and Ryan, but there were protests to attend, speeches to give, candidates and legislation to back. Cliven told the story of the Battle of Bunkerville to friendly audiences, usually at Tea Party or Patriot events. At a meeting of the Independent American Party in St. George, Utah, Cliven seemed disappointed that fewer than 120 people showed up, and that the crowd contained no people of color, which he called "our black and our brown." He offered the Mormon belief that the US Constitution was divinely inspired.

"If our Constitution is an inspired document by our Lord Jesus Christ, then isn't it scripture?" he asked.

"Yes," the crowd replied.

"Isn't it the same as the Book of Mormon and the Bible?"

"Absolutely!"

Six months after the standoff, an Independent American Party candidate for Congress named Kamau Bakari reached out to Cliven and asked if the rancher would appear in a campaign advertisement. Cliven agreed. Bakari's campaign supplied a script. The rancher and Bakari, who was black, wore cowboy gear and made conversation as they saddled up a horse.

"I know black folks have had a hard time with slavery, and you know, the government was in on it," Cliven said. "I worked my whole life without mistreating anybody. A man ought to be able to express hisself without being called names."

"I hear you, Cliven, and I believe you," Bakari said. "A brave white man like you may be just what we need to put an end to this political correctness stuff in America today."

And after the standoff, it did seem the rules had changed. One week before the standoff's one-year anniversary, Cliven and Ammon traveled to Carson City with more than one hundred people to support a state bill the Bundys had helped draft. The bill would require the federal government to obtain permission to use land within the state's borders and would create a state registry of water, mineral, timber, and grazing rights. The Bunkerville standoff had sparked the Sagebrush Rebellion back to life, at least on the state level, as eleven western states had introduced similar bills.

Cliven's fight had also inspired ranchers here and there to "go Bundy," meaning letting their cattle graze on BLM land without a permit. In northern Nevada, forty supporters accompanied one ranching family as they trucked about three hundred cattle to a BLM allotment and released them. The BLM simply struck a new deal with the family and several other ranchers, allowing them to graze if they paid a trespass fine.

AFTER THE STANDOFF, LAVOY FINICUM BEGAN QUESTIONING HIS OWN relationship with the BLM. He began reading more widely about politics and economics, sitting in the living room chair that Jeanette had bought and reupholstered for him. He kept a changing stack of books under the chair, an eclectic range of titles that included G. Edward's Griffin's *The Creature from Jekyll Island*, first published in 1994, which posited the Federal Reserve as an instrument of totalitarianism. Finicum called and met with Cliven a number of times and began inviting small groups of Patriot-minded people over to the Finicum house for meetings.

Two weeks after the standoff, Finicum had sat in his chair and recorded a video of himself delivering a measured rebuke to his longtime media favorite Glenn Beck, who had criticized the Bundys and their followers.

"You say violence is never the answer," Finicum said. "When it comes to our home, our family, our life, liberty, and property, do we not have a God-given right to defend them physically, if necessary?"

Finicum created a YouTube channel and uploaded the video. Two weeks later, he created another video responding to President Obama's jibes about Cliven's "Negro" speech. Every few weeks or months, Finicum posted new videos, sometimes from scenic spots on his grazing allotment, sometimes with Esperanza, or his dog, or one of his daughters. He always wore a cream Stetson. In one video, he sat atop a one-hundred-pound crate of rolled oats and discussed how to prepare for a disaster, explaining how two people could store a year's supply of food under a queen bed.

On Independence Day in 2015, LaVoy and Jeanette self-published his apocalyptic novel. A month later, after more than a year of soul-searching, Finicum announced that he had sent a letter to the US Office of the Solicitor General canceling his grazing contract with the BLM. He'd never had any issues with the BLM before, and he got along with the local rangers, believed they were good people. But how could he justify making a legal agreement with a federal agency he knew was unconstitutional?

The BLM's response was restrained. The agency began to assess fines against his cattle. Finicum heard BLM officials had met with the Mohave County sheriff and were trying to evaluate the mindset of his neighbors in Cane Beds, wondering if they had the makings of another Bundy standoff on their hands.

One evening in mid-October 2015, Finicum was about to take a load of cattle to his winter range when he paused to stand in a pasture and record a short interview, the late-day sun illuminating his face. Usually sedate on camera, Finicum was openly agitated this evening. He struggled to find words and smacked his hands together in frustration. He'd been reading about a ranching family in Oregon. A father and son who'd been sentenced a week earlier to prison time for doing controlled burns on BLM land. Their last name was Hammond.

"Dadgummit, it's gotta stop. It's gotta stop." Finicum glared at the camera. "BLM, here I am. You want to come pick on somebody? Come pick on me. It's time somebody stands up."

In Blanchester, Ohio, about forty miles northeast of Cincinnati, a twenty-seven-year-old man named David Fry watched Finicum's video about the Hammonds.

Fry clicked to the comments and attached a link to a story about the Nestlé company lacking the proper permits to extract groundwater in California. He wrote:

> nestle hadn't renewed their permit for 27 years to extract water but the government allowed it. yet . . . the MINUTE

any one of the ranchers don't pay their grazing permits they come after you like a pack of dogs!

Five weeks earlier, Fry had become an unlikely LaVoy Finicum fan after he watched the rancher talk on YouTube about canceling his grazing contract. He liked the way Finicum presented himself: calm but firm, controlled but defiant. Fry, who lived in his parents' home and worked in the office of the dental practice they managed, shared only the defiance. He'd struggled with the law and his own mind for years.

Fry's mother was a native of Japan, and his father was an American Marine. Fry had learned to speak Japanese first, and then English when he was three years old, and his voice still held the trace of an accent. He'd been one of the few nonwhite kids in his school. Slight and angular-faced, Fry wore his black hair in a long ponytail. He always liked computers and gaming, and in his late teens, he grew obsessed with dark events and spent hours doing online research, reading about the infamous Tuskegee syphilis experiment, looking at pictures of aborted fetuses. He spent time in mental-health facilities. He was arrested more than once for smoking marijuana, was fined for not wearing a life jacket while river rafting, blew up at a cop who pulled him over. His anger became focused on law enforcement and government, his fears on Jewish conspiracies and nuclear meltdowns. He began writing a blog he called *Dead America*.

He sensed a kindred spirit in Finicum. Fry wrote on Finicum's YouTube page and a brief correspondence ensued:

> **FRY:** I refuse to pay my tickets for not wearing a life jacket in a 3 foot deep river and smoking marijuana!! Fuck you government!
>
> **FINICUM:** Thanks for your support David.

FRY: No, sir. thank YOU! you give people like me hope. I really mean that. Yah bless you! Halleui Yah!

FINICUM: Share and spread the word, there is power in numbers, it will take each one of us to save this Country and the Constitution.

A week later, Fry took to YouTube himself, creating a channel titled *DefendYourBase*. His first video was a LaVoy Finicum–style act of defiance. He stood on the gravel driveway of his parents' home and lit afire a letter from a collection agency that was trying to collect the fine he owed from the river-rafting penalty.

"This is how every American should treat these unjust laws," Fry said.

LIKE FINICUM AND FRY, MANY PATRIOTS DECIDED TO TAKE CONTROL OF their message. They created YouTube channels, blogs, and Facebook pages. Laid up with a broken foot after falling off a roof she was repairing, Shawna Cox pounded out a book about the Bundy stand-off. Titled *Last Rancher Standing*, it was an enthusiastic and stream-of-consciousness retelling, punctuated with quotations from the US Constitution and the Book of Mormon.

Patriots had always had their own information channels, going back to the early days when John Birchers and Posse Comitatus traded self-published pamphlets. Now, thousands of like-minded people had met each other in Bunkerville, and as a result, many found both their voices and a wider audience. Modern technology allowed any-one to share views. Those who didn't want to write anything longer than a social media post often turned to video, usually posted on Face-book or YouTube. After the standoff, Cliven continued his series of educational videos on the Bundy Ranch blog, with titles like "Where do the Feds Get Their Power?"

A few Patriots backed up their reports with extensive documentation, including Gary Hunt, a California man in his late sixties who had begun self-publishing a Patriot newspaper called *Outpost of Freedom* in 1993, eventually transitioning to the internet. His coverage of "The Bundy Affair," as he called it, was investigative reporting from a Patriot point of view, pieced together with leaked documents and insider interviews and details collected on the ground. On the other hand, Hunt's credibility was undermined by views that hewed somewhat to the extreme even by Patriot standards, including his apparent belief that Timothy McVeigh got a tough break.

Many Patriots played it fast and loose with the facts, hitting "record" on their cell phones and letting fly all manner of theory, supposition, and stuff they'd heard. Former Lt. Col. Roy Potter couched his statements in such a knowing tangle of Kabbalistic and black-ops gobbledygook that it was nearly impossible to challenge him. Sometimes even the most conspiratorial Patriots acknowledged that they were attracted to stories that might not stand up to the light of day, stories they simply wanted to believe. They found ways to justify this. Many stories on Infowars were provably incorrect or even ridiculous, they acknowledged, but the *ideology* behind them was sound. The arc of the moral universe was long, they believed, and while not every Infowars story turned out to be accurate, over the long haul, Alex Jones was right.

THE FREE STATE FILMS DOCUMENTARY PROJECT FIZZLED AFTER ITS CROWD-funding campaign collected only $5,817.

But the other documentary team, the one called Longbow

Productions, persisted. The working title for the film was *America Reloaded*. Between June 2014 and April 2015, the film crew had interviewed one Bundy relative and supporter after another. Anna had set up the interviews. The producer came off as a little ditzy, didn't seem to know much about the standoff or the Patriot movement, but she was enthusiastic and appeared to side with the Bundys.

In August, the crew traveled to a cabin in Idaho to interview Eric Parker and the friends who'd journeyed together to Bunkerville. A lawyer had advised Parker against speaking out, but Anna coaxed him into the interview.

"This is not about getting people in trouble," she said. "This is about spreading your message."

Parker felt reassured by the size of the crew and video equipment at the cabin. During the two-hour interview, the director, Charles Johnson, asked repeatedly if Parker had been willing to die for the cause and if he'd been prepared to shoot.

"How do you acquire your target?" Johnson asked.

"There's no picking the target," Parker said. "I wasn't chambered, and my finger wasn't on the trigger."

When Anna called Ryan Bundy, he was suspicious. Other interviewees had told him the documentary crew was asking lots of very specific questions about firearms.

"We deem those questions to be inappropriate," Ryan said. "The Second Amendment gives us the right to keep and bear arms, and it doesn't matter whether we have a BB gun or something bigger."

"Right!" Anna agreed.

But Ammon was in favor of working with Longbow and talked his family into sitting for interviews. In December 2014, Cliven and Ryan met the Longbow team in a suite at the swanky Bellagio hotel in Las Vegas. The six-person crew pointed high-definition cameras and an array of lights at the white leather chair where Ryan sat for the interview. Ryan still felt uneasy.

"Is this an interview and a documentary?" he asked. "Or is this an interrogation? That is our question."

"I understand that," Johnson said. "The only thing I ask from you is very simple: I'll ask you a question, and I ask you to tell me the truth. I want a truthful documentary."

"Alrighty," Ryan said. "Let's proceed then."

IF THE BUNDYS HAD KNOWN WHAT TO LOOK FOR, THEY'D HAVE SEEN A NUMber of warning signs that the Longbow team wasn't a real documentary crew.

Some of the hints were technical. The crew posed a squinting Carol in dappled sunlight and sat Cliven in front of a garish Bellagio painting. They recorded interviews in whipping wind that rendered statements inaudible. They pointed cameras at license plates while ostensibly capturing B-roll.

Other tip-offs were ethical in nature. The crew left microphones running when the interviewees asked them to turn them off. They had hidden cameras and microphones, in addition to the official ones. They supplied one interviewee with alcohol. They offered Booda Cavalier a payoff and offered Ryan Bundy tickets to the Wrangler National Finals Rodeo in Las Vegas.

But despite their crash course in the news media, the Bundys weren't versed in documentary filmmaking. The Longbow team had a lot of expensive-looking equipment, including a drone that they used to video the Bunkerville party marking the anniversary of the standoff. And Charles Johnson said things that sounded director-ish, such as: "Quiet on set!" It was enough.

Johnson, of course, was an FBI agent. Over a sixteen-year career, he'd investigated bank robberies, white-collar crime, domestic terrorism. After the standoff, he was pulled into the Bundy case and asked to develop an undercover operation. The problem was: undercover work was usually done to catch a target planning a criminal act. In this case, the offense had already been committed. So the FBI team had come up with the plan of creating a fake documentary crew and simply asking the Bundys and their followers to tell their stories. Johnson enjoyed photography in his spare time and had taken videography courses.

The FBI created the Longbow Productions website, email addresses, phone numbers, and business cards. Agents decked out a van with cameras, lights, and sound equipment. They also brought snacks and liquor to the interviews, though many of the subjects were non-drinking Mormons. Johnson developed a script of questions, and the Longbow team spent about ten months conducting interviews.

But, as Johnson had noted to his colleagues in the very first interview at Bundy Ranch, they felt like the last ones to the dance. The only interviewee who said anything inflammatory was Greg Burleson, who took a couple shots of bourbon, no chaser, during the interview. The fidgety Arizona man brought an assault rifle to the interview, though he left it in the car, and freely offered that he'd been disappointed the standoff didn't turn violent. He'd gone to Bunkerville, he said, to put federal agents "six feet under."

Booda Cavalier gave an incognito interview in Las Vegas, his face wrapped in a green scarf, and made lots of dubious claims, including that "high-level people" inside the BLM and FBI were feeding him information and running background checks at his request. "Without giving too much away, we definitely ran you guys and found out you're not related to FBI, BLM, or ATF," Cavalier told the FBI agents. "So that shows us that your motives for your production were possibly true, and you were not a security threat."

Despite thousands of miles of traveling and hours of interviews, the Longbow team wasn't coming up with a whole lot. The Bundys, as Johnson had feared, were kind of an open book. They'd told their stories dozens of times already, and few new details were coming out. But Johnson kept trying, asking the same questions in different ways.

"Did you think you might have to take a life?" he asked Ammon.

"I never did once think I'd have to take a life," Ammon said. "I was never armed."

WHEN THE FEDS APPROACHED TERRI LINNELL FOR INFORMATION ABOUT the Patriots, they didn't pose as documentary filmmakers.

In March 2015, the woman called Momma Bear was sitting outdoors at a table on her mountainside property inland of San Diego when two men in suits walked up and introduced themselves as US marshals. One did all the talking.

He said: *How do you feel about murderers?*

Linnell said: *Well, of course I don't like murderers. Who are you talking about?*

The marshal said he was referring to John Farrell Villarreal, a twenty-two-year-old South Carolina man accused of shooting two people who'd picked him up as he was hitchhiking to Georgia on Christmas Eve 2014. One victim had died and the other was in a wheelchair. Linnell had met Farrell Villarreal at a Patriot rally in Washington, DC, seven months before the shooting.

Like any Patriot, Linnell was wary of federal law officers. And her experience in Toquop Wash had only sharpened her suspicion that the government was keeping tabs on her dome house, mostly by the helicopters buzzing overhead but also by the nearby telephone pole that she believed was being serviced far too often.

Still, Linnell was a gregarious woman, and curious, and she was appalled by the murder. She decided she had no problem talking to the marshals about Farrell Villarreal.

Linnell told the marshals: *Have a seat.*

As the conversation progressed, however, it became clear that the marshals were interested in more than the murder case. They began asking questions about Farrell Villarreal's militia ties and gave her a list of names she mostly didn't recognize. Still, she kept speaking to them. She liked the marshal who did all the talking, and she agreed to meet him again.

Over the summer of 2015, Linnell met repeatedly with federal officers. Her primary contact became an FBI special agent who said her name was Carly. They usually met at a Panera Bread in a shopping center, and Carly said she belonged to the joint terrorism task force in San Diego. This alarmed Linnell, but eventually she came around to the idea that the Patriots and the terrorism task force should be working together. Linnell had cooperated with police as a neighborhood watch organizer. This was similar. Both sides had the same goals.

So when Carly asked Linnell to go to Oath Keeper meetings and report on the leader, she complied. Then a Three Percenter group opened up in Linnell's region, and she joined. Linnell worked her way up within the group, but Carly told her to not take on a leadership position, so she didn't.

Before long, even for Momma Bear, it began to seem natural to be working both sides of the fence.

EARLY IN 2015, LISA AND AMMON HAD ANOTHER BABY, AND IN THE SUM-mer, they moved the family to the hills of Emmett, Idaho, northwest of Boise, buying a house on a five-acre property with an orchard that contained 240 apple trees. Ammon wanted his kids to grow up out of doors, as he had. After the tumult of the past year, it felt urgent to get his family out of the city and lead a quieter life.

Ammon and Lisa loved their pastoral new home, but Ammon found it wasn't that easy to put the standoff behind him. He flew once a week from Boise to Phoenix to spend a day at Valet Fleet Service, and airport security pulled him aside every time to search and interrogate him. His boarding passes had special letters stamped on them, and while security didn't explain, Ammon became convinced he'd been placed on a terror watch list. After all, Harry Reid had called him a domestic terrorist.

Ammon never adapted to being frisked and having his bags searched, item by item. And as the months passed and he didn't hear from the Longbow Productions team, he became convinced they were federal agents, which meant Ammon had persuaded his family to let wolves in the door. He didn't take these vexations lightly. He believed the government was hounding him, punishing him without due process.

While his father and brothers and sisters had remained in Dixie and pursued simpler lives, Ammon had chosen to venture further into the world, living in a big city, building a substantial business. He'd lived the life of a modern American, traveling and dealing with a wide variety of people. He was a man of standing. The past year and a half had changed all of the Bundys, but perhaps because Ammon's life was more mainstream, the events had jolted him harder than the others, spun his worldview more violently. Ryan *expected* to clash with the authorities. Ammon had never been charged with a serious crime, and it appalled him to be considered a danger to society. So Ammon fell farther, had farther to fall. His views darkened.

Ammon hadn't carried a gun at Bunkerville, but he was glad others had. Over time, as he reflected on those events, he'd realized that firearms were a crucial part of the equation. When the family and neighbors were just carrying signs and giving speeches, the feds had felt free to arrest them, take their cattle, throw them down, taser them. When men with guns showed up, these activities ceased. When men with guns showed up, the news media began to tell the Bundys' story. But it took men with guns.

Ammon increasingly commandeered the Bundy Ranch blog, posting a series of videos and articles about the range wars and also about his troubles with airport security. Newly bearded, he spoke to the camera in a YouTube video.

"We have been labeled a threat to society, a threat to the rest of Americans," he said, looking desolate. "I just want to point out that history proves that the true threat to the citizens are their own governments. If the people do not keep an eye on their government, keep them checked and balanced, it always ends in mass murders of their own people."

After Ammon moved to Idaho, Cliven began nagging him about a hard-pressed ranching family in Oregon, the same family that LaVoy Finicum was concerned about.

Cliven said: *What do you know about these Hammonds? I feel like what happened to us is happening to them.*

Ammon didn't engage.

He said: *Dad, I can't fight another battle.*

On the evening of November 2, 2015, Ammon was lying in bed at home, and his cell phone buzzed on the bedside table. He grabbed it and clicked on the message, which contained an article about the Hammonds.

Ammon scanned the story. It had been a long day, and he was tired. It wasn't his responsibility. But he also couldn't believe that everything that had happened was for nothing. This wasn't over. It couldn't be over. He lay in bed, his mind pushing and pulling against itself.

And then a compulsion overwhelmed him. He had to know everything about the Hammonds and their fight with the government.

He got out of bed and went downstairs to his laptop.

Part III

Chapter 7

ROAD TO OREGON

Ammon stayed up all night, reading about the Hammond case. He couldn't sleep. He read as many articles as he could find, and a good chunk of the court transcripts.

Dwight and Steven Hammond were father and son ranchers in Harney County, the largest county in Oregon but one of the least populated. Hammond Ranches, Inc. owned about 12,000 acres of remote range and used an additional 26,420 acres of BLM grazing allotment. In the mid-1990s, the Hammonds were arrested for obstructing federal employees who were building a fence to keep Hammond cattle out of the Malheur National Wildlife Refuge, an important rest area for migratory birds. They weren't prosecuted, but the incident marked the beginning of a long, Bundy-like series of run-ins between the federal land agencies and the family.

In 2001, the Hammonds set 139 acres of BLM land ablaze. In the high plateau of eastern Oregon, ranchers and land managers regularly set fires to eradicate invasive plant species. The Hammonds said they started the blaze to control destructive juniper. Federal prosecutors said the Hammonds did not seek advance permission and set the fire to cover up evidence that they'd killed a herd of deer. In 2006, Steven Hammond set another fire, this time to keep a wildfire from spreading to the ranch. The government said he'd done so knowing that firefighters were camped nearby and could have been endangered.

After several years of legal proceedings, the Hammonds pleaded guilty to federal arson charges in 2012. They faced sentencing under the federal Antiterrorism and Effective Death Penalty Act of 1996, which mandated a five-year prison sentence for arson. The judge disregarded the mandatory minimum—declaring that five years would be cruel and unusual, a punishment that "would shock the conscience"—and instead sentenced Dwight to three months and Steven to one year. The Hammonds served the time and returned to Harney County. But federal prosecutors appealed the sentences, saying they were unlawful under the 1996 statute. They won, and in October 2015, the Hammonds were resentenced to finish the mandatory five-year terms. They were scheduled to report to prison after the holidays.

People in Harney County were outraged. They speculated that the BLM was after the Hammond ranch, especially because the agency didn't renew the Hammonds' grazing permits and included a provision in a related settlement that gave the federal government the first shot at buying some of the Hammond land.

AROUND 3 OR 4 AM, AMMON WAS EXHAUSTED, EMOTIONAL. THE HAMmonds' story felt so much like the Bundys'. Another urge seized him; he wanted to write about the Hammonds. But his brain felt clouded, so he prayed, and his head cleared. He began writing, and as the words flowed, he started to understand what the Lord wanted. It was the same feeling he'd experienced during the BLM roundup in Gold Butte: a clarity of direction. The Lord was working through him, trying to accomplish His objectives through an imperfect man. Ammon composed a 2,700-word letter and attachments that summarized the case and included photos and maps.

Ammon was inspired to spread the word about the Hammonds. Because if he didn't, what was happening to the Hammonds would replicate itself, county after county, across the United States. If Americans allowed the Hammonds to be unjustly punished, the federal government would be emboldened to take more land and resources. The Constitution was hanging by a thread. And if the United States fell, the world would fall.

He finished the letter, and Lisa proofread it. He sent it to an email list, several thousand strong, that the Bundys had collected after the Bunkerville standoff. He also posted it to the Bundy Ranch blog and Facebook page a little after noon. Then he received his next direction: he was to go to Harney County and meet the Hammonds in person.

Ammon told Lisa he was going to be gone for a couple of days. He wanted her to understand his urge to help the Hammonds even though he and Lisa faced challenges of their own. They had six kids now, including an infant, the orchard, the business in Phoenix, the new house in Idaho.

Lisa believed the Bundys had done enough. They'd shown other ranchers how to stand up to the feds. Those families could take it from here. Besides, she and Ammon still had twenty boxes to unpack from their move to Idaho. But she had faith in Ammon's judgment, in his ability to discern spiritual prompts, and in his courage to follow them. She gave her blessing.

Ammon received a number of responses to the mass email, including some from people who shared their own research about the Hammonds. Ryan Payne called from Montana that night. He'd received the email, and he was heading to Harney County too. He'd call when he got there.

Ammon didn't know Payne very well; during the standoff, his father and brothers had spent more time with the wayward militiaman.

THE NEXT DAY, AMMON DROVE TO OREGON, HIS THIRD TIME IN THE STATE. US Route 20 took him through mostly federal land. The last hundred miles was beautiful high desert, and remarkably empty—mountains and valleys, small rivers and shallow lakes, a tiny village that was little more than a few campers and a diner. Useful land, too, dotted with cows that enjoyed plenty of grasses and water sources. Much better cattle range than Gold Butte.

His destination, Burns, Oregon, was a cowboy-and-timber town in the north-central part of Harney County. With a couple thousand residents, it was too small for a Walmart. It had wide streets and boot scrapers bolted to the sidewalks outside local businesses. It had peaked in population and prosperity forty years earlier, when logging in the Malheur National Forest north of town supported a full third of the local economy. But federal conservation efforts in the 1980s led to the decline of logging. Now, the lumberyards and mills sat empty, and government provided 45 percent of Harney County's jobs. The county's other major employer was agriculture, and residents feared environmental restrictions would kill ranching too.

Ammon found Hammond Ranch, about fifty miles south of Burns.

Steven Hammond, age forty-six, was there, working in the machine shop. Ammon introduced himself, and the younger Hammond said he knew about the Bundys. Steven needed to move some cattle and invited Ammon to help. Ammon spent the rest of the day with Steven, and the two men talked about their families' struggles. After the sun had set, Ammon told Steven that he believed he was supposed to help the Hammonds somehow. But the rancher said he didn't want Ammon's help. He was going to serve his sentence. To Ammon, he seemed like a broken man, no more fight left. The feds had beaten him.

Ammon drove to Burns and met Ryan Payne. The militiaman was planning to spend the night in his truck, but Ammon had booked a room at the Silver Spur Motel that had two beds, so they shared. The next morning, they went to the Hammonds' home in Burns and met the family matriarch, Susan. Ammon had brought her a box of apples from his orchard. Her husband Dwight was out working, Susan told the visitors, trying to make as much money as he could before he had to report back to federal prison. Unlike her son, Susan seemed full of spunk. Ammon told her how the American people had forced the feds to stand down in Bunkerville, and Susan seemed to like Ammon's message.

Ammon and Payne next went to the Harney County Sheriff's Office, an unadorned brick-and-stucco building in the middle of Burns. Ammon had called ahead for an appointment, and it appeared that Sheriff Dave Ward had prepared for the meeting. On the sheriff's desk was a printout of the letter Ammon had written two days earlier, and Ammon wondered how the sheriff had discovered it. Ward was friendly and self-effacing, a good listener, his earnest blue eyes locked on Ammon's throughout the meeting. He knew about the Bundys and seemed to sympathize with their cause. He'd been on the job less than a year and hadn't met the Hammonds and didn't know much about their case. Ammon and Payne told Ward that they expected him to protect Dwight and Steven Hammond if the feds tried to illegally imprison them. They said the feds lacked the constitutional authority to own land in Harney County, and they'd give him documents to prove it.

The meeting lasted more than an hour, and Ammon felt good about how it went. This sheriff, he believed, could be an ally.

SHERIFF WARD LEFT THE MEETING FEELING UNEASY.

When Ammon had called that morning to make an appointment, Ward had recognized the Bundy name, remembering the confrontation in Nevada a year and a half earlier. Before the meeting, he did more research. The last thing Harney County needed was a militia/federal standoff. Ward wasn't a Las Vegas sheriff with hundreds of officers to deploy. Ward had four deputies and ten thousand square miles to patrol, the ninth-largest county in the United States.

Sheriff Ward and Ammon had much in common; both were country boys from churchgoing families who had played football and wrestled in high school. Ward owned 160 acres and ran a small herd of cattle, and if he could afford more land or obtain a grazing permit, he happily would have become a full-time rancher. He was a strong believer in the First and Second Amendments and told Ammon so. Ward was a year older than Ammon and had served in the army, doing combat tours in Somalia and Afghanistan. Before running for sheriff, he had worked as a ranch hand, a corrections officer, a patrol deputy, and a probation officer.

In the meeting, Ward liked Ammon, found him easy to talk to. But the man's message was extreme. Ammon kept saying the federal government couldn't own large chunks of Harney County and it was Ward's duty, as the highest law-enforcement officer in the land, to inform the feds that they had no jurisdiction over the Hammonds.

Sheriff Ward had received materials from the Arizona-based Constitutional Sheriffs and Peace Officers Association, which promoted the county supremacy concept. But Ward rejected the theory. On public lands within Harney County, he shared concurrent jurisdiction with the feds: they upheld federal laws, and he upheld the local and state laws. Ward was no cheerleader for the federal government, and he had his own opinions about the fact that the feds possessed most of Harney County. But he didn't think the concept was illegal. And he believed there were imperfect but appropriate avenues—the court system, the political system—for citizens who felt the government had done them wrong.

Ward had told Ammon and Payne that he'd look into the Hammond case, but he didn't want a Bunkerville-style confrontation. They should work to resolve the situation without civil unrest, he said.

Payne, who was wearing a sidearm, hadn't done much talking up to that point. He'd stared at Ward like he was trying to bore a hole through the sheriff, an empty-eyed gaze Ward had observed in certain combat veterans.

Payne had interjected: *If you don't do your job, Sheriff, thousands of people will come here to do it for you. And we cannot control what they may or may not do.*

OVER THE NEXT WEEK, AMMON SPENT HOURS ON THE PHONE WITH THE Hammonds and Sheriff Ward. He gathered more information, learning when the Hammonds had purchased the ranch, the rights they'd paid for, the various conflicts with the federal land agencies. He updated Ward on his findings. The conversations with the sheriff were friendly, though Ward did repeatedly point out that Ammon was taking on a leadership role by stirring up people's emotions around the Hammond case, and if things went bad, he'd be held responsible.

Ammon continued to believe that the sheriff had sympathy for his point of view. In mid-November, Ammon circulated an even longer synopsis of the case.

"The abuses to this family are much greater than I originally explained to you," he wrote to his followers. "They have quietly suffered much more than even the Bundys can fully understand."

Ammon also turned up the heat on Sheriff Ward, directing his followers to express their discontent about the Hammond case.

Typically, Ward had a single 911 dispatcher handling both emergency and nonemergency calls. Suddenly, ten times the normal volume of calls began pouring into the dispatch center, far more than Ward could return. His email inbox was flooded with messages, including this one:

Nov. 17, 2015

Sheriff Ward, with all due respect, your alternatives in handling the Hammond case have narrowed to:

Number 1, protect your constituents from an abusive and corrupt government cabal.

Number 2, see your county invaded by some of the most determined and organized and armed citizens alive in this country today.

The Bundys have sent out a nationwide alert. And if you have any doubts about what that means, I suggest you ask the sheriff of Clark County, Nevada. We are high-stakes players, Sheriff, and are perfectly willing to raise the bet.

Neil Wampler, Los Osos.

Ward forwarded the more aggressive emails to the FBI, including some death threats. He met with FBI and US Attorney officials in Bend and brainstormed how to handle the situation. Someone tossed out the idea of taking the Hammonds into custody early, but Ward was vigorously opposed. The feds had agreed to let the Hammonds turn themselves in after the holidays. Taking them early would only stoke more resentment.

IN MID-NOVEMBER, 2015, TWO WEEKS AFTER HIS FIRST TRIP, AMMON returned to Burns. He and Payne and other supporters visited Dwight and Susan Hammond, and the old couple seemed more hopeful. Susan had begun saying "I love you" when she ended phone conversations with Ammon. During the meeting, the Hammonds told everyone their story, and Dwight broke down in tears several times, burying his face in his hands.

Some of Ammon's followers wanted to take a Battle of Bunkerville approach to protecting the Hammonds—establishing a perimeter of protesters and militia around their home, barring the feds from taking Dwight and Steven into custody. This strategy had worked in Bunkerville, and it could work here. But the Hammonds weren't willing to support Bundy-like tactics. They preferred the idea of holding a rally.

Ammon and Ryan Payne also went back to the sheriff's office. This time they brought about ten supporters with them, including the rancher Cliff Gardner, a longtime opponent of the BLM, and members of the Idaho Three Percenters, the Oath Keepers, and the Pacific Patriots Network. Ward's office had room for only three chairs and his own desk, so he took the group upstairs to the courthouse law library, which had a big table and more space. Several of the visitors were wearing guns. The courthouse was a gun-free zone and even had a sign that said "No firearms." Someone told Ward that the group had left an armed man in front of the building.

Ward believed the group was trying to bait him into an argument over the Second Amendment, so he ignored the weapons. He wanted to lower tension, not inflame things. But he felt apprehensive. No deputies were available, so he retrieved a corporal who was guarding the jail. All the chairs in the room were taken, so the corporal stood in a corner, and Ward noted that the militiamen posted a man in the opposite corner, a tactical move.

Ward listened as each of Ammon's compatriots spoke about the injustices being waged against the Hammonds. By now, the sheriff had a deep familiarity with the case. Since his initial meeting with Ammon and Payne, he had reviewed police reports, court transcripts, and grand-jury indictments, had spoken with prosecutors and Dwight Hammond. He tried to tell Ammon's group that the previous sheriff had conducted a thorough investigation of the case. He disagreed with the mandatory minimum sentencing law that required the Hammonds to return to prison, but it was the law of the land, passed by Congress, signed by the president. He couldn't pick and choose which laws he enforced.

Ammon's group wasn't satisfied. The meeting went on for a couple hours. Ward was less obliging this time, and Ammon grew frustrated. The two men had spoken for many hours over the past few weeks, he said, and the sheriff's stance had not budged.

Ward said: *And neither has yours.*

SHERIFF WARD COULDN'T SLEEP THAT NIGHT. AT 2 AM, HE GOT OUT OF BED and drove to his office and composed a letter about the Hammond case. He wrote that misinformation was rampant and then detailed how the case had proceeded through the system. He drew no broad conclusions, but the letter seemed to indicate that he believed the Hammonds had received due process. "It is my belief that the Hammonds are decent hard working citizens of Harney County and deserve my attention in this matter," Ward's letter concluded. "I have read and will continue to read and look into any injustice found in this matter."

The sheriff began responding to the thousands of emails he'd received from Ammon's followers, pasting the letter into each response and attaching some court documents. He hoped to persuade some that Ammon's take on the Hammond case was questionable, though he knew he wouldn't sway the diehards.

When Ammon saw the letter, he was crushed. Ward had presented himself, Ammon thought, as a constitutional sheriff. But Ward's letter sounded to Ammon like the sheriff was saying that the Hammonds had received their day in court, so everybody should get over it. To Ammon, the letter read like a brush-off.

Ammon was increasingly on edge. In one of their many conversations, Sheriff Ward had said the FBI was watching Ammon's every move in Harney County. The Hammonds had told Ammon they were worried federal agents would shoot all of them, bullets to the backs of their heads. The fear was contagious.

Ammon stood underneath the deck of his house in Emmett and made a short video that he posted to the Bundy Ranch Facebook page. In the video, Ammon looked tense and forlorn, his eyes watchfully flitting around. He said Dwight Hammond had just called and said he couldn't talk to Ammon anymore. Federal agents had called the Hammonds' attorney, Dwight had said.

Ammon read from notes he'd jotted on a scrap of paper.

They informed him that they would "transfer pain to the Hammond family" if any further contact with Ammon

Bundy continued, that "they would bring misery to the whole family." He said his family and friends are being threatened. He said he felt that my life was also in danger. And then he informed me that he would not be able to continue to keep communicating to me, that he was afraid to do so and this would be the last time we would talk.

I tried to instill courage in him, and faith, and to stand and do what's right. But he is extremely afraid, and fears for his life and fears for his family's life.

In the video, Ammon told his supporters that they didn't need to come to Burns yet, but he wanted them to be prepared to do so. The Hammond family may have felt too threatened to ask for help, Ammon said, but they needed it anyway.

Ammon was hurt by the Hammonds' rejection. He had believed he could convince them to stand as the Bundys had. But he understood that they were beaten down to the point where they could fight no more. The federal government's tyranny over them was complete, Ammon believed.

He recalled his own transformation during the Bundy Ranch conflict, how it had been hard for him to come to the conclusion that the government was not going to protect his family, that he needed men with guns to do it instead. For a family like the Hammonds, established members of their community, this was a difficult idea to swallow. But Ammon wasn't giving up. If the people allowed the government to oppress the Hammonds, he believed, it would happen to all Americans eventually. This was bigger than one family. He would stand for the Hammonds, whether they wanted him to or not.

IN EARLY DECEMBER, WARD WENT TO THE OREGON STATE SHERIFFS' Association annual conference in Bend. While he was gone, Ryan Payne showed up at the sheriff's office visitor's window and asked for Ward. The sheriff's lieutenant recognized Payne from his previous visits with Ammon. On his last visit, Payne had been armed. Today, he was wearing a heavy coat, and the lieutenant couldn't tell if he had a gun underneath.

As Ward wasn't available, the lieutenant took Payne to Ward's office to talk.

Payne said: *Do you support the United States Constitution?*

The lieutenant said he fully supported the Constitution.

Payne said Sheriff Ward did not. The federal government's punishment of the Hammonds was unconstitutional, as was its control of public lands in Oregon. But Ward was unwilling to do anything about it. Payne spent some time on these subjects, getting worked up. Then he made a bizarre suggestion to the lieutenant.

Payne said: *If Sheriff Ward won't support the Constitution, you need to remove him from office and take over yourself. By any means necessary.*[*]

The lieutenant was stunned. Was Payne asking him to kill Sheriff Ward? What Payne had said was ridiculous. The lieutenant decided it wasn't necessarily a direct threat to Ward, but more of a statement of belief, not something that warranted an immediate arrest.

The lieutenant escorted Payne out of the sheriff's office. He stood at the door and watched until Payne had walked across the street to his truck in the parking lot. As soon as Payne was out of sight, the lieutenant called Sheriff Ward in Bend.

---

[*] Lt. Brian Needham later testified that Ryan Payne had added the words: "including by death." However, an FBI agent offered conflicting testimony, saying that Needham did not include those additional words when he reported the conversation a few days later.

RYAN PAYNE COMMITTED TO THE NEW MISSION EARLY, PLUNGING IN AS HE had with Bunkerville. He moved to Burns in early December, staying at a house that belonged to locals who supported the Hammonds.

Payne had lost none of his grandiosity. In one email, he wrote:

> But the display of tyranny in this particular case is so appall-
> ing, the people being directly subjected to it so undeserving,
> and the oppressive weight so heavily and completely applied;
> upon not only the Hammonds, but their entire community;
> that to decide to allow it to persist should trouble the soul
> such that death might be a welcome relief.

For some time, Payne's militia network—renamed Operation Mutual Defense—had been shopping around for the "next big event," as Payne called it. Most Sundays during the fall of 2015, he had held a conference call with four other OMD board members. They discussed various flashpoints OMD could mobilize around, includ-ing LaVoy Finicum's brewing war with the BLM and the resettlement of refugees in the United States. As the fall of 2015 wound down, it became clear that the Hammond case was the most promising OMD mission, mainly because Ammon Bundy was throwing his weight behind it. But after the Hammonds said they didn't want help, the other board members lost their enthusiasm for the operation. They voted to take no action. One member reportedly resigned from OMD, worried that Payne was going to take an aggressive approach, and he didn't want to be associated with it.

The board member was right. Payne had bigger ambitions than organizing a simple rally for the Hammonds. Waving signs and flags wasn't his style. Not after Bunkerville. The Bundy Ranch standoff and Camp Liberty had been about Americans making a stand for other

Americans, being ready to die for them. That's why people had paid attention.

But the Hammonds didn't want the militia surrounding their home. So Payne cast about for other ideas, an action of greater consequence. Something more than a rally.

OTHER PATRIOTS BEGAN TO TRICKLE IN TO OREGON AS WELL. MANY HAD met in Bunkerville, and others were new. They got rooms at the Silver Spur Motel, and several bunked in the house where Ryan Payne was staying.

Sheriff Ward had begun tracking the Patriots. It wasn't hard to spot them. They tended to advertise their Patriot status with Three Percenter patches on their coats, Gadsden flags on their trucks, and guns on their hips. Plenty of Harney County residents had firearms, but few open carried even though it was legal. The Patriots traveled in bunches, so if Ward recognized one, he could often identify the others by prowling Facebook pages. He referred the names to a BLM analyst who also was working the Bunkerville case. By mid-December, they'd compiled a still-growing list of forty-five outsiders who'd come into Harney County on behalf of the Hammonds.

One of the more visible new arrivals was Jon Ritzheimer, a volatile motorcycle mechanic from Phoenix, Arizona. Earlier in the year, the thirty-two-year-old Marine Corps Reserve veteran organized a series of anti-Islam demonstrations in Phoenix. He'd posted YouTube videos that showed him shooting a copy of the Quran and threatening to arrest a Michigan senator for supporting a nuclear deal with Iran. He had created an apparel company called Rogue Infidel that sold anti-Islam T-shirts. In November, he joined the OMD advisory board. Like Ryan Payne, he employed portentous and high-flown language.

217

Unlike Payne, who only occasionally gave interviews or appeared on a video, Ritzheimer hungered for attention. On YouTube, he regularly worked himself into a furious lather or melodramatic tears. If there had been a Patriot reality show, Ritzheimer would have been cast first.

FOR AMMON, THE FINAL WEEKS OF 2015 WERE A CHAOS OF PHONE CALLS, emails, texts. He organized meetings, gave lectures about the Constitution, printed hundreds of flyers, and generally tried to harness the energy of the Battle of Bunkerville and direct it toward Burns. He created a petition, signed by thousands, demanding that Oregon officials, including Sheriff Ward, act on behalf of the Hammonds.

Plenty of locals thought the Hammonds had gotten a raw deal, but they didn't think outside armed militia was the solution. Even some of the people who initially backed Ammon began to wonder if the Bundy crew was too radical. After all, lots of people here worked for the federal land agencies. The BLM alone employed ninety-four people in Harney County.

Conflicts bubbled up. Some federal employees reported that they'd been followed, while others received threats. A Utah man disrupted a state court proceeding, demanding that the judge impanel a grand jury for the Hammond case. Signs popped up around town: "Militia go home!" Ryan Payne saw a "Go home Bundys" sign on a house and knocked on the door, looking for a debate.

At Christmastime, Sheriff Ward was shopping in a ranch-supply store with his eight-year-old son when he noticed Jon Ritzheimer, who seemed to be tailing him through the store. The sheriff also spotted Patriots following him on his way to work in the mornings. A few days later, someone punched a hole in the sidewall of his wife's car. The most bizarre incident occurred when a group of militiamen, one armed, approached Sheriff Ward's elderly parents at an American Legion yard sale. Ward's mother didn't take kindly to their criticisms of the sheriff. Afterward, Ryan Payne went to the sheriff's office and complained to Ward that the seventy-four-year-old woman had threatened them.

Ward found his mother, asked if she'd menaced the Patriots.

The woman said: *I most certainly did not! I said, if you intend to harm my son, we will arm ourselves and fight you.*

WHEN NO OFFICIALS RESPONDED TO HIS PETITION, AMMON WASN'T SURE what to do next. The Hammonds were set to report to prison on January 4, 2016. Patriots and locals were planning a rally for January 2. They would gather for speeches in the parking lot of the Safeway store in downtown Burns. Then they would march north past the sheriff's office and courthouse, to the Hammonds' home in town, and head back to the store. Organizers had spoken to the Safeway manager, who agreed to stock the store with extra flowers that supporters could buy for the Hammonds. And they were planning to throw coins at the sheriff's office, to signify that he had "sold out" to the feds.

Ammon helped plan the rally, but he knew it wasn't enough. A rally would attract attention for a day, and then everyone would go home and the Hammonds would be forgotten. As the days passed, a vision crystallized: Ammon knew what he was supposed to do. It was a difficult obligation, one that would take a great amount of fortitude and might exact a heavy price. So he wrestled with it, but it became clear, just as the path to the Battle of Bunkerville had opened up before them as the Bundys took each step.

He knew some people would think he was crazy, but he was certain the Lord was working through him to accomplish His purposes, so that Americans would have something to pass on to their children.

Ammon would gather a multitude in Harney County and not just for a rally. For a hard stand.

In conversations and meetings during late December, a number of ideas were thrown out as to what exactly that hard stand should be. One idea was to put cattle back on the Hammonds' old grazing allotments and then guard them. Another proposal was to set controlled burns on the range without a permit. Another was to take over public land, an occupation.

Ryan Payne began scoping out federal facilities in Harney County, casing them to determine if they'd be a good spot for an occupation. There were plenty to choose from, as the federal government owned three-quarters of the county. At least once he visited Malheur National Wildlife Refuge. There, US Fish and Wildlife Service and other federal land agency employees worked in a cluster of thirteen buildings—a lookout tower, a machine shop, a garage, a natural resource lab, workshops, and a museum—a little less than two miles from the vast and shallow Malheur Lake. One day in December, Payne and three other men stopped at the refuge compound and used the bathroom. They spent time looking around, watching who came and went. The federal employees recognized Payne. His photo had been posted on a wall, and they'd been told to look out for him.

Later that month, Ammon floated the idea of an occupation with a group of Harney County supporters, not giving specifics. They favored a more traditional protest.

Word began to leak out that Ammon and Payne were planning an aggressive stand, something akin to Bunkerville.

A Bundy supporter messaged Jon Ritzheimer: "I need all patriots here on or before Jan. 2 for the wink . . . wink . . . rally."

But the details were unclear.

Pete Santilli told his listeners: "A lot of stuff that's going to be happening out there, I can't go into the exact details, because I don't have all the details. I'm on a need-to-know basis."

Ammon got a message from a supporter in Washington State: "I'm getting conflicting messages on the 2nd. On one hand, it's being called a rally and a protest. And on the other, it's a call to action. People are confused."

Ammon punched out an immediate response, keeping his cards close to his chest: "I would never show up to a rally without my arms."

ON DECEMBER 30, 2015, EMPLOYEES AT MALHEUR WERE SENT HOME EARLY and told not to come back until instructed.

Rumors had been flying around Harney County, speculation based on gossip and social media postings. The Bundy militia was going to take over the Harney County Courthouse. The militia was going to take over a BLM district office in Burns. Now, intel had surfaced that the militia had seriously targeted Malheur.

In a typical year, Malheur Lake covers about forty thousand acres and is two and one-half feet deep. The wetlands attract more than three hundred migratory bird species, including 2.5 million ducks. The refuge was originally created from unclaimed lands around the lake. In the 1930s and '40s, the government bought or was deeded several ranches, and the refuge grew into its current territory—viewed from above, a formless patch of lakes, rivers, wetlands, and salt flats. In summertime, the refuge was crowded with birders. In the winter, a diverse group of conservationists had the refuge buildings mostly to themselves.

In December 2015, those federal employees were busy. An archaeologist was in charge of managing the four hundred prehistoric and historic sites on the refuge lands, working closely with the local Paiute people. An ecologist was managing the hay and grazing program, maintaining hundreds of miles of irrigation ditches and conducting winter wildlife surveys. A firefighter was planning a series of pre-scribed burns designed to limit future wildfires. A fish biologist waged never-ending war against invasive carp fish, the biggest threat to the refuge's wildfowl.

Supervisors at the refuge decided better safe than sorry—they'd send everyone home a few hours early, giving them an advance start to the New Year's holiday weekend, three days before the planned rally on Saturday, January 2. Most likely, the supervisors believed, everyone would be back at work on Tuesday. After all, Malheur was Fish and Wildlife land, and the Hammonds' beef was with the BLM. So why would protestors target Malheur?

THE BUNKERVILLE GANG CONVERGED ON BURNS FOR THE RALLY, BACK together like college friends at a wedding.

Eleven months earlier, Pete Santilli had moved to Cincinnati, where his girlfriend was from, and they'd run *The Pete Santilli Show* together out of a makeshift studio in her apartment. But Santilli wasn't about to miss another Bundy event, so they drove across the country in a van stuffed with video equipment. After Bunkerville, he'd invested in gear that would allow him to better cover remote events. He'd also picked up a mesh vest printed with green fluorescent words: PRESS: PETE SANTILLI. He checked into Room 123 at the Silver Spur Motel on December 30, expecting to head home after the Saturday rally.

Shawna Cox's husband had suffered from heart problems a few months earlier, and she was unsure about leaving him for the rally. But her husband told her to go, knowing she wouldn't be happy missing out. On New Year's Day, Cox and her cousin drove from southern Utah to Burns in her 2006 Town & Country minivan. They brought sleeping bags, planning to just bed down in the van and head back the next day. But when they got to Burns, the temperature was minus thirteen degrees and dropping fast, so they got a hotel room. Before going to bed, Cox took some rally notices and hit the streets, stapling the flyers to poles and walls around Burns.

Neil Wampler in California also drove up with a friend on New Year's Day. He hadn't kept in touch with the people he'd met in Bunkerville—that wasn't him—but he followed the movement closely. He wanted to relive the exhilaration he'd felt when the cows ran down Toquop Wash.

LaVoy and Jeanette Finicum had spent a frigid, windy New Year's Eve gathering cows with several of their children and then sleeping in a big tent on their winter grazing allotment. They branded the next morning and had just driven the fifty miles home when LaVoy received a call from Ryan Bundy about the rally in Burns. LaVoy agreed to drive up. He'd protested the Hammond case on YouTube even before Ammon had. Always prepared, he took his sleeping bag, cold-weather gear, a change of clothes. He said he'd be back in a couple of days. He drove his four-month-old Dodge Ram 2500 crew cab truck and picked up Ryan Bundy along the way.

Ryan brought a lever-action carbine to Oregon. Brand Nu Thornton brought no guns but did pack his ram's horn shofar. Booda Cavalier left Cliven and Carol at Bundy Ranch and came to Burns. Later, they all said they didn't know exactly what Ammon was planning, and none of them came prepared for more than a day or two.

Since Bunkerville, some had reunited at various smaller standoffs and rallies, including the all-terrain vehicle ride in Recapture Canyon and public-lands standoffs at precious metals mines in Oregon and Montana. But Burns was the first big reunion. Several of the men who'd been clean-shaven at Bunkerville had since adopted the Patriot movement's signature big-bearded look, including Ammon, Ryan Payne, and Wampler. Thornton had grown his white beard longer.

223

Finicum remained clean-shaven. His shaving kit was among the few items he'd packed for the trip.

Cliven stayed home, but he did have someone hand deliver a letter to Sheriff Ward and the Hammonds, suggesting that Dwight and Steven turn themselves in at the county jail, where Ward could protect them from the feds by placing them in protective custody.

THE OATH KEEPERS DECLINED TO COME. STEWART RHODES SAID HE SYMPA-thized with the Hammonds but regarded their situation as very different than the conflict at Bundy Ranch. In 2014, Rhodes had believed the Bundys were in danger of being "Waco'd." The Hammonds, on the other hand, had been convicted by a jury of their peers and were agreeing to go to prison. They didn't want Patriot help, so he wouldn't force it on them. Rhodes also said Ammon should be clearer about whether he was planning a rally or an armed confrontation.

"Oath Keepers will not be involved in an armed standoff being manufactured by hotheads who want a fight," Rhodes said in a New Year's Eve video posted to the Oath Keepers YouTube channel. "This is gonna be a bad fight."

Rhodes didn't specifically identify who the "hotheads" were, but no doubt he was thinking of Ryan Payne, who had called Oath Keepers "deserters"—and said deserters should be shot—after Rhodes had pulled his men out of Bundy Ranch.

Rhodes might have also been thinking of Jon Ritzheimer, who posted a video of himself on the same day sitting in a truck in Harney County, a Three Percenter sticker on the rear window. The video was purportedly a goodbye to Ritzheimer's wife and two kids, in case he died defending the Hammonds.

"Your daddy swore an oath," he intoned, brandishing a pocket Constitution. "He swore an oath to protect and defend the Constitution."

It was an operatic performance, full of pregnant pauses and steely gazes and overwrought tears. Ritzheimer's message seemed intended for a larger audience than his daughters. Without giving details, Ritzheimer made it abundantly clear that the Patriots were planning something more perilous than a rally. At one point, he discussed Dwight and Steven Hammond's decision to go to prison without a fight.

"Dwight's so old he may die in there, and I'm hoping he sees this video," Ritzheimer said. "It's real simple, Dwight. You want to die in prison labeled as a terrorist by the oppressors? Or you want to die out here with us as a free man? I want to die a free man."

If Ritzheimer had been looking for a bigger audience, he found it with the "Daddy Swore an Oath" video, as it became known. Within days, a couple hundred thousand people had watched it.

In his dealings with the Patriots, Sheriff Ward's style could be characterized as the anti–Dan Love approach. Despite the intimidation tactics he and his family experienced, Ward did not overreact, believing that the Patriots were trying to goad him into a mistake that they could exploit. He beefed up the ranks of law enforcement in Burns but minimized their visibility.

To fortify his department for the January 2 rally, Sheriff Ward borrowed the services of eight state troopers. The rally organizers had publicized a route map for their march, so Ward put together a patrol plan that would ensure that his officers would be nearby but would not come into direct contact with the protesters. If the situation escalated, the state police had two SWAT teams at the ready, one staged to the east in Juntura and the other to the west in Bend.

The march was going right by the sheriff's office, which unsettled Ward. He'd heard the Patriots might try to take the building, so he approached the situation with a soldier's mindset, drawing on the force protection training he'd received in the army. The jail was the most secure facility at his disposal, so he moved all of the inmates to an adjoining county's jail and stored his office's firearms and ammunition in the Harney County Jail building, in case the sheriff's office was breached. He also made sure the parking lot was emptied of police vehicles, so none would be vandalized. He deployed his corrections officers to provide security for the sheriff's office and 911 dispatchers. If the protesters took the sheriff's office, the officers were instructed to grab the dispatchers and barricade themselves in the jail. *Do not confront, do not inflame,* Ward said.

If all the protesters did was to throw coins at the sheriff's office steps, as planned, Ward decided they would donate the money to a local youth center.

ON THE MORNING OF JANUARY 2, PEOPLE BEGAN TO ASSEMBLE IN THE FRIGID Safeway parking lot for the rally. While the crowd gathered, Ammon met with a couple dozen insiders in a back room of Ye Olde Castle, a faded diner and antique shop next to the grocery store. Key players included Ryan Bundy, Ryan Payne, LaVoy Finicum, Jon Ritzheimer, and Blaine Cooper.

After coffee and chitchat, the meeting began with a prayer. Ammon stood up and gave a short speech about how he'd come to involve himself in the Hammond case and his growing frustration that the redress of grievances had generated no official response. Then he revealed his plan. He said he'd come to the conclusion that Hammond supporters should go to the Malheur National Wildlife Refuge and take it over. Malheur was symbolically appropriate, Ammon believed, because it was an instrument by which the federal government had controlled land that rightfully belonged to the people. And it was a practical choice because it contained a number of buildings where the Patriots could sleep and eat.

The listeners didn't immediately react. Just as many in Bunkerville had had no idea what Toquop Wash was, some of the people at the meeting weren't familiar with Malheur.

Then Ryan Bundy stood up. He said he backed his brother.

LaVoy Finicum stood up and talked about his own ranch in the Arizona Strip and how he'd canceled his contract with the BLM. He barely knew Ammon but said he was in too.

Not everybody liked the plan. The room was split. It was decided that those in the meeting who wanted to occupy the refuge would depart immediately as an advance team. Ammon would stay at the protest in Burns and tell everybody else about the occupation.

The meeting broke up. Ammon went outside and crossed the street to the Safeway parking lot, where the rally was beginning. Ammon and another three hundred or so people marched in the parade. They threw pennies at the sheriff's office. They carried flags to the Hammond house and laid flowers on the snowbank in their yard. Dwight and Susan came out, and Susan hugged several marchers.

They headed back to the Safeway parking lot. A militiaman from central Oregon who had helped organize the rally was congratulating everyone on a peaceful demonstration and suggesting that they all head to the fairgrounds to learn how they could take more steps to help the Hammonds.

Ammon climbed atop a nearby snowbank and interrupted the rally organizer.

"Those who need more information, you should probably go to

the fairgrounds," Ammon said. "Those that understand that we need to make a hard stand, those who know what's going on here and have seen it for many, many years, those who are ready to do something about it, I'm asking you to follow me and go to the Malheur National Wildlife Refuge, and we're gonna make a hard stand. There are already agents who are on the roads and are gonna block the roads and they do not want us to go out there. But we're gonna go out there anyway."

Someone asked if the police could keep them from going to the refuge.

"No, they can't legally keep us from going out there, but when has that stopped them?" Ammon said.

Someone said, "What are you trying to do?"

"We're gonna make a stand," Ammon said. "We're going to insist the Constitution is protected here in this county."

UP TO THEN, SHERIFF WARD WAS FEELING PRETTY GOOD ABOUT THE RALLY. The protesters had thrown the coins at the sheriff's office and moved on without incident, though the personnel inside said the windows were rattling and one protester had chucked an entire roll of coins so hard that it dented the stucco. Ward was sitting in a police vehicle with two of his officers, watching a live feed of Ammon and the other marchers when he got a call. It was a deputy he'd stationed on a mountain south of Burns.

The deputy said a convoy of men in vehicles had just passed him, headed south. Toward the Malheur refuge. The group included Ryan Payne and at least one of the Bundy brothers.

On Ward's live-feed screen, Ammon stood on a snowbank giving a speech, saying something about a "hard stand."

The hair on the back of Ward's neck went up.

Because Ammon had kept the plan mostly to himself, the advance team wasn't ready. The ragtag crew of men left Ye Olde Castle and spent the next hour or so gathering vehicles and coats and weapons before heading to Malheur. Many of them didn't even know where it was.

A local man named Butch Eaton who'd become friendly with the Patriots over the last few weeks had been standing in the Safeway parking lot, waiting for the rally to begin. Eaton was age forty-six, with a thick orange beard that almost tickled his belly. He'd been a carpenter for twenty-five years but retired due to chronic obstructive pulmonary disease. Three days earlier, he'd changed his Facebook profile picture to a shot of a colonial militia from the 2000 Revolutionary War movie *The Patriot*. The Hammond case had become important to him, and he thought Ammon's followers were extraordinary men, like Mel Gibson's movie militia: God-fearing patriots who'd left their own families to stand up for American rights.

Ryan Payne walked up to Eaton in the parking lot.

Payne said: *Are you ready to go?*

Eaton figured Payne was talking about starting the march. But Payne ushered him into a truck with two other Patriots. An assault rifle lay on the bench seat.

They took off, first to the fairgrounds, where other trucks joined them. Then the convoy of half a dozen vehicles headed south out of town, and Eaton guessed their destination. He'd gone to several meetings over the past few weeks, and there'd been talk of protesting at Malheur. The convoy passed a number of patrol cars on the side of the road.

Someone said: *They know we're coming.*

But no one tried to stop them, and they drove the thirty-one miles to the refuge unimpeded.

229

They got to the refuge, made a sharp turn into the entrance, drove past a metal fire tower, and headed down into a depression that contained a pleasant little snow-covered campus of stone-clad buildings with terra-cotta roofs, smoke coming from some of the chimneys. Behind those buildings were sheds and boats and trucks and snowplows.

The men got out of the truck, and someone said: *Don't fire until fired upon.*

The advance team moved through the compound with purpose, rifles at low-ready, as they made sure the buildings were clear of outsiders. Eaton, Blaine Cooper, and Brand Nu Thornton were the only unarmed men. The main building was locked, so they kept moving. Other buildings were open, but nobody was inside. Someone found keys to the main building. It took ten minutes to search the compound. Thornton blew his shofar, which Eaton took as a signal that they'd cleared the area.

The men began unloading generators and camping supplies from their vehicles. They talked about stationing someone in the fire tower as a lookout. Someone said the rally in town would be over soon, and more folks would be arriving.

Eaton had seen enough. He hadn't planned to be part of this. These men had a wholehearted belief in what they were doing. Eaton knew his conviction wasn't as strong as theirs. He wasn't sure what would happen next, but he believed these men were going to lose. He was a sick man and didn't want to go to jail, and he didn't want to die out in the desert either.

He walked up the long drive to the main road. A truck was parked across the entrance drive, blocking it. LaVoy Finicum stood next to it, a six-shooter on his hip.

Eaton kept walking. It was about seven degrees, and the cold air seared his damaged lungs. He made it a couple of miles, and then called his wife to pick him up. She did, and as they were driving back to Burns, a long line of cars passed them, heading toward the refuge. Eaton told his wife what had happened, and she told him to call 911.

She said: *You better call and let them know you were there, because it's better they know now than if they find a video and say, "Hey, who's that bald, red-headed son of a bitch?"*

Eaton did what she said.

Chapter 8

A HARD STAND

For Ammon's followers, the Malheur occupation was an act of faith. There was a goal, but no plan, at least not one they knew much about. There was little hierarchy, other than the loose confederation of insiders that included Ryan Payne, Shawna Cox, LaVoy Finicum, and the Bundy brothers. Ammon was the leader, of course, but only inasmuch as people were willing to follow him out to the refuge.

Ammon estimated one hundred people gathered at the refuge on January 2, 2016, approximately one-third of the number that had marched for the Hammonds earlier in the day. Many didn't stay overnight. The next day, a reporter who toured the refuge counted only about two dozen people on the premises, and Pete Santilli confirmed that number. People came and went; at any moment, there were some who were sleeping at the compound, more in town, some who'd gone home for the weekend, some on patrol. It was hard to get an accurate count.

Speaking to journalists and supporters, Ammon outlined his vision in more detail the first night. The refuge, he said, would become a base of operations for Patriots from all over the country. The refuge buildings offered warmth and lodging, and food would be provided as well. Ammon asked people to bring weapons and join them there. He knew it was likely that they'd eventually get kicked off the refuge or arrested, but those developments would allow him to fight the range wars in court. If the feds never came for him, he believed he'd eventually claim the land through a legal mechanism called "adverse possession." They would stay until they had liberated the lands from federal control.

"We're going to be freeing the lands back up, and getting the ranchers back to ranching, getting the miners back to mining, getting the loggers back to logging," Ammon said. "We're the tip of the spear."

Harney County would begin to thrive again, Ammon said, but it would take years to reach this ambitious goal, so they were settling in for the long haul. The occupiers would not leave the refuge until the people of Harney County could use the public lands as they desired, without fear.

Ammon was focused on the range wars, but only a few of his backers were schooled in the particulars of public land use. LaVoy Finicum, of course. Shawna Cox. Ken Medenbach, an Oregon man who'd spent almost three decades challenging the feds by repeatedly putting up cabins on public lands and living in them. It had been a long, lonely battle, and Medenbach was overjoyed to be part of a group occupation. Many of the others who followed Ammon to the refuge knew little about the range wars but felt more generally aggrieved by the government and saw the Malheur occupation as a chance to strike back. If they were killed—martyred—the American people would surely rise up.

As he had at Bunkerville, Ryan Payne ran security. He established communication systems and checkpoints on all the entry roads. He rotated shifts of patrols. Guards climbed the observation tower near the front driveway to keep an eye on the roads.

Some of the occupiers expected the whole thing to be over by the end of the long holiday weekend and were surprised when the refuge workers didn't return and SWAT teams didn't show up.

Shawna Cox had no inkling about the plan. She had heard that the protest was supposed to start in Bend before moving to Burns, so she got up early and started driving there. Ammon called and told her they'd scrapped the Bend idea and were now just going to protest in Burns. Cox turned the minivan around. Then, after the rally, Ammon announced his plan to take Malheur.

Cox said: *What's a maloor?*

But she was game and joined the stream of vehicles headed toward the refuge. Upon arriving, she greeted the advance team, almost all of whom she knew from Bunkerville. The buildings were mostly open, including the firefighters' summer bunkhouse with half a dozen bedrooms, a roomy kitchen with two of every appliance, couches, laundry facilities. The TVs worked, and the power and heat were on. But the beds were stripped and there was no food. The bunkhouse became the central gathering place, mainly because of the big kitchen.

Cox found a bag of frozen potatoes in the back of someone's truck and marshaled several people to start peeling. Then she headed right back to Burns to get some groceries, including milk and butter to make potato soup. She also bought some overalls and snow gear. By the time she got back, reporters had descended on the refuge. Cox chopped the peeled potatoes and began making the soup. The kitchen windows steamed up, and people could smell the food, so they began to crowd into the little building, and the reporters videoed Cox cooking, sticking cameras right over the pot and fogging up their lenses.

The whole scene struck Cox as funny. The Patriots had taken over the refuge, and the world was watching, yet the news reporters were asking her questions about potato soup.

SHERIFF WARD BELIEVED AMMON WANTED TO PROVOKE A CONFRONTATION, and he was determined not to play into Ammon's hands. Not that Ward had much control over events at the refuge—that was the feds' problem, for the most part. But Burns was thick with Patriots too, which was the sheriff's responsibility. More Patriots were staying in town than at the refuge, and the day's events had stirred them up.

The day the refuge was occupied, Sheriff Ward was snowed out of his house. He sent his wife and kids to stay with somebody else and prepared to spend the night at his lieutenant's house. As night fell, several Patriot vehicles kept circling the block. Ward and his lieutenant felt exposed behind the house's big picture windows. So they grabbed a couple of AR-15 rifles and sat there, knowing the drive-bys were probably just more posturing on the part of the Patriots but also wondering if the night would end in a firefight. Because anything felt possible now. A group of armed Patriots had taken over the Malheur refuge.

FROM THE BEGINNING, MALHEUR FELT MORE RADICAL THAN BUNKERVILLE.

Cliven Bundy's clash with the BLM had been cast as a family standing its ground, defending its rights, its property. Even to those who disagreed with this characterization or tagged Cliven as a welfare cowboy, the idea of a family fighting for its livelihood was relatable.

But taking over a federal facility? That was an offensive move, and it had disrupted life in Harney County. In Burns, the BLM office shut down, idling eighty federal employees. The Harney County School District called off classes. The courthouse was fortified with a temporary chain-link fence, concrete barriers, and guards with rifles.

The occupation was far too militant for many. Oath Keepers had already bowed out after Stewart Rhodes deduced that Ammon was planning more than a rally, though that decision may also have been influenced by bad blood from Camp Liberty. In addition, several independent militias who'd helped organize the rally for the Hammonds felt betrayed by Ammon's secret plan and refused to join him at Malheur.

The Church of Jesus Christ of Latter-day Saints issued a statement condemning the "armed seizure." The Mormon Church was "deeply troubled by the reports that those who have seized the facility suggest that they are doing so based on scriptural principles."

The Burns Paiute tribe was more blunt. Paiutes had occupied the entire area, including the refuge, for much of the previous six thousand years. The tribal chair said the US land agencies were good protectors of the Paiute's cultural rights on the refuge. The occupiers, one tribal council member said, "just need to get the hell out of here."

The Hammond family, the reason why everybody had come to Oregon in the first place, issued a statement distancing themselves from the occupation, and Dwight and Steven Hammond turned themselves in to a federal prison in California on schedule, two days after the occupiers commandeered the refuge.

Former Bundy allies backed away too. A committee of Hammond-supporting locals thought the occupation was too aggressive. Even Pete Santilli seemed torn. On the one hand, he scrapped his plans to return to Cincinnati and covered the occupation with the same confrontational glee he'd brought to Bunkerville. On the other, he repeatedly told people—on the show and off—that the occupation was a bad idea. Instead of bunking at the refuge overnight, he kept his room at the Silver Spur, turning it into a makeshift radio studio.

Most troubling was the characteristically candid statement that Cliven Bundy himself gave to Oregon Public Broadcasting, in which he asked a question that was on the minds of many observers.

"I don't quite understand how much they're going to accomplish," he said. "I think of it this way: What business does the Bundy family have in Harney County, Oregon?"

Back home in Bunkerville, the rest of the family watched the occupation play out on a livestream. The Bundy women were supportive in public, but several had the same question as the rest of America: What were Ammon and Ryan *doing*? Defending the family ranch was one thing. But taking over a wildlife refuge? Ryan's wife wasn't exactly surprised that her husband had gone along with the occupation. That was the man she'd married. Once he'd decided upon a course of action, there was no talking him out of it. Whether he was fasting or fighting the government, his resolve seemed to be unbreakable. Still, she couldn't help questioning this move.

Dave Bundy, like Cliven, did not go to Oregon. His night in jail and brief entanglement in the federal justice system back in 2014 had scared him. He wanted to help his brothers, but he had his own family to worry about.

LaVoy Finicum had come to the refuge mainly as a show of allegiance with the Bundys. Driving from Burns with the advance team, he'd felt like Caesar crossing the Rubicon: Whatever happened next, there was no turning back. En route to the refuge, he saw a bald eagle on a fence post. The bird spread its wings and launched into the sky, and the Arizona rancher took it as an omen that he was doing the right thing.

LaVoy called Jeanette. She'd had no fear of his trip to Burns when she thought it was just a rally and march. Taking over a federal facility was a different matter altogether.

She said: *What are you* doing?

After the LDS Church condemned the occupation, two days after it began, Ammon decided to take control of the message. Only he and Finicum should speak to reporters from now on, he said. The occupiers blocked the refuge driveway and stopped giving news reporters tours of the buildings. Ammon held a press conference on the driveway at 11 AM each day. He often gave a statement and turned away abruptly, rebuffing reporters' questions. LaVoy Finicum was more genial and often stuck around to talk. He remembered people's names. Along with Ammon, Finicum became the face of the Malheur occupation. At Bunkerville, Finicum hadn't spoken to reporters and had headed home as soon as his ride to Toquop Wash was over. Many people weren't even aware that he'd been there. But he'd spent the last year and a half organizing meetings and making YouTube videos about his views, and he'd become comfortable taking a more public role.

Jeanette understood why Ammon wanted LaVoy representing the occupiers. Finicum was measured, well-spoken, amiable, calm. Jeanette had not met Ammon, but watching him on TV, she thought the two men shared a similar on-camera persona. Both had a lightness about them, a softness of personality, undergirded with firm conviction.

The Malheur occupation was a global news story, and lots of reporters wanted to find out more about this LaVoy Finicum character. In contrast to its sluggish coverage of Bunkerville, the *New York Times* immediately dispatched two correspondents to the scene, and their initial front-page story contained a quote from Finicum:

I want to leave as soon as possible, but I will stay as long as necessary.

In Arizona, the Finicums' landline rang constantly, either a reporter, a friend, or one of their eleven frantic children. News crews traveled to Cane Beds, and Jeanette was thankful her house was so hard to find and her neighbors so practiced at being tight-lipped. When reporters knocked on doors just up the dirt road, neighbors acted as if they'd never heard of the Finicums.

Journalists called the foster-care organization the Finicums worked for, and the service notified Jeanette that they were pulling their four current foster boys out of the house. Jeanette understood that the organization couldn't place boys with a family that was associated with militants. But the boys were crushed. One had been living with the Finicums for almost two years.

After their initial phone call, Jeanette had a difficult time reaching LaVoy in the first couple of days, partly due to cellular reception at the refuge and also because her husband was busy. When they finally connected, she was upset. If LaVoy wasn't coming home, he at least needed to pick up her calls. It wasn't fair to leave her at home wondering if he was okay.

She said: *You will pick up every time I call. You will not leave me hanging. You promise me that.*

LaVoy said: *I promise, Jeanette.*

From then on, even if he was in the middle of an interview, LaVoy answered when Jeanette called. Some of those early conversations were heated, Jeanette pleading with LaVoy to come home. LaVoy explained that he had to do this. Ranchers were coming to the refuge, asking for his help. It reminded him of his mission years. Jeanette came around, decided to support what he was trying to accomplish.

A few days into the occupation, LaVoy's parents and several of his daughters and grandchildren drove to Oregon to visit him. Jeanette stayed home, still busy packing up the foster boys. Not everyone wanted kids and family there, but LaVoy felt it was good to maintain a family reunion atmosphere—cooking, campfires, lots of talk. The occupiers had begun to settle into routines and were starting to believe the cops were really going to stay away. After all, the authorities hadn't even cut off the power.

But right about the time the Finicum daughters arrived at the refuge, a source told the occupiers that arrest warrants had been issued for the Bundy brothers and LaVoy. According to the intel, the FBI was preparing to storm Malheur and take everybody out in body bags. A current of fear jolted the occupiers. LaVoy told his daughters and parents they should leave, only a couple hours after they'd arrived.

That night, LaVoy became even more prominent when he stationed himself on the refuge drive, sitting in a lawn chair, his rifle across his knees, swathed in a heavy brown blanket and a blue plastic tarpaulin over his head. The cameras couldn't get enough of "Tarp Man," as he became known on social media. Reporters approached, crouching next to him with microphones, lifting the blue tarp to speak to him. LaVoy's head would emerge like a hatchling breaking through an eggshell. He spoke about his family, his ranch, and his love of the country. He also made it clear that he would not allow himself to be arrested.

"I have been raised in the country all my life, I love dearly to feel the wind on my face, to see the sunrise, to see the moon in the night," LaVoy said. "I have no intention of spending any of my days in a concrete box."

"There are people watching this who would say you're a terrorist, you've occupied land that's not your own, and you've got a death wish," an MSNBC reporter said.

"I have no death wish," LaVoy said. "I love life."

HEADLINES CALLED IT AN ARMED OCCUPATION, WHICH WASN'T EXACTLY inaccurate. But that description didn't capture how loose it was. Police and feds kept their distance, and occupiers drove back and forth to town at will.

Dozens of visitors flowed in and out of the refuge every day, more on weekends. Many were locals who wanted to find out for themselves who these occupiers were; some of the area ranchers who visited were gratified that somebody cared about their plight. Using a whiteboard and dry-erase markers, the Bundys and LaVoy Finicum gave seminars about their interpretation of constitutional law and the proper forms of government. One local boy came to the refuge and interviewed Brand Nu Thornton for a school assignment.

The guards at the driveway were told to let everyone in, but sometimes that blanket order was overruled, as when an Arizona group devoted to bringing awareness to veteran suicide rates set up an army tent across the road from the refuge driveway. They said they were there to extract the volatile Jon Ritzheimer before he hurt himself or somebody else. They ended up getting into a fistfight with a couple of the Malheur occupiers and were banned from the refuge. Some guards were unsure what they were supposed to do if the feds came. Ammon said to bring them to him. But no feds showed up.

A constant flow of individuals felt called to the refuge, not to join the occupation but to offer advice and help. A pro-gun public relations specialist from Utah came and advised the Bundys to keep what she called "ugly guns"—black rifles with folding stocks, for example—out of public view. The Bundys agreed.

And then, as if to test the new no-ugly-guns rule, two dozen militia members from Oregon, Washington, and Idaho pulled up to the refuge the next day, just as LaVoy Finicum was finishing a press conference. Several carried assault rifles, and the news cameras lingered on one shifty-eyed and jittery man who inexplicably carried his AR-15 at low-ready, like he was patrolling a bloody war zone. This was the exact opposite of the image Ammon wanted to portray. He'd been insisting he wasn't running an armed occupation. The new arrivals said they were going to establish a perimeter around the refuge to ensure the safety of people on both sides. Finicum asked them to put away the long guns. Ammon went further, asking the militiamen to leave the refuge, and they complied, although many remained in Burns.

A Kansas woman named Odalis Sharp brought seven of her ten children to the refuge, where they sang gospel songs for the occupiers. The occupiers were familiar with the Sharp Family Singers, as they billed themselves, because the family had also spent time at Camp Liberty in Bunkerville. They didn't know that in 2011, Sharp's eldest child had been placed in foster care after reports of alleged abuse and neglect. To the occupiers, Sharp seemed to be settling in for the long haul at Malheur, planning to raise her children there.

But the Sharps were the exception. The refuge saw dozens of visitors on some days, but few remained overnight and fewer moved in. Partly because after dark seemed the most likely time for the FBI to stage a raid.

The occupiers debated whether children should be allowed to stay at the refuge. Some worried about their safety, but others believed that having children present was making a statement that the occupation was not a combat zone. They aspired to be peaceful, to cast the feds as warlike, but this attempt was undermined when guys like Jon Ritzheimer talked constantly about getting slaughtered by the feds.

As the days passed, it became clear that a Bunkerville-style flood of thousands of backers was not materializing. Around forty people were staying at the refuge, a number that changed as people came and went. Nevertheless, Pete Santilli, who had repeatedly called for ten thousand Patriots to come to Bunkerville, upped his target number tenfold. Even though Santilli had decided to stay at the Silver Spur, not the refuge, he repeated the new number over and over.

"What we need," Santilli said, "is one hundred thousand unarmed men and women to stand together."

Low on cash, Terri Linnell was waiting for her husband's next paycheck before making the long drive from Southern California to eastern Oregon. But then Carly, the FBI special agent who had recruited Linnell to report on Oath Keepers' meetings, called and said the government would pay for her trip. Carly said the Bundys were mixed up with some very bad and dangerous folks. The FBI needed eyes and ears inside the refuge.

Linnell took a couple of days to pace around her mountainside property and mull Carly's offer. She wrote about it in a notebook, listing each potential pro and con. Was there anything wrong with telling the FBI the truth about what was happening at the refuge? No, Linnell decided. Besides, despite what Carly had said, Linnell couldn't imagine Ammon Bundy associating with bad guys. Would the Patriots suspect she was reporting to the FBI? Unlikely, as Linnell was a longtime and well-connected Patriot. Her biggest concern was that the feds would raid the refuge while she was there, but Linnell figured she could help keep people safe. Linnell asked Carly if she could serve as a liaison between the FBI and the Bundy brothers, but the special agent said that wasn't how the FBI operated.

In the end, Linnell agreed to Carly's proposition. At the Panera Bread restaurant where they always met, Linnell signed a one-page contract pledging that she would not break the law as a confidential informant. She and Carly didn't discuss a payment amount, but they haggled over other details. Carly wanted her to fly, but Linnell insisted on driving. Linnell also was adamant that she would bring a gun, which Carly wasn't happy about. Carly gave her $1,000 in cash for expenses and told her to hang on to her receipts for additional reimbursement.

On January 13, Linnell posted her plans on Facebook:

I'm leaving in a Jetta, don't know when I'll be back again.
Oregon or bust lol
—Momma Bear

Neil Wampler was having the time of his life.

The friend who'd driven him to Burns was not keen on the occupation and went back to California, leaving Wampler without a car. But Wampler was perfectly happy to remain at Malheur for awhile. He slept in a shared room in the firefighters' bunkhouse and stationed himself in the kitchen during the days. He liked cooking because eventually everybody would circle through for food, which allowed him to meet a lot of folks. Like Bunkerville, there was no shortage of provisions. Ranchers dropped off beef. People ran to the grocery store and came back with eggs and ham. A Washington State cranberry farmer brought four buckets of oysters he'd harvested himself, and the occupiers barbecued them. A local hay farmer butchered and smoked a hog and brought it to the refuge, and he and Wampler discussed filing a writ of habeas corpus to free the Hammonds.

Someone donated beer, which became an issue. The leaders were mostly abstinent Mormons, and they didn't want people getting drunk, especially if they were on security duty. On the other hand, the occupation was an experiment in liberty and the leaders didn't want to tell adults they couldn't enjoy a beer. A balance was struck. The beer was locked in a special cooler and a two-beer-per-day rule was established.

At night, people played music and sang songs and told stories. The Bundy brothers sometimes talked about growing up on Bundy Ranch, how Cliven had given them permission as teenagers to hunt and sell feral bulls that weren't part of his herd. The boys had cut the top off a Ford Bronco and installed a winch. They'd lasso a bull and then drag it home, and often as not, the two-thousand-pound beast would turn on the Bronco, ramming and nearly toppling it. The Bundys knew how to spin a yarn, and their audiences loved the stories.

The refuge was like a little village, a return to tribal living. Everyone knew each other. Everyone was taking a break from normal life, from jobs and family. Meals were taken together. The occupiers were expected to find work to do, spreading gravel on the driveway, splitting firewood, filling the bird feeders. Some occupiers took on roles that were more symbolic than practical. Brand Nu Thornton blew his shofar. One man clopped around on his horse, Hellboy, lofting an American flag.

As with any village, any tribe, some of the denizens were misfits, which tested the occupation's all-are-welcome ethos. One young guy from Burns pulled a guard-duty shift in the observation tower but turned out to be a methamphetamine user and a felon. Another got thrown off the refuge because he was talking about burning down the buildings and sabotaging the heavy equipment. If an occupier seemed too high-strung or aggressive or just plain unhinged—and there were a few—they were deemed "Section 8," a military term meaning mentally unfit for service. The last thing the occupation needed was to harbor another Jerad or Amanda Miller.

Wampler adopted a retiree's routine. He got up early, made breakfast. He'd take a midmorning walk around the compound. Lunch was casual, just a matter of laying out coleslaw, potato salad, sandwich makings. He'd take a midafternoon nap. Then it was time to make dinner and clean up afterward. The days were punctuated with lots of cigarette breaks, lots of conversation. Wampler discovered that not everybody shared a strong grasp of the occupation's goals. He called these people "low-information Patriots." One morning after breakfast, he went for his walk and came across a young man on guard duty holding a rifle. Wampler chatted with him and mentioned the Bundys.

The kid said: *Who are the Bundys?*

Oregon Public Broadcasting interviewed Ryan Bundy, who said the occupiers would be calling for a community meeting.

"If the county's people tell us to leave, we'll leave," Ryan said.

Sheriff Ward saw Ryan's quote and decided to call the Bundys' bluff. He held a town hall meeting on January 6. Around four hundred people showed up, probably the most ever for a Burns town hall meeting. Ward asked for a show of hands: Who wanted the occupiers to leave? Ward estimated that 85 percent raised their hands. Several residents urged him to meet with the occupiers and ask them to leave.

The next day, Ward arranged a meeting with Ammon. Neutral territory on a desolate back road east of the refuge. Ward brought backup, and Ammon brought Ryan Payne. A number of journalists showed up as well. The meeting was short and amicable and awkward. Both men spoke in soft tones, Ammon scuffing his boots on the asphalt, hands jammed in his pockets.

Ward wanted Ammon to feel he'd accomplished something, which would give him a way out. So Ward started the meeting on a positive note, saying that Ammon's activities in Harney County had shone a light on the range wars. People were paying attention. Ward had spoken to both of the state's senators as well as the governor. Now it was time to leave before something bad happened.

"I'm willing to get you an escort all the way out of the state," Ward told Ammon.

Ammon wasn't interested. He wanted to talk about the redress of grievances—specifically, why Ward hadn't responded to it.

Ward wouldn't address the document.

"I'm here because the citizens of Harney County have asked me to ask you folks to peacefully leave," Ward said.

Ammon countered, saying that a couple hundred local people had visited the refuge.

"We pose no threat to the community," Ammon said.

"You guys have both told me that you can't guarantee the things that other people that come here might do," Ward said.

"We mean no harm to anybody," Ammon said.

"I believe you," Ward said. "But it only takes one unstable person to show up."

In Blanchester, Ohio, David Fry saw LaVoy Finicum on the news, talking about the Oregon occupation. After his early interactions with Finicum via YouTube in the fall, Fry had been inspired to start making his own videos and had refused to pay his fine for river rafting without a life jacket.

Now, seeing Finicum at Malheur, a voice spoke to Fry. A voice he'd heard before in his head, a few times in his life. A female voice, but not that of his mother, Sachiyo, and not any woman he'd ever met. Fry knew that doctors had said the voice was a symptom of mental illness, but he liked to think of it as a more benign presence, a sort of angel. Now, the voice told him that LaVoy Finicum would not survive this experience.

Fry knew if he didn't go to Oregon right away, he'd never meet Finicum in person. The next day, he gathered about $700 in cash and packed his HP Mini laptop and some extra battery pack chargers in his silver 1988 Lincoln Town Car. He punched the refuge address into his

Motorola Droid phone. His parents begged him to stay home, but Fry's mind was made up.

Fry followed the directions on his phone all the way to Oregon. The roads were covered with snow and ice, and what should have been a thirty-two-hour drive turned into a four-day haul. Fry slept in the Town Car every night except his last night on the road, when he finally checked into a motel. Before he got to the refuge, he bought canned goods and extra toothbrushes to give to the occupiers.

When Fry finally pulled into the refuge driveway on January 8, a pickup truck was blocking it. Two men approached, shined a flashlight in his face, asked what he was doing. Fry said he'd driven from Blanchester, Ohio, and was there to bring supplies and help out. The men radioed the refuge and backed up their truck so Fry could pass. Another vehicle came up the drive to escort him down to the refuge.

The men took Fry to the bunkhouse, where about twenty people were hanging out. He didn't see the Bundys or Finicum that first night. Fry's father and brother had both been Marines, and Fry was familiar with guns and hunting. But he'd never been around militias before, and he didn't know what to expect. Everyone was welcoming, and they offered him food. The occupiers were dying to get some news, but they'd disconnected all of the computers, fearing the government would be able to spy on them. Most of their phones had AT&T or Sprint service plans, which weren't working at the refuge. Fry, as it turned out, had Verizon, which worked. So he let them use his phone to check out what Alex Jones was saying about the occupation on Infowars. He slept on a couch in the bunkhouse.

The next morning, Finicum came to the bunkhouse. Fry was surprised to see that Finicum was bald—he wore a cowboy hat in his videos. Fry greeted him, and the rancher recognized his name from their YouTube interactions. Finicum asked if Fry knew anything about computers, and Fry said he did.

Finicum said: *I was just praying that somebody would come this way who could help me with some computer stuff. I guess that's you.*

Fry felt pretty good about that. At Finicum's request, he reconnected the computers to the internet cables but found that the service wasn't working. So Fry hooked up his smartphone to a router and was able to provide Wi-Fi to the entire bunkhouse.

When he wasn't serving as the occupation's tech guy, Fry shot videos about the everyday life of the refuge and posted them on his YouTube channel, *DefendYourBase*. He recorded his strolls around the icy refuge paths. He videoed the wildlife, including a row of quails running across the snow and a conversation with a ground squirrel. He shot video of the food, including a pork dinner and a breakfast burrito. He recorded TV reporters doing standups. He also recorded more significant moments, such as meetings with visitors, including area ranchers, who'd come to learn more about the occupation.

After the first night on the bunkhouse couch, Fry moved to the firehouse, which the occupiers were using as a media center. Finicum gave him a sleeping bag and a foam mattress, and Fry found a spot on the floor between a desk and a file cabinet. He had not brought a gun, but when he found a Second Amendment sticker in a box, he stuck it on his Town Car's bumper. He became known among the occupiers for a strange sleeping habit. Sitting on a couch, he'd just fold himself over, still in a sitting position, and fall asleep with his head on his knees.

Fry liked most of the people he met, but he still felt out of place. He was a half-Asian computer geek from Ohio, not a rancher or a militiaman. He wore sweats and wire-rimmed spectacles, not camo. He was friendly but odd, accustomed to not fitting in. A few days after Fry got there, an Oregon Public Broadcasting reporter figured out who Fry was and plumbed his social media history. Some of Fry's past posts included what sounded like pro-Nazi and pro-ISIS statements.

"ALL I WANT FOR CHRISTMAS IS FOR ISIS TO NUKE ISRAELHELL!" he'd written recently on Google's social network.

When the Oregon Public Broadcasting story came out, Ryan Payne blew up, especially about the ISIS part. He wanted Fry gone. Fry protested that the posts were nothing more than sarcastic jokes. He said he hated Nazis, thought the government was veering toward fascism. Finicum stepped in and made peace between them, and Fry was allowed to stay.

A few of the occupiers talked about how much they hated Muslims, and that bothered Fry. Around the campfire, one guy said the only good Muslim was a dead Muslim. Fry didn't know how that belief could possibly be compatible with the liberty-minded goals of the occupation. He thought about leaving, even wrote a goodbye letter, but ended up throwing it away.

He only occasionally interacted with Ammon or Ryan. The Bundy brothers were polite but distant and stern, and they stuck to their inner circle. They weren't like Finicum, who had the ability to make everybody feel singled out and special. Fry didn't hold it against them. The Bundys were busy men. Important.

EACH MORNING, THE LEADERS HAD AN INFORMAL MEETING, OFTEN AMONG the stuffed-and-mounted bird specimens in the refuge museum. A western snowy plover and a whitefaced ibis stood witness as everybody threw out ideas about what needed to be done. If the group agreed, somebody volunteered to do the task. At night, Ryan and Ammon talked with each other about what had gone well that day, and what hadn't.

Ammon was told that the Bundy Ranch Facebook page was getting six million views a day. Everything he did was scrutinized. He couldn't make a misstep. He carefully planned casual-looking trips to

Burns, and he didn't carry a gun, didn't travel with bodyguards. He got his hair cut in town, went to a Chinese restaurant, met with people in their offices. Three times he drove home to Emmett to see his family and go to church. The police left him alone.

About a week into the occupation, as things were settling down, Ammon and the leaders began planning a series of events designed to sustain attention to the cause. They renamed the Malheur refuge, calling it the Harney County Resource Center. They erected vinyl signs and attached stickers to government vehicles. Ryan Bundy and Ken Medenbach drove to the temporarily abandoned BLM district office near Burns and screwed a "Closed Permanently" placard onto the front sign.

A couple days later, surrounded by cameras and reporters, Ammon and several others cut a barbed-wire fence to allow a local rancher's cows access to refuge lands. Ranch hands fixed the fence within a day or two, and the ranch owner complained, saying someone else at the ranch had given Ammon approval for the publicity stunt, not him. A few days later, Ryan Bundy held a ladder against a utility pole as Finicum climbed it to remove surveillance cameras the FBI had put up to keep an eye on the occupation. When critics accused the occupiers of trashing the refuge, the occupiers responded with videos that showed them cleaning the buildings and asking the Paiute tribe to help them preserve artifacts stored at the refuge.

Behind the scenes, Ammon and Shawna Cox were trying to piece together a registry of land rights, using records they'd found at the refuge. They'd started at the northern boundary of Harney County and were working their way down. Once they knew who the Malheur lands were supposed to belong to, they planned to transfer the properties back to those private owners. Over and over, Ammon explained his plans to different groups of Harney County citizens, at in-person meetings and in Skype calls, and some began to believe Ammon could pull it off.

In those meetings, the Bundys urged the ranchers to do as Cliven and LaVoy Finicum had done: tear up their contracts with the federal land agencies. The occupiers said they would create "rapid response teams" that could back up ranchers who defied the feds.

Ammon said: *We will protect you.*

Sheriff Ward heard that some ranchers were coming around to Ammon's message. This was worrisome. If Ammon could convince even one rancher to defy the federal land agencies, it could spark another Bunkerville-sized crisis. If he could organize a group of ranchers . . . who knew what would happen?

Every so often, LaVoy Finicum and the Bundys would hint that they were close to revealing their exit strategy, but it never quite happened. After the first week, Ward was happy to see that media coverage seemed to be leveling off. The occupiers tried to spark attention through public acts of defiance—the Harney County Resource Center signage, the fence cutting—but the FBI agreed with Sheriff Ward that the hands-off policy was best. Leave them alone, and the occupation would melt away like a spring snow.

Not that law enforcement was doing nothing. A unified command post that included federal, state, and local personnel was set up in the school district administration building catty-corner to the sheriff's office. Additional officers operated out of the Burns Municipal Airport, which took on the feel of a temporary military base, with portable buildings and armored vehicles. FBI agents across Oregon were mobilized to Harney County. They collected intelligence from Patriot informants. They placed "ping orders" on several occupiers' phones, allowing them to tell when and where a call was made. They flew surveillance aircraft over the refuge. They installed a set of cameras on a utility pole near the compound, one that could read the license plates of passing cars and the other for standard surveillance and evidence gathering. The cameras were supposed to help law enforcement prepare for whatever came next, whether that was a prosecution or a raid, but Ryan Bundy and LaVoy Finicum had quickly taken them down.

The first in-person interaction between the Bundys and the FBI happened eight days into the occupation. Two FBI agents who were Mormon were asked to go to the LDS church in Burns for Sunday services and see if any Bundys showed up. The agents agreed to the task, but said they'd go as themselves, not undercover. Ryan Bundy showed up, and the agents introduced themselves and gave their real names.

One agent said: *I'm a Mormon. I'm an FBI agent. I'm here for the Malheur occupation.*

Ryan introduced himself, and they shook hands. They sat a few seats apart during the service, and that was that.

In mid-January, the FBI got some troubling intel. A trio of sovereign citizens had arrived at the refuge, including a Denver man who called himself a "Superior Court Judge of the Continental uNited States of America." He told the occupiers how to set up "common-law courts" and "people's grand juries," extralegal techniques sovereign citizens had attempted to use in the past to prosecute various public officials. He said if any of the occupiers wanted to be a federal marshal, he could swear them in. Word was, the sovereigns would be issuing "indictments" to some Harney County officials and possibly attempting to arrest them. Sheriff Ward was on the list.

The FBI also heard that the occupation leaders had been talking to the sheriff in Grant County, just north of Harney. Glenn Palmer was known as a true constitutional sheriff who believed in the concept of county supremacy. If Palmer agreed to protect a Bundy-led occupation in his county, it would at the very least legitimize the occupation. If he went even further and decided to, say, deputize the occupiers, it would set up a locals-versus-feds nightmare scenario.

On January 15, an official in the Oregon governor's office called a Grant County commissioner to discuss the situation. If the occupiers made a run for Grant County, they speculated at one point, they'd be driving through a lot of remote, isolated, wooded highway. This was something to think about. Later that night, the governor's office staffer summarized the conversation in an email to colleagues.

"There is a lot of open road traveling between Harney and Grant Co.," he wrote. "Doesn't it seem like an opportunity for law enforcement to stop the occupiers on their way and make some arrests?"

LOCALS WEREN'T THE ONLY ONES RIVETED BY EVENTS AT MALHEUR. A global audience was tracking the unfolding conflict on social media, and things got weird fast.

Within days, popular Twitter hashtags included #VanillaISIS, #YallQaeda, and #TaliBundy. Hundreds of Twitter users were creating micro-fiction about the after-dark goings on at Malheur, tagging posts as #BundyEroticFanFic. A representative sample:

Ammon hesitated. "Isn't this against the laws of nature?"
"Laws?" panted Dwight, "We make our own laws, Ammon."

Another:

"Did you bring condoms?" Jed whispered.
"Not to worry, we're protected by the 1st and 2nd Amendment," Ammon replied.

Bundy spectators howled when Blaine Cooper sent out a call for "snacks" and "cold-weather socks" on Facebook. Carol Bundy contributed a longer wish list of almost one hundred items, including tampons, gaming supplies, mayonnaise, and Neil Wampler's favorite cigarette, Pall Mall Menthol 100s. Many observers found it ironic that the occupiers were asking that the provisions be delivered through the US Postal Service to a post office in Harney County. Stories targeted the Bundy followers' lack of preparation for a long-haul occupation, and jokesters sent glitter, diapers, and baby food.

After his "Daddy Swore an Oath" video went viral, Jon Ritzheimer had become a favorite target. People discovered his anti-Islam videos and sent him boxes of Qurans. Others sent dildos and a bag of gummy candies shaped like penises. Ritzheimer piled the boxes on a table and made a short video marveling at the various items of "hate mail" the occupiers had received.

"Rather than going out and doing good," he said, "they just spend all their money on hate and hate and hate and hate." Ritzheimer paused, then, without warning, swept all the boxes off the table. "So we're gonna clear the table, and we're gonna continue to do work and do good for our country."

The *Daily Mail*, a British tabloid newspaper, dug into the military records of the men who'd taken over the refuge and discovered a few exaggerated claims of service and distinction, and one outright fabrication. Booda Cavalier, Cliven's bodyguard who had often identified himself as a Marine combat veteran, had not served in the Marines. Shortly after reporters questioned him about the lie, Cavalier drove off the refuge. Word was he'd holed up in a local motel, drinking.

A week later he was back, claiming to have gone to Arizona for a court date. Confronted about his military record, Cavalier admitted he didn't serve in the Marines. He said he'd concocted the lie when he came to Bunkerville because he wanted to be Cliven's bodyguard and he knew the old rancher valued military service. He just wanted to protect Cliven, he said. Cavalier was a smooth talker, and the occupiers took him back in.

Two weeks into the occupation, Ken Medenbach took a Malheur refuge truck to town for grocery shopping, happy to show off the new Harney County Resource Center stickers he'd put on the sides. Someone spotted the government truck and the state police arrested him on suspicion of unauthorized use of a vehicle. Up to that point, he was the only occupier arrested.

When Neil Wampler had seen Medenbach taking the truck off the refuge, he'd told him it was a bad idea. Events like this made Wampler wish Stewart Rhodes had not distanced the Oath Keepers from the occupation. The Bundys and Finicum and Ryan Payne were strong leaders, Wampler believed, but there was a need for midlevel leadership that the Oath Keepers could have provided, someone to establish some rules like: Don't take the refuge trucks to town. Instead of the relatively disciplined Oath Keepers, the occupiers' midlevel leadership consisted of guys like Booda Cavalier, Blaine Cooper, and Jon Ritzheimer.

Then a dark episode from Wampler's own past surfaced, giving the occupation's critics even more ammunition. The *Oregonian* newspaper was digging into the various occupiers' histories and had discovered a Neil Wampler who at age twenty-nine had murdered his own father in California. A reporter asked Wampler about it, and he denied he was the same man. But the reporter verified it was him through records and witnesses and published an article on January 20. Wampler then wrote a short editorial to his hometown newspaper confirming the story.

In 1977, in a drunken rage, Wampler had hit his father in the head with a sixteen-inch eye bolt, killing him. Wampler hitchhiked to a liquor store and called the police. He confessed to the murder and served four years in prison. He quit drinking and claimed to have lived a peaceful life since then.

Wampler hated that his crime was distracting from the occupation's goals, if not validating critics' worst fears about the kind of people who were attracted to Malheur. He left the refuge and began hitchhiking home. It took the disheveled ex-hippie a lot longer to catch a lift than it had when he was a young man, and eventually he gave up and caught a train back to Los Osos.

WHEN WAMPLER LEFT, TERRI LINNELL TOOK HIS PLACE ON THE EARLY breakfast shift. Momma Bear had arrived at the refuge in mid-January. She brought a Glock pistol for the drive, but at her FBI handler's suggestion, she didn't carry it at the refuge at first. She was assigned a bed in the bunkhouse. She took chow-hall duty: cooking, doing dishes, chatting with everybody.

Once a day or so, Linnell would grab her cell phone, step out of the bunkhouse, and dial Carly's number. Linnell didn't look for a private spot or make a big deal of the call in any way. She made the calls right outside the bunkhouse, near her car. Being seen making a furtive phone call would have been a dead giveaway that Linnell was a confidential informant.

During their daily phone calls, Carly always asked about the same half-dozen individuals: the Bundy brothers, Ryan Payne, Jon Ritzheimer, Blaine Cooper, and Pete Santilli. She asked where the "armory" was, and Linnell said people had firearms, but she was aware of no armory. The agent asked about weapons and visitors. Linnell said ranchers from other counties were asking the occupiers to help them. She said children were staying at the refuge, including the Sharp Family Singers, and it was making some people uncomfortable.

None of this bothered Linnell much, but she was dismayed by

the presence of sovereign citizens. She'd run across sovereigns before and knew they were trouble. When she got to the refuge, three sovereigns were there, a self-proclaimed judge and two men who called themselves federal marshals. Linnell heard that the judge was planning to swear in some other occupiers as marshals. Some of the occupiers had no experience with sovereigns and seemed enthusiastic about the idea. Momma Bear decided she'd better put a stop to it. No American should impersonate a police officer or judge, whether she agreed with their politics or not.

So when the "judge" declared loudly that he wasn't a United States citizen, Linnell stared at him across the chow hall.

Linnell said: *Well, I'm a proud United States citizen, and I believe only a US citizen should uphold and defend the Constitution of the United States from all enemies, foreign* and *domestic.*

The "judge" protested, but Linnell wasn't having it. After that, nobody volunteered to be sworn in, as far as Linnell knew, and the trio of sovereigns left soon thereafter. Linnell reported them to Carly.

Sometimes the FBI agent told Linnell about things that were happening at the refuge, things Linnell had no clue about. Eventually, Linnell realized that someone else at the refuge was working for the feds. Someone closer to the leaders than she was. Maybe more than one.

THE DAYS WENT ON, AND THE FEDS STAYED AWAY. NEVERTHELESS, THE occupiers ramped up their military training, practicing how to stop a car by laying a nail-studded fire hose across a road. And then how to remove the driver from the vehicle for interrogation. They designated a shooting range and fired thousands of rounds of ammunition during training sessions. They learned survivalist techniques, basic medic skills, hand-to-hand combat.

One day in late January, a group of trainees gathered at the boat launch area near the lake to undergo training with a mysterious foreigner who called himself John Killman.

"Contact front! Contact front!" Killman yelled in a hard-to-place European dialect.

The row of militiamen raised their rifles at an unseen enemy.

"You have a malfunction! You have a malfunction!" Killman yelled.

The militiamen lowered the rifles and brought up handguns, stepping forward, knees bent.

Killman was excitable. He'd bark at the trainees, grab and shake them to make a point, yell at women that he was trying to teach them so they "will not get raped!" People struggled to nail down his accent. Some thought he was French, others South African. He'd shown up in late January and was Facebook friends with several occupiers.

Other training sessions were primarily led by Ryan Payne as well as an Arizona man named Mark McConnell. McConnell was part of a civilian border-patrol group in Arizona and had become something of an inner-circle guy since arriving in Oregon early in the occupation.

Ryan Bundy had a bad feeling about Mark McConnell. There was something dark about the man, he thought. He warned Ammon about his misgivings, but Ammon continued to employ McConnell as a bodyguard. It was the essential conundrum the Patriots faced: they needed all the bodies they could muster, but a single Section 8er or infiltrator could derail the whole thing.

ON THE EVENING OF JANUARY 19, 2016, A FEW HUNDRED PEOPLE CAME TO Burns High School to vent about the occupation. Fifteen minutes into the meeting, Ammon and Ryan Bundy, along with another ten or so occupiers, edged into the gymnasium, past uniformed police. They tried not to cause a disturbance, but the crowd tensed up anyway. Ryan sat with Jon Ritzheimer. Ammon sat on the other side of the gym, picking a seat high on one side of the bleachers. He was flanked by Booda Cavalier.

Despite the ridicule and public relations setbacks, Ammon believed community sentiment was beginning to bend his way. US Representative Greg Walden of Oregon had given an emotional and sympathetic twenty-five-minute speech on the House floor about the range wars, which made Ken Medenbach burst into tears because someone in Washington was finally listening. Also, the public schools were back in session after a week-long hiatus. Ranchers were paying attention to Ammon's message, seriously considering ripping up their BLM contracts. Ammon had said repeatedly that the occupiers would leave the refuge when area residents were ready to take up the fight. Local allies had initially felt betrayed when he took over Malheur, but as the weeks passed, some had begun to appreciate the attention the occupation had brought to the range wars. Now those locals said they were ready to take on parts of the occupiers' mission.

But if Ammon expected a positive reception in the high school gym, he was mistaken. He sat silently as speaker after speaker addressed him directly, blaming him for inciting fear in local schools, for damaging local friendships, for hijacking the Hammond case for his own political ends. Chants of "Go home" broke out.

One woman said the occupation had raised important issues but told him, "Get the hell out of my county."

With sheriff's deputies and Oregon state troopers posted inside and outside the gym, many people at the meeting wondered why the Bundys weren't arrested on the spot. Sheriff Ward believed that would have been too dangerous, given how many people were around. Also, the occupiers were almost daring him to try to take them into custody in front of the cameras, and he wasn't going to fall into that trap.

Instead, Ward took the microphone and simply repeated the request he'd been making of Ammon for weeks now: *Go home to your family.*

Neither of the Bundys nor their followers spoke, though Ritzheimer raised his hand but never got a turn at the microphone. As the occupiers joined the crowd flowing toward the exits, individuals continued to plead for them to go home.

Ryan said only: "If we left now, there would be nothing accomplished."

Ammon just headed for his vehicle.

The same day, Oregon governor Kate Brown spoke to FBI director James Comey about the armed radicals who had taken over the Malheur refuge almost three weeks earlier. The refuge was isolated, she said, but that didn't mean the occupation was benign. The town of Burns was overrun with the militants and their supporters, residents felt intimidated, and state and local law enforcement were straining to cover the situation.

At the request of the FBI, Brown had mostly held her tongue about the occupation with the public and press, but the refuge was the feds' responsibility, and it was time for the US government to take action.

The next day, she doubled down on her demand in letters to Comey, Attorney General Loretta Lynch, and President Barack Obama.

She wrote: "I request on behalf of my fellow Oregonians that you instruct your agencies to end the unlawful occupation of the Malheur National Wildlife Refuge as safely and quickly as possible."

Immediately, the FBI stepped up efforts to reach out to Ammon. An FBI negotiator left a dozen messages on Ammon's phone. Ammon went to the Burns airport to meet the negotiator. As with most of

Ammon's excursions, a group of supporters accompanied him and recorded the encounter. If Ammon was arrested, they wanted it on camera. The negotiator wasn't at the airport, but an FBI agent got him on the phone, and Ammon stood outside in the cold wind near the airport's barricaded entrance, talking for nearly an hour. He put the phone on speaker mode, so the reporters, FBI agents, and his supporters could hear. It was a one-way conversation, the negotiator patiently listening as Ammon told him what they were doing at the refuge and why, a litany he'd repeated a hundred times by now.

They ended the call with a promise to speak the next day, but Ammon reconsidered. The federal government had no authority over public lands in Harney County, he believed, so why was he speaking to the FBI? Instead, the following day, he and the entourage went to the barricaded courthouse and asked to speak to the sheriff. He got a lieutenant, and they had a brief conversation, punctuated by blasts of Brand Nu Thornton's ram's horn shofar.

Ammon asked the lieutenant whether Sheriff Ward had given the FBI authority to operate within Harney County.

"The FBI are taking care of the refuge situation," the lieutenant responded. "It's federal property, and . . ."

Ammon shook his head as several occupiers took exception to this statement.

"No, it's not federal property," Ammon said.

The men stared at each other across an impasse as unnavigable as Zion Canyon once was.

THREE WEEKS INTO THE OCCUPATION, JEANETTE FINICUM DROVE TO THE refuge to visit. She'd seen LaVoy in person only once since he'd left. On January 13, LaVoy and Ryan Bundy had driven home together, a wonderful surprise. They held a meeting in Cedar City to try to persuade a group of Dixie ranchers to reject the BLM, and then headed back to the refuge the very same day.

So Jeanette went to him, and she stayed for three days, spending the night in the little sleeping quarters LaVoy had carved out. LaVoy was busy as the occupiers geared up for a press event on Saturday, January 23, 2016. A New Mexico rancher, who had traveled to Oregon for the affair, signed papers declaring that he was following the lead of the Bundys and LaVoy in severing ties to the Forest Service. The Sharp Family Singers harmonized, and a notary public attested to the rancher's signature. LaVoy gave the rancher a sheet containing members of the occupation's rapid-response team, in case the feds gave him trouble.

"We will stop everything and come to your aid," LaVoy said.

Nearby, environmentalist protestors were giving the occupiers a hard time, and LaVoy was tense. When a reporter asked LaVoy about his own grazing controversy, he uncharacteristically waved off the question and stormed away. But Jeanette came up and hugged him. Someone snapped a photo of them at this moment, standing in the snow, LaVoy offering a smile that was a little tighter than usual, Jeanette relaxed and beaming, her head tucked into the crook of his shoulder, storm clouds gathering behind.

Despite his moment of exasperation, LaVoy was excited. The revolution was catching on. In addition to the New Mexico rancher, nine other ranchers in Utah and Oregon had agreed to renounce the federal land agencies, and the Utahns had hired a lawyer to represent them.

When LaVoy got the call about the ranchers, he yelped: *Woo-hoo!*

The next day, Sunday, they went to church in Burns, and then Jeanette left to drive the New Mexico rancher to the Boise, Idaho, airport on her way back to Cane Beds. She and LaVoy had made plans to meet the following week in Idaho at another ranchers' meeting. LaVoy was also excited about a meeting in Grant County on Tuesday where three hundred people were planning to come. Sheriff Glenn Palmer had met with Ryan Payne and Jon Ritzheimer, who signed the sheriff's pocket Constitution.

The vast majority of public-lands ranchers were continuing to back the system that had governed the rangelands of the West for so long. But here and there, tiny rebellions were breaking out, Ammon's improbable master plan catching fire like a scattering of lit matches on a dry pasture.

THE NIGHT JEANETTE LEFT, LAVOY FINICUM GOT A PHONE CALL FROM three Oath Keepers, including Stewart Rhodes.

Oath Keepers stationed in Burns had reported that the FBI was ramping up in town, Rhodes said. Finicum said a drone had been hovering over the refuge throughout the previous night or two. The Oath Keepers said the drone probably had a thermal sensor and was detecting the location of the Patriot security forces in advance of a raid. The feds' next step probably would be to cordon off the refuge and cut off the Patriots' communication systems. The feds would isolate them, Rhodes said, like they did with the Branch Davidians at Waco.

"Kinda looks like they're getting ready to put a hurt on us," Finicum said, chuckling.

The Oath Keepers stressed that it was important not to get arrested.

"You guys are too valuable to all the ranchers in the whole entire western half of the country," one said. "You're basically the George Pattons of the resistance."

"Don't put us there," Finicum objected. "We're just rednecks."

"You're no longer just a redneck," the Oath Keeper said. "You've taken a lead."

The Oath Keepers had a suggestion. Since Sheriff Ward had proven to be unfaithful to the Constitution, the occupiers should "pop smoke"—move to a different county, one where they'd get support from the local law.

"If a constitutional sheriff and ranchers are willing to stand united together, you'd have massive support," Rhodes said. "They have never yet jumped down on a sheriff. Whenever a sheriff has stood up, the feds have always backed down. It'd be a huge game changer."

They should leave that night, the Oath Keepers said, or tomorrow night at the latest. The feds probably would make their move midweek, when many of the militia members staying in Burns had to go home for work.

Finicum said he was grateful for the Oath Keepers' advice and he'd take their suggestion to the others.

Overnight, the Patriot networks buzzed with speculation that the occupiers were leaving the refuge.

The next day, Finicum recorded and posted a short video to dispel the rumors. He stood outside one of the refuge buildings and spoke to the camera. The occupation was successful, he said. Ranchers were rejecting the federal government's control of the lands.

"We are not leaving," he said. "We are here to do a job. Our course is fixed. Steady as she goes. These buildings do not ever return to the federal government."

The next day, Tuesday, January 26, Finicum and seven other occupiers set out from Malheur refuge toward the little Grant County town of John Day. The occupation leaders were scheduled to meet with hundreds of citizens and Sheriff Glenn Palmer, who they believed was sympathetic to their cause.

As was often the case with the Malheur occupation, plans for the trip to Grant County were still shifting at the last minute. David Fry was supposed to video the proceedings, but he was fixing someone's computer when Finicum texted him, and he missed the message. So Shawna Cox grabbed her Canon camera and some trail mix and jerky and jumped into Finicum's new Dodge pickup. The Sharp Family Singers were planning to entertain the crowd, so they had headed up early to prepare. But Victoria Sharp, an eighteen-year-old soprano, was still in the shower when they left. So she rode with Finicum too, wearing blue-silver glitter eye shadow for the performance, her long brunette hair still wet.

At 3:30 PM, Finicum set out on the ninety-nine-mile trek from the refuge to John Day, with Ryan Payne in the passenger seat, Ryan Bundy directly behind the driver's seat, Victoria Sharp in the middle rear seat, and Shawna Cox to her right. The second occupier vehicle, a brown Jeep driven by Mark McConnell and carrying Ammon and Booda Cavalier, was supposed to depart fifteen minutes after Finicum, but McConnell decided to leave around the same time and settled in behind the truck.

The vehicles traveled through Burns and into a canyon that took them up and out of the Harney Basin and into an elevated band of Malheur National Forest, nothing but firs, pines, and snow lining the two-lane route. In the truck, the men talked and Cox worked on her cell phone, calling, among others, Jeanette Finicum. In the Jeep, McConnell jawed with Booda, who was sitting in the front passenger seat. Ammon wasn't feeling well and dozed off in the back seat.

A little after 4:20 PM, twenty miles north of Burns and still about fifty miles from the travelers' destination, several unmarked police vehicles whipped out onto the highway from a side road, lights flashing, sirens whooping.

McConnell pulled over immediately. Police with rifles piled out of the vehicles behind him, and laser dots jumped around in the Jeep. The police yelled for the men to stick their hands out the windows. Ammon and the other men complied. The police told them to get out of the Jeep, one by one, and get on their knees on the snowy shoulder of the road, hands in the air. Ammon followed orders, afraid to even grab his cowboy hat. He left it on the seat. On his knees in the snow, he edged backward on the road toward the team. He was handcuffed and searched, along with McConnell and Cavalier. McConnell was carrying a semiautomatic pistol, and Ammon and Cavalier were unarmed.

Some police vehicles bypassed the Jeep and pursued the truck. Inside the truck, Finicum had been determined to keep going, but Ryan Payne argued that Finicum should stop, and finally he did. Payne rolled his window down, letting in a blast of twenty-five-degree air, and stuck both hands out the window. A projectile hit the truck on his side, a bang echoing from the vehicles behind the truck, and Payne yanked his hands back inside.

Payne said: *They mean business.*

He opened the door and got out of the truck, hands above his head, and surrendered, yelling to the officers that there were women in the vehicle.

Nobody else wanted to get out of the truck. Cox tried to call an Oath Keeper for help, but she had no service. She put her Canon camera on video and hit the "record" button to document the scene. Ryan Bundy did the same with his cell phone, angling it out the window to record the men behind him.

Finicum rolled down his window and hollered out at the lawmen clustered around the black vehicles behind him. He wasn't out of control, wasn't raving, but he was deeply angry he'd been pulled over.

He'd never received even a traffic ticket in his entire life, much less been taken into custody, and he was outraged.

"You wanna shoot me, you can shoot me!" he yelled. "I'm going to meet the sheriff. The sheriff is waiting for us. You do as you damn well please. Here I am." He pointed at his forehead. "Right there! Right there, put a bullet through it. You understand? I'm going to go meet the sheriff. You back down, or you kill me now."

An officer yelled: "Send the woman out!"

"I'm going to ask them if they want to go out," Finicum yelled. He swiveled to the back seat, inquired calmly: "You want out?"

"What for?" Cox said. "What are we getting out for?"

Ryan Bundy bellowed out the window: "Who are you?"

"Yeah, who are you?" Finicum said.

The answer came: "Oregon State Police."

"Okay, well, I'm going to go meet the sheriff in Grant County," Finicum yelled. "You can come along with us, and you can talk with us over there."

A trooper continued yelling commands.

"You're wasting oxygen, son," Finicum said.

"If we duck, and you drive, what are they gonna do?" Cox said.

"They could shoot your tires out," Victoria Sharp offered.

Finicum slouched in the driver's seat, his right leg jiggling with tension, hand draped across the wheel, gazing out the window like he was waiting for a drive-through attendant to deliver his food. A pop song came on the radio, low, and he reached to turn up the volume, and then turned it up more:

When the days get short, and the nights get a little bit frozen . . .

Finicum pondered his dilemma. Behind him, Ryan Bundy still

269

held his cell phone out the window, recording the police behind the truck.

We hold each other.
We hold each other.
We hold each other. MM-mmm.

Finicum seemed to come to a decision. He turned down the music and yelled out the window once more.

"You want a bloodbath, it's gonna be on your hands! You better understand how this thing's gonna end. I'm gonna be laying down here on the ground with my blood on the street, or I'm gonna go see the sheriff."

Ryan Bundy said, to no one in particular: "We should never have stopped. We should never have stopped."

"I'm gonna keep going," Finicum told his passengers. "You ready?"

He eased off the brake, and the big pickup moved off. Finicum upshifted the manual transmission until he was going more than seventy miles per hour. Wind whipped through Ryan's open window until he rolled it up.

Ryan said: "What about Ammon and those guys?"

"I'm gonna go get help," Finicum said.

Everyone's voice was a little tenser. On his knees on the truck floor, Ryan looked back at the police vehicles trailing the truck.

"They're coming up fast," he said.

Ryan peered ahead and saw a roadblock, three vehicles obstructing the two lanes ahead, facing them, red and blue lights flashing, and nothing but big snowbanks on each side of the road. Finicum let off the gas, tapped the brakes, slowing to less than sixty miles per hour. A bullet hit the side-view mirror with a snap, and Ryan ducked.

"Hang on," Finicum said.

Another shot snapped, and another, spaced.

Finicum wrenched the steering wheel left across the oncoming lane, trying to dodge the roadblock, and the truck plowed into the snowbank, throwing up a white tsunami and narrowly missing an FBI agent running through the deep powder. The truck came to a halt, stuck in the snow.

Finicum shoved his door open with both hands and leapt out, flinging his arms high in the air, moving fast despite the deep snow, stepping away from the truck.

"Go ahead and shoot me!" he yelled.

Two shots sounded as something burst through the truck's roof, throwing sparks and shrapnel, and Ryan's window shattered. Ryan grunted in pain.

Victoria Sharp screamed, going falsetto: "No!"

Outside, Finicum kept yelling for the officers to shoot him, and they yelled back for him to get on the ground. Three more shots: *crack, crack-crack.*

Victoria screamed again.

"Damn it," said Cox, who rarely swore, her voice rising with alarm. "Are they shooting him? Did they shoot him? You assholes!"

The shattered glass in Ryan's window crumbled, fell. Like the women, he was trying to make himself as small as possible, while also covering as much of them as he could with his own body. He shoved on the door, but the snow outside held it fast.

"I can't get out," he said, his voice sounding oddly conversational.

"Is he dead?" Victoria said, and then started screaming, almost unintelligibly, that she was trained in emergency medicine and wanted to help Finicum.

"Are you hit?" inquired Ryan, who had in fact himself taken a slug, or something, in his shoulder.

Victoria was unscathed but kept screaming. More explosions rang out, and more. Victoria screamed again.

Cox said: "Shut up."

Ryan was trying to get a glimpse of Finicum without raising his head too high above the window. Finicum was lying in the snow, a truck-length away.

"I think they just killed LaVoy," Ryan said, and his voice was still low and composed but now carried an edge of dread.

THE TRAFFIC STOP HAD BEEN IN THE WORKS FOR A COUPLE OF DAYS. THE FBI had known that raiding the refuge would very likely result in another Waco or Ruby Ridge disaster. Luckily, the occupiers were constantly leaving the refuge. It would be safer, it was decided, to find out ahead of time when one or more of the occupiers would be leaving the refuge and have a team in place to pull them over, preferably at a remote spot with little chance of bystanders getting in the way.

A mix of state troopers and FBI agents were assigned to the traffic-stop team. They reviewed information packets, which the FBI called "baseball cards," about the key leaders, including photos, criminal histories, significant statements they'd made. In briefings, the officers watched YouTube and news videos starring the main targets. They saw LaVoy Finicum's "Tarp Man" interviews, in which he said he wouldn't spend his life in a concrete box. They knew he carried a shoulder rig. Among the occupiers, Finicum and Ryan Payne were considered the most likely threats.

When the FBI brass heard that the entire group of key players was heading to Grant County, they knew this might be their best chance to take them down all at once. The traffic-stop team developed a plan, reconnoitered the route north of Burns, and chose a spot that was isolated and lacked cell phone service. The occupiers had eyes all over

Burns that might have spotted a bunch of police vehicles heading north on the highway. To avoid such a tip-off, the traffic-stop team used unmarked police vehicles or armored cars and sent them one by one to the arrest spot. The plan called for one group to pull over the vehicles and another to barricade the road to the north with vehicles and spike strips. Contingencies were discussed: Which units would pursue if one vehicle didn't stop, if both stopped, if both kept going, if someone took off on foot through the woods, as well as how to make sure an innocent vehicle didn't get caught in the crossfire. Two government planes would track the targets and record the scene from above.

The initial stop went as planned, and the individuals in the rear vehicle, a brown Jeep, complied with the arrest. The lead vehicle, a white Dodge pickup truck, was a different matter. When the driver of the truck yelled that the traffic-stop team would have to shoot him, the team moved to what they called the "gas plan," which meant firing a pepper-spray capsule at the truck. The forty-millimeter foam-and-plastic round contained oleoresin capsicum powder, and it ricocheted off the passenger side of the truck. Ryan Payne got out and surrendered, but the other occupants did not. Minutes later, the driver of the truck made a break for Grant County, and the traffic-stop team radioed the blockade team that he was heading their way.

Suddenly, despite all the planning, the blockade team felt very exposed, walled in by snowbanks, a three-ton vehicle headed straight at them.

One state trooper said: *We gotta get out of here.*

He ran up the snowbank on the side of the road, and immediately got stuck thigh deep. He churned and crawled and made it to a tree. Some of the other troopers and agents moved further behind the vehicles but remained on the road.

The truck came around a curve. It wasn't stopping. A trooper behind one blockade vehicle squeezed off three spaced shots, hitting the front of the oncoming truck twice and the driver's side once. The truck wasn't stopping. The trooper off the road watched. He felt relatively safe, but if the truck rammed the front two blockade vehicles, the two FBI agents crouched behind them would be crushed.

He yelled again: *Get out of there!*

One of the FBI agents took off running, heading up the same bank the trooper had struggled to climb moments before. A bad decision, because the white truck swerved across the road and into the same snowbank, missing him by maybe six inches.

The driver burst out of the truck, hands up, and the trooper near the tree line recognized him immediately from the baseball cards as LaVoy Finicum, cowboy hat and everything. Finicum yelled—"Go ahead and shoot me!"—and, as if in response, two gunshots cracked. Finicum struggled to churn his way through the deep snow, just as the trooper had.

The trooper drew his pistol and yelled: *State police! Keep your hands up! Lemme see your hands!*

Finicum was yelling too. He stumbled and then righted himself. He reached across his body with his right hand, lifted his arms again. He didn't seem to see the trooper, and then caught sight of him. He looked pissed but put his hands shoulder level, still yelling: *just shoot me.*

The traffic-stop team had pulled up and exited their vehicles with rifles. Finicum was increasingly contained.

Feeling very exposed in his black gear in the white snow, the trooper was trying to focus on Finicum while moving out of the line of fire of the unknown occupants in the back seat of the truck. He was calculating the risks of holstering his pistol and pulling out his Taser, wondering whether the Taser darts would penetrate the wool-denim jacket Finicum was wearing.

Another trooper from the blockade waded across the tracks of the stranded truck, his AR-15 rifle leveled at Finicum. Up the road, one of the troopers who had pursued Finicum from the initial traffic stop also was closing in with an AR. This made the trooper now positioned at the tree line feel safe enough to holster his pistol and yank out his Taser.

Finicum turned to the nearest trooper with the AR, and then back to the trooper with the Taser, who couldn't get the laser sights to work. Finicum looked down and reached across his body again with his right hand, and then lifted his hands again. Then Finicum turned away from the trooper with the Taser, toward his truck, and his shoulders hunched forward. It looked to the trooper like Finicum was moving his jacket aside, a familiar movement to the trooper, one he'd practiced a thousand times himself. Finicum seemed to be going for his gun, a cross-draw off the hip or shoulder. The trooper left the shelter of the tree line and ran across the snow at Finicum, Taser in his outstretched arm, trying to get closer so the Taser would work, and chastising himself for picking the worst possible moment to holster his pistol, because Finicum was going to spin and shoot and get the drop on him.

The troopers near the road must have been thinking the same thing, because three shots rang out. Finicum fell to his knees and then dropped onto his back, his hands empty, no gun.

From the moment Finicum's truck came to a halt in the snow to the moment he fell took fifteen seconds. His arm lifted once, and fell. It was another minute or two before he was perfectly still.

As LaVoy Finicum died, the people in the back seat of the truck prayed, broken glass everywhere, the diesel engine still rumbling, and red laser dots dancing around the truck's interior.

"Please protect us, God, please protect us, please protect us, please protect us," Cox said.

Hunched down low, Ryan Bundy was angry at himself, at the whole occupation. They'd let down their guard, thinking everything was fine and dandy. They'd been suckered.

A series of shots resounded and projectiles crashed through the window on Cox's side, some sort of silver shells hitting the dashboard and ricocheting around the front seat. Blue smoke began to waft. They began to choke and cough.

"Those were gas rounds," Ryan said.

Cox buried her nose in her down jacket, breathing through it. Victoria did the same, jamming her face into Cox's jacket. Ryan covered his nose with his flannel shirt sleeve.

"Should we get out?" Cox said, her throat clenched.

"No, don't get out," Ryan said.

They discussed waving a white flag out the window. Ryan was still recording with his cell phone, and he began to narrate what had happened. Someone outside yelled for them to get out on Ryan's side, so Ryan shoved the door open and clambered out, arms raised. He saw Finicum in the snow, still wearing his cowboy hat.

"LaVoy's dead," he told the women in the truck.

The officers barked commands at him. Ryan had his cell phone in one raised hand. He let go of it, and it disappeared into the snowbank.

To the feds, Ryan said: *You just started a war.*

Chapter 9

THE FINAL
FOUR

Ammon lay on the road in cuffs. The troopers and FBI agents didn't give any details, but he could tell something had gone wrong up ahead. Eventually, Ammon, Booda, McConnell, and Ryan Payne were moved to a police vehicle. Two sheriff's deputies brought Shawna Cox and Victoria Sharp in a big van, and the four men were loaded in. The women said Ryan had been taken away in an ambulance to be treated for his wounded shoulder, and that Finicum was dead.

Ammon cried. Payne banged his head against the van window, yelling at the traffic-stop team.

The deputies drove toward Burns. The prisoners thought they

were going to the Harney County Jail, but the deputies passed through town and headed west. Ammon realized he still had his cell phone and managed to make a surreptitious call to Lisa. He told her Finicum was cooperating with the authorities when he was shot. The deputies noticed the phone and confiscated it. But the word was out.

AT THE COMMAND POST TWELVE MILES AWAY IN BURNS, SHERIFF WARD had watched the live feed from the surveillance planes. For a heart-stopping moment, as Finicum's truck plowed into the snowbank, Ward thought the vehicle had hit the FBI agent who was running off the road.

Ward thought: *We gotta get that truck off that guy!*

Then the pickup's driver got out, and the troopers closed in on him, and the driver fell to the snow.

Ward's heart sank. For two months now, he'd done everything he could to defuse the situation. He hadn't reacted to the vehicles tailing him to work. He'd refused to arrest Ammon when he came to Burns. He'd even had to pacify local residents who wanted to go to the refuge themselves and eject the occupiers. He hadn't wanted unnecessary bloodshed in Harney County, and he certainly hadn't wanted to create a martyr.

AS NIGHT FELL IN BURNS, PETE SANTILLI HEARD THAT SOMETHING HAD happened to the convoy. He swung into action, live-streaming from his van as he drove from the Harney District Hospital, which was on lockdown, to the FBI operations at the Burns airport. He reported that two people had been shot on the way to Grant County, though he didn't reveal the names. He reported that Ammon Bundy was in custody. He reported that the FBI was calling occupiers and telling them to leave the refuge immediately.

Santilli approached a group of officers outside the barricaded sheriff's office and said he wanted permission to go to the refuge and rescue the women and children. He talked and talked, and the police nodded and said they appreciated his offer, and Santilli kept talking.

"I'm making a genuine offer to go get the women and children and get them out of there," said Santilli, who didn't seem to notice that the semicircle of officers was edging closer to him.

One of the officers casually took ahold of Santilli's left arm, and another took his right, and it dawned on Santilli what was happening.

"I'm under *arrest?*" he said in disbelief, as he was led away, still talking.

IN THE REFUGE BUNKHOUSE, A DOZEN PEOPLE GATHERED AROUND DAVID Fry's cell phone, watching and listening to Santilli's livestream. Some disregarded the reports of death and arrests as just another product of the Patriot rumor mill.

Fry believed it. He recorded a couple of his own livestreams, in total darkness, using a low, conspiratorial voice.

"Sounds like they arrested a couple of our guys, and maybe even shot one of them and killed him," he said. "So this is probably the last transmission you'll get from me."

Fry had seen the text he'd missed from Finicum asking if he would come to Grant County to video the meeting. It was weird, Fry thought. If he'd been in the truck with LaVoy, who knew what would have happened?

Then Blaine Cooper got a call from Lisa Bundy, who told him the rumors were true. Ammon had managed to call her from a police van.

He and the others had been arrested, Ryan Bundy had been shot, and Finicum was dead.

Cooper told everybody in the bunkhouse.

Chaos erupted. Crying. Yelling. Women gathered their children and bolted, leaving behind clothing, guns, cash, electronics. Vehicles tore out of the refuge. The two-dozen or so remaining militia members put on their tactical gear and armed up. Fry found a shotgun someone had left behind in the bunkhouse and began carrying it. The same thing was on everybody's mind: Waco.

JEANETTE FINICUM WAS IN THE GYM BLEACHERS AT FREDONIA HIGH School, watching her daughter play basketball. She'd gotten home from Oregon late the night before, and she was telling LaVoy's parents and brother about her trip. Someone came up and told her that something was wrong at the refuge.

Jeanette checked her phone. It was dead. Someone gave her a charger, and she went out to the school hallway to plug it in. When her phone powered up, she tried to call LaVoy. No answer.

Then the phone rang. Ammon's wife, Lisa. She was hysterical.

Over and over, Lisa screamed: *They killed LaVoy! They killed LaVoy!*

Jeanette dropped the phone, and LaVoy's brother held her for a long time in the school hallway.

THREE HUNDRED PEOPLE, MOSTLY BUNDY SUPPORTERS, WAITED FOR THE occupiers to arrive at the senior center in Grant County. As time passed, the Sharp Family Singers, minus Victoria, performed gospel songs. Rumors began to fly that there'd been a roadblock, shooting, arrests. Sheriff Glenn Palmer left, heading to check out the scene at the traffic stop. Shouting broke out, some questioning whether the sheriff had set up the Bundys.

SEVERAL OCCUPIERS WEREN'T AT THE REFUGE THAT NIGHT. NEIL WAMPLER was already home in California. Brand Nu Thornton was home in Las Vegas. Terri Linnell also had driven back to her home near San Diego three days earlier because her daughter was visiting, and she had told the occupiers that she'd return to the refuge in a week.

Jon Ritzheimer was in Arizona, visiting his wife and two young daughters. Four hours after the shooting, Ritzheimer took to Facebook to announce he was turning himself in to the FBI. He recorded himself saying goodbye to his daughters on a Facebook video.

"Daddy's gotta go again, okay?" he said, on his knees in his living room, hugging the girls.

"In the Oregon again?" one said, sticking her lower lip out.

"I'm not going back to Oregon again," Ritzheimer said. "Daddy's gotta go. He's gotta go away for a little while."

THE REMAINING OCCUPIERS' PHONES KEPT BUZZING—AN FBI NEGOTIATION expert calling them, one by one, trying to persuade them to leave the compound.

David Fry wasn't going anywhere. He was the occupation's tech guy, the video guy. If he left, he thought, who would record the inevitable slaughter?

Fry wasn't part of the security team, so he wasn't there when they gathered in the bunkhouse kitchen late in the evening to vote on whether to flee to Idaho. A Georgia man named Jason Patrick had taken charge. He favored staying. Patriot networks had put out a call to arms, and Patrick believed thousands of militia members were on their way to Oregon. Patrick wanted the occupiers to sit tight and basically continue the mission as Ammon and Finicum had envisioned.

But the dozen or so people at the meeting were scared, grim faced, arms crossed, and the conversation kept getting sidetracked. They'd heard that Finicum had been killed with his arms in the air, on his knees, basically executed. Some believed the same thing would likely happen in an FBI raid. The FBI considered the occupiers to be terrorists. They would shoot to kill.

"The sound tactical decision is to leave," one man said. "A guerrilla force does not hold ground against overwhelming odds. Any type of military that you study will show that guerrilla outposts that are attacked are immediately abandoned."

One man wanted to become a roving guerrilla retribution squad. But Patrick tried to shut down this idea.

"Say we roll out to Idaho, and we're the guerilla warfare team," Patrick said. "Where's the fight?"

"Where's the *fight?*" the man responded. "Wherever there's a federal building or a federal employee."

"Are you saying full-on attack?" someone asked.

"Yes!" the man said. "Regroup, go and find out who works for the feds and start executing them. Execute them, their families, everyone. Make it a statement: If you work for these crooked fucks, you die."

"And you think that's more tactical than just standing peacefully here?" Patrick asked. "Right now, the reason we're winning is we're standing and defending. We are the David in the David and Goliath story. You go guerrilla tactics now, and the narrative changes to domestic terrorists that have gone full tactical."

Blaine Cooper, wearing a tactical vest and carrying an assault rifle, suggested they take the refuge fire truck and make a run for it.

"Five armed guys get in the fire truck, and everybody follow us," he said. "If they try to fuck with us, lay the lead down. We regroup in Idaho."

Others thought that was a sure way to get arrested, given what had happened when Ken Medenbach took the refuge truck to Burns. An agitated militiaman from Washington, sitting on a stool with rifles propped between his legs, said he had no vehicle to follow in.

"I got dropped off here!" he said. "I don't have a house! I don't have a fucking job no more!"

"I don't either," Cooper said. "I lost my house, I lost everything, brother. You're not the only one."

"All I have is what I'm fucking wearing and you guys here," the other man said. "And all I see is a bunch of salty motherfuckers that are talking with their tails between their legs. We came here for one fucking reason! And that's to fight!"

"I came here to defend the Constitution," Patrick said calmly. "Not fight. To stand in defense of the Constitution."

Patrick asked if they were ready to take a vote. They were.

"Okay, all in favor of leaving and going on a convoy to Idaho, say 'Aye.'"

Silence.

"All opposed, 'Nay,'"

"Nay!" numerous voices said.

"Unanimous decision," someone said. "We're staying."

Despite the vote, a sizable group fled shortly after the meeting. Around 10 PM, a neighboring rancher spotted a half-dozen cars bumping across his pasture, bypassing blockades the feds were putting up on the roads leading to the refuge.

Within twenty-four hours, almost all of the occupiers would be gone.

Protocol demanded that an outside agency investigate the officer-involved shooting. Several hours after Finicum died, a team of detectives from various Deschutes County, Oregon, law-enforcement organizations arrived at the shooting scene. The investigators took a circuitous route in order to avoid running into any angry Patriots in Burns. They interviewed the traffic-stop officers and walked through the snow, studying footprints, looking for blood and shell casings, and checking the officers' stories against the physical evidence.

Two state troopers had reported that they had shot Finicum—one fired once, and the other twice. The investigating officers photographed the troopers and seized their weapons, clothing, and gear. The five FBI agents at the shooting scene said they had not discharged their weapons.

Law enforcement blocked off a forty-mile stretch of the highway between Burns and Grant County. A state trooper drove to a nearby town and rented a portable light tower to illuminate the shooting scene.

The interior of Finicum's truck bore a dusting of pepper-spray powder, and several of the windows in the four-door crew cab were broken. On the floorboard behind the driver's seat was a .38 Special revolver, loaded with five rounds. Under the back seat were two loaded Smith & Wesson .223-caliber rifles, both purchased by Finicum in 2009.

Finicum's body was still sprawled in the snow with adhesive pads stuck to his torso from the paramedics. His hands were cuffed behind his back. After the passengers had exited the truck, the officers had moved in and placed the handcuffs on him. A state trooper had rolled him over and saw a black pistol grip in the interior left pocket of his denim jacket. It was a loaded Ruger 9-millimeter semiautomatic pistol with one round in the chamber. Two ammo magazines were found in his right inside jacket pocket. He wore a small dagger in a leather sheath on his belt.

After the scene was processed, Finicum's body was taken to the medical examiner's office.

AS THE NIGHT WENT ON, THE REFUGE HELD FEWER AND FEWER PEOPLE. Some just slid away in the dark. One man pulled out in his truck at midnight, and, too embarrassed to admit he was heading home, he told the guard at the front entrance that he was going to establish a "forward observation post" to keep an eye on the feds.

David Fry continued to record livestream after livestream on his *DefendYourBase* channel, some less than a minute long, one almost an hour. He no longer whispered in the darkness. He strode around, entering buildings, then leaving, riding in the back of a pickup truck, petting a dog.

The other remaining occupiers were defiant or serious, but Fry seemed almost jovial, narrating the proceedings like a deranged game show host. He slung a bandolier of shotgun shells around his neck and pulled his long black hair into a ponytail. Sometimes he turned the camera on himself for a moment, and he blinked and grinned, and his vestige of a Japanese accent was more pronounced than usual.

"All right, guys, they got vehicles surrounding us, we're completely surrounded right now," he said. "Looks like this is it! This is gonna be the final stand here, guys!"

Law enforcement had moved in, he said, vehicles blocking off all the entrances to the refuge. They could see the clusters of headlights off in the dark. There was no way out. But he didn't want to leave. He wasn't going to jail.

"Where's all the Americans?" he asked. "Where's all our

supporters? We didn't get too many. Now you guys are gonna get to watch us *die!* Live on *DefendYourBase* livestream!"

Sixteen miles west of Burns, the van bearing the prisoners pulled over at a rest stop. Each prisoner was loaded into an individual government vehicle, mostly dark SUVs. Pete Santilli joined the convoy in handcuffs. Victoria Sharp departed it and was taken to a grocery store, where her mother would pick her up.

The long convoy raced across the expansive dark spaces of central Oregon. It was a five-hour ride from Burns to Portland, a rural drive, and the drivers went fast, no doubt mindful that plenty of Patriots were angry about the death of LaVoy Finicum.

Cuffs on her hands and feet, Shawna Cox needled the driver: *Is it okay for you to go eighty miles per hour through these little towns?*

An FBI agent sat next to her in the back seat, and he took out a recorder and began asking her questions about the refuge.

Cox said: *I don't want to talk to you about all that, but if you want to tell me about your family and friends, you go right ahead. I'm a good listener.*

The agent didn't respond, so Cox started singing hymns.

When they hit Portland at 2 AM, police blocked every stoplight, waving them through like a presidential motorcade, all the way to the Multnomah County jail. The initial criminal charge was conspiracy to impede a federal officer through the use of force, intimidation, or threats. It was a felony that carried a maximum six-year prison sentence and fines. Everyone looked grim, raw, haunted in their booking photos, everyone except Ammon, whose visage still conveyed the amiable, reasonable persona of a small businessman from Phoenix. It could have been his Valet Fleet Service website photo.

Around that time, the prisoners realized one of their number was missing. The driver of the Jeep, Mark McConnell, hadn't been arrested.

HOURS AFTER THE SHOOTING, AN AUDIO RECORDING OF AN INTERVIEW WITH Victoria Sharp was posted on YouTube. The teenager said the police had riddled Finicum's truck with bullets, that they'd shot at least one hundred and twenty times, that forty police vehicles were involved in the stop, that there were men in tactical gear coming out of the woods, that it was a setup, a murderous ambush, that Finicum was killed in cold blood.

"Let's just get this clear," the anonymous interviewer said. "Mr. Finicum's hands were in the air when he was shot."

"Yes," Victoria said. "His hands were still up after he was dead."

"Okay, so they shot him and he went down, and they shot him again on the ground?"

"Yeah, they shot him at least six times," she said.

Victoria Sharp's story was the first extensive recounting of what had happened. Though many details were later proven wrong, her account was widely reported on Infowars and other Patriot networks, and Victoria, who had brown doe eyes and a sweet soprano voice, became something of a goddess of truth in Patriot circles.

The next morning, Mark McConnell surfaced in a video he posted to Facebook in which he recounted his version of the traffic stop. He acknowledged he hadn't seen what happened at the roadblock, but he said he'd cobbled together an account from various sources, "taking pieces here, pieces there." McConnell said Finicum was the aggressor.

"He was not on his knees," McConnell said. "He went after them. He charged them. LaVoy was very passionate about what he was doing up here."

McConnell said he loved and admired Finicum but thought taking off from the traffic stop was foolish. In addition to the fact that McConnell was not in custody, the video fueled Patriot rumor-mill speculation that he'd been a federal informant, that maybe he'd even tipped the feds off about the exact timing of Finicum's trip to Grant County.

THE NEXT MORNING, A FORENSIC PATHOLOGIST CONDUCTED AN AUTOPSY ON LaVoy Finicum's body at the state medical examiner's office in Clackamas.

Finicum's clothing and possessions demonstrated his preoccupation with survivalism and preparedness. He was wearing cowboy boots, two pairs of gray socks, Wrangler jeans, a brass-buckled belt, thermal underwear, a Levi's denim jacket, a white fleece sweater, and a snap-buttoned black cotton shirt. In addition to the Ruger pistol and dagger that already had been collected as evidence, he carried a folding pocket knife, matches in a plastic container, reading glasses in his shirt pocket, cough drops, earmuffs, and a watch. He appeared to be in good health, trim, no sign of drug use, no tattoos. A toxicology test revealed the presence of ibuprofen.

The pathologist found three gunshot wounds. One bullet had entered Finicum's left shoulder and went through. Another hit the left upper back, fractured two ribs, and perforated his left lung. The third entered his right lower back and ricocheted around, causing profound damage, puncturing his right lung, diaphragm, kidney, colon, liver, the right ventricle of his heart, and left lung, in that order, before exiting.

When the government autopsy was complete, Jeanette Finicum went to Oregon to drive the body home in a van. She stopped in Salt Lake City and had a private pathologist conduct a second autopsy, as her attorney had directed.

As Finicum's body was being examined and theories were brewing on Patriot networks, the FBI took the unusual step of releasing a twenty-six-minute aerial video of the shooting. The low-resolution, silent video cut back and forth between the vantage points of the two FBI planes. It started with the traffic stop of Finicum's truck, the seven-minute standoff, and then the one-mile chase, ending with the crash into the snowbank. Finicum burst out of the truck, a tiny black figure against the white snow, arms raised high. His right arm seemed to reach across his body, then go up again, then down, then up. He turned away from the two oncoming troopers, facing the truck, and appeared to be reaching under his jacket, exactly where the Ruger was found. And then he fell to the snow.

The video cleared up a few misconceptions. Finicum's arms were not raised when he was shot, as Victoria Sharp had said, and he certainly wasn't on his knees, as many were reporting. Neither was he "charging" the police, as McConnell had said. In fact, his back was turned when he was shot.

But the video was grainy, and Finicum and the troopers were like bugs crawling across a computer screen, so any interpretation of the raw video was just that, an interpretation. Finicum's body *appeared* to be in the position and movement of a cross-draw. If he was attempting to pull his gun, it was not a smooth draw. He appeared to be fumbling, perhaps hindered by the fact that the Ruger was in an interior pocket, not a holster. Or, possibly, he was trying to draw fire from the troopers without actually pulling the gun.

Skeptical Patriots noted that Finicum generally carried a revolver, a six-shooter, just like the hero of his book, *Only By Blood and Suffering*. They said they'd never seen him with a 9-millimeter pistol. Maybe the troopers or feds planted the Ruger when they realized they'd killed an unarmed man?

The ATF's National Tracing Center in West Virginia ran a search on the Ruger's serial number and got a hit. The weapon was made in Brazil and had been sold in 2011 by Judd Auto Service in Fredonia, Arizona, to a local man. A deputy sheriff in Arizona tracked down the buyer, who said he'd never liked the gun, so he'd sold it to another man two years later. The second buyer said he'd sold it to yet another man. The third man confirmed he'd bought it about a year earlier and that he was Finicum's stepson. He'd given it to Finicum as a gift. Case closed.

Still, Patriots had their own take on the video. They theorized that Finicum's hands had gone down repeatedly because he lost his balance in the deep snow. They maintained he was starting to lift his hands again when the troopers shot him. They questioned why the FBI, with all its vast resources, had such shitty cameras in their surveillance planes, and why those cameras had no audio. Some even believed that the feds were planning to slaughter everyone in the truck, but they decided not to when they realized Victoria Sharp was inside.

As the occupiers scattered and the refuge descended into disarray and paranoia, David Fry remained an outsider.

The people he'd spent the most time with were gone—Shawna Cox in custody in Portland and LaVoy Finicum dead. The remaining militia members were suspicious of his motives and loyalty and wouldn't talk to him. At 4 AM on that first sleepless night after Finicum's death, the new substitute leader of the refuge, Jason Patrick, told a reporter that he barely knew Fry, that the young Ohioan was likely just "gawking," not a true believer in the cause.

"He's not going to help us when the FBI rolls in," Patrick said.

The remaining holdouts at the wildlife refuge had agreed they shouldn't stay in the buildings any longer. They knew by now that the charges against the arrested occupiers had something to do with preventing the feds from doing their jobs. They didn't want to continue breaking that particular law, so they parked their cars and trucks in the gravel parking lot at the end of the front driveway and stayed in their vehicles all night, waiting for a federal ambush that never came. Nobody got much sleep.

The day after Finicum's shooting, they rummaged through the refuge buildings. The fleeing occupiers had left behind belongings, reminiscent of the feds who'd abandoned so much equipment in their rush to demobilize the federal command post in Toquop Wash in 2014. The refuge buildings were littered with cell phones, tablets, firearms, toiletries, clothing, camping equipment. And food, including freezers full of beef and elk. The remaining occupiers gathered what they thought they could use and hauled the items to the new camping area. There, they erected a pop-up canopy tent between the encircled vehicles and enlarged the shelter by draping a tarpaulin from the canopy tent to a truck. They commandeered heavy equipment that belonged to the refuge, blocking one entrance with a loader and using an excavator to dig two trenches next to the parking lot to make it more difficult for the feds to attack. They dubbed the new parking-lot site Camp Finicum.

But their numbers were shrinking fast. About a dozen had remained the morning after Finicum's shooting, but more trickled away as the day went on. Many were besieged with calls, as relatives, friends, and FBI negotiators all pleaded with them to leave.

The FBI stopped and questioned departing occupiers at the checkpoints surrounding the refuge. A half dozen were allowed to pass through, but three were arrested. Despite his dubiousness about David Fry's allegiance and his exhortations to the other militants to continue the Bundys' mission at the refuge, even Jason Patrick left. He skirted the nearby federal roadblock by walking six miles overland from the refuge. Two militia members picked him up at a prearranged meeting spot, but they were promptly stopped at a secondary FBI checkpoint, where Patrick was arrested.

Two days after Finicum died, the occupation had dwindled to four people. Rifles slung over their shoulders, the final four paced around the cluster of vehicles and tents in the refuge parking lot, talking, smoking, eating, making phone calls. Besides Fry, there was Jeff Banta, a carpenter from Nevada who had arrived only the day before Finicum was shot, and Sean and Sandy Anderson, a married couple who'd recently moved to Idaho from Wisconsin. Sean owned an outdoor supply company and Sandy was a hairdresser. Sean, who had an outstanding bench warrant from two years earlier, didn't want to go to jail.

Fry's reasons for staying seemed to shift with his moods and mental state. He wanted the feds to agree to let Sean Anderson go free. He didn't want to be taken into custody himself. He wanted to continue Finicum's crusade. He feared the feds would execute him. He wanted someone to live-stream the bloody raid he was sure was coming, and he knew his three companions lacked his technical skills.

So he continued to record one livestream after another on his YouTube channel. Mostly, these were cutting-room-floor snippets in the life of Camp Finicum, created not for viewer interest but as potential evidence, like a surveillance camera in a convenience store, an ever-present witness of violence that hadn't yet occurred. Sometimes the camera was pointed at the blue sky for long, actionless minutes. At night, Fry trained the camera on a crackling campfire, and the audio caught snippets of after-dark conversation about the Constitution, about families, about the afterlife. In one video, the Andersons slow danced in the mud as the Staind song, "Tangled Up in You," blared from the open doors of a pickup truck. In another, Sean Anderson finally lost his patience with the drone hovering overhead and, off-camera, popped four gunshots into the night sky.

Periodically, Fry's angular face loomed into the frame, looking intent as he adjusted controls or read comments from YouTube viewers. He responded to some comments and seemed to revel in having thousands of followers. Other postings upset him, as when one watcher wrote: "We Americans just can't stand Terrorists. Domestic terrorists need to be put down like rabid dogs."

Fry read the statement and responded on the video: "See, this is why I have to shut off the live feed, because you guys allow Americans to sit here and badmouth us. You guys fucking disgust me. Except for the good people, of course."

UNTIL NOW, LISA HAD ALWAYS FOUND THE FAITH TO OBEY AMMON'S DIVINE revelations, always gathered the strength to subdue the initial stab of fear she felt when he proposed one of his audacious plans. And things had always worked out. But this? LaVoy was dead. Ammon and Ryan and others were in federal custody, facing felony charges. The feds had surrounded four terrified souls at the refuge. They needed help, just like the Bundys in 2014.

Lacking instructions from Ammon, who was in shackles on his way to Portland, Lisa got on the Bundy Facebook page and wrote a call to arms.

"Ammon would not have called for the patriots to leave. We have lost a life but we are not backing down. He didn't spill his life in vain. Hold your ground ... ranchers come and stand!"

The next day, she found out that Ammon had received different guidance. Ammon appeared briefly in a federal courtroom in Portland, and outside the courthouse afterward, his attorney read an announcement from Ammon to the news media. The statement praised Finicum as "one of the greatest men and greatest patriots I have ever seen," and instructed the remaining occupiers to "stand down. Go home and hug your families." In case the occupiers believed they were being duped, Lisa recorded a short audio segment reiterating Ammon's statement.

Lisa traveled to Portland to see Ammon. The court had appointed attorneys for all the defendants, except Ammon, who hired his own lawyers. Ammon instructed his attorneys to make the federal prosecutors an offer. He would plead guilty to a federal conspiracy charge if the government dismissed charges against the others and let everyone leave. The prosecutors rejected the deal.

Two days after the arrest, Lisa sat on an unmade hotel room bed, fear in her hazel eyes, and spoke to Ammon on her cell phone as one of the attorneys recorded video of the call. The attorney told Ammon he wanted him to try yet again to make a statement persuading the final four occupiers to leave.

"Please presume that anything you say can be used against you, like we've discussed," the attorney warned.

Ammon gathered his thoughts and then asked again that the holdouts stand down.

"This was never meant to be an armed standoff," he told his followers. "We only came to expose abuse and educate people about their rights as protected by the Constitution of the United States. Please do not make this something it was never meant to be."

As Ammon continued to instruct his followers, Lisa looked hopefully at the female attorney sitting next to her on the bed and whispered: "He sounds good." Then she cast her eyes to the floor.

David Fry ignored Ammon's instructions. He had followed LaVoy Finicum to Oregon, not Ammon Bundy. He wasn't going to leave because, for one thing, he didn't believe Finicum would have left.

As the days and nights dragged on, Fry was afraid to snatch more than a few minutes of sleep now and again. When he did doze off, he'd wake up to check a livestream or to answer his phone, which was always ringing. He was afraid not to answer every single call from the FBI, for fear that they'd think he was asleep and decide to attack.

Every couple of days, the holdouts would go to the bunkhouse to take showers and collect food. On one of those ventures, Fry found a nylon zipper case with a big black book in it with LaVoy

Finicum's name embossed on the cover. It was a compendium of the Holy Bible and the other Mormon scriptures. He grabbed it to give to Finicum's family.

As the final four collected additional items from the abandoned refuge, Camp Finicum's infrastructure grew to include half a dozen vehicles in a rough circle, plus ice chests, tents, and sleeping bags. The Andersons slept on a futon they'd found in the refuge welding shop. Fry dozed in a recliner chair. Jeff Banta found a heavy-duty mummy sleeping bag and slept on the ground. Banta was a loner, a lean and philosophical man who'd come to Oregon hoping to meet the Hammonds and perhaps get a job helping out on their ranch after the men reported to prison. Banta used a machete to cut and gather cattails from the nearby pond and spread them on the ground so the holdouts weren't walking in mud. He used his carpentry skills to build two sleeping quarters. Every day, Camp Finicum became a little more substantial. Banta grew to care about Fry and worried about the younger man's mental state.

A four-person team of FBI negotiators continued to call. Each morning, one would check in, and longer calls would usually take place later in the day. Fry took a liking to the negotiators, and their conversations roamed from his pets to UFOs, though he was stalwart in his refusal to leave Camp Finicum. Other times, he mused about "taking out" FBI agents if they raided the encampment. Sometimes he suggested that he might kill himself, or commit suicide by cop.

Banta believed the negotiators were trying to trick him into incriminating himself. He didn't trust the FBI to follow through on the negotiators' promises. A few days after Finicum's death, Banta requested that the FBI bring in a neutral party. Banta's choice for this role was not a relative or friend. He wanted Franklin Graham, the son of famed Christian evangelist Billy Graham. Franklin Graham ran his ninety-seven-year-old father's evangelistic organization in North

Carolina and struck Banta as someone who could be trusted. The negotiators said they'd give it a shot.

The holdouts and the feds contended with each other. The FBI cut off Fry's phone service and left a Verizon flip phone in the cab of the excavator blocking the refuge. The new phone couldn't access the internet, but Fry found another smartphone in the refuge and resumed his livestreams.

A couple of days later, Fry's phone rang. It was an FBI negotiator, and he transferred the call to Franklin Graham. The evangelist spoke to each of the final four, asking them about their daily routines. Banta was composed. The Andersons talked about the Constitution. Fry was interested in theology.

"He seems like a pretty good guy," an unusually tranquil Fry said in a livestream moments after the call.

After that initial conversation, Graham called the holdouts nearly every day.

TEN DAYS AFTER LAVOY FINICUM'S DEATH, ABOUT ONE THOUSAND PEOPLE gathered at a Mormon church in Kanab, Utah, for his memorial service. Dressed in white, Finicum's body lay in an unadorned, open casket built by family members out of pine. Jeanette walked behind the casket. A processional of cowboys rode on horseback. Afterward, Finicum's two eldest daughters spoke to news media and followers.

"Going forward, we are calling for a private, independent investigation to find out exactly what happened to our dad in an ambush on a lonely, desolate stretch of highway in the dead of winter in eastern Oregon," one said, crying and covering her mouth.

"Murder!" yelled a man in the crowd.

Three days earlier, the Finicum family had released a statement that outlined a comprehensive theory designed to explain LaVoy's actions in the last moments of his life, specifically why he kept lowering his hands. According to Shawna Cox, someone had shot at the truck immediately after it slammed into the snowbank. The family believed LaVoy got out to draw gunfire away from the other occupants of the truck. And he might have been wounded by one of those early shots, which could explain why his hands went down—an involuntary reaction to the trauma. Given all of this, the family was demanding the release of the video on Shawna Cox's camera, which she'd left in the truck.

Jeanette let her daughters do the talking. They were articulate women who had worked their way through college, and she clung to them. In addition to her grief, she'd been thrust into a new, high-profile role as the wife of a Patriot martyr. She was terrified and completely unprepared. LaVoy had been a survivalist who believed the federal government was acting unconstitutionally, but until Bunkerville, really until the last few months of their marriage, he hadn't been very political and hadn't enjoyed the spotlight. Even at church functions, among people he'd known for years, he tended to stand in the back of the room, leaning against the wall. He didn't belong to a militia and hadn't been deeply involved with the Patriot world until he'd gone to Oregon, and that was only a month earlier.

Now, among the friends, neighbors, and family at the memorial service were many newfound LaVoy Finicum admirers. They had latched on to LaVoy as a symbol of their beliefs, despite the fact that many had first heard of the rancher only a few weeks earlier, when he gave his Tarp Man interviews at the refuge. His "LV" brand was popping up everywhere, on flags, T-shirts, truck stickers, websites. The problem was, LaVoy was gone, and Jeanette felt like she was living in a foreign country. She didn't speak the Patriot language or understand the Patriot culture. Three Percenters and Oath Keepers and militias were all vying for position in the Patriot hierarchy, wanting to forge a relationship with her, and Jeanette believed some simply wanted to capitalize on her husband's new status. They gave her "intel" on other groups or told her about individuals who had supposedly helped the feds get LaVoy. Jeanette would agree to speak to someone and then an anonymous package would show up, a five-page dossier on the individual. Cloak-and-dagger stuff, like she was living in a movie.

She believed the government had murdered her husband, and she didn't know who she could trust.

WHILE THE FINICUM DAUGHTERS SPOKE, CLIVEN BUNDY SAT ASTRIDE HIS horse, loosely clasping a lariat, his face solemn and unreadable. Ammon and Ryan were in jail in Portland. Two days earlier, a federal grand jury had returned an indictment of sixteen people, which included the final four occupiers of the refuge.

Brand Nu Thornton blew his shofar at the memorial service. He'd left the refuge the day before Finicum's death, planning to go home to Las Vegas to take care of things and then return two days later. Then Finicum was killed, and most people fled the refuge, scared the feds were looking for them. A number of former occupiers had holed up in three safe houses in southern Utah counties with Patriot-friendly sheriffs. Few had any money to speak of, and Thornton was spending a lot of his own cash to help feed them. Everyone was paranoid, talking constantly about who might be arrested next, whether the SUV parked outside the safe house contained feds or surveillance equipment. Thornton, who hadn't been indicted, believed that blowing his shofar had delivered him from his enemies, as the book of Numbers, chapter ten, verse nine, from the Old Testament instructed. It also helped that he hadn't been photographed carrying a firearm at the refuge.

Terri Linnell also attended the funeral, emotional and angry. Hours before Finicum had been shot, Linnell had met Carly at their usual Panera near San Diego, and the FBI special agent hadn't given her a clue that something big was in the works. When Linnell later learned that Finicum was dead and the others arrested, she was livid. Still, the next time she met Carly, a few days later, she took the FBI's money. Three thousand dollars, a stack of one hundred dollar bills in an envelope. Linnell had worked as a cocktail waitress once and was pragmatic about money; just because someone gave you a big tip didn't mean you owed them anything.

A few days after the funeral, Linnell got a call from a Patriot connection who asked if she could accommodate two former refuge occupiers who were trying to evade arrest. No public warrants had been issued for either occupier, so Linnell believed she couldn't be accused of harboring fugitives. She picked them up in Mesquite, and they stayed in her house for two weeks. After all, Momma Bear was still a Patriot, despite her work for the FBI.

Even so, if her compatriots found out she was a confidential informant, Linnell knew she'd be shunned. Or worse.

FIVE DAYS AFTER ATTENDING FINICUM'S MEMORIAL SERVICE, CLIVEN BUNDY headed for Oregon. Over the previous two weeks, he'd grown increasingly vocal. He'd called Finicum's death a murder. He'd sent Sheriff Dave Ward another letter demanding that he remove all feds from Harney County. He'd encouraged the final four occupiers to continue their stand at the refuge, which clashed with Ammon's instructions. Now he planned to visit Ammon and Ryan in jail and also to go to Harney County.

The Bundy Ranch Facebook page announced Cliven's travel plans with an all-caps bulletin:

WAKE UP AMERICA! WAKE UP WE THE PEOPLE!

WAKE UP PATRIOTS! WAKE UP MILITIA! IT'S TIME!!!!! CLIVEN BUNDY IS HEADING TO THE HARNEY COUNTY RESOURCE CENTER IN BURNS OREGON.

Cliven never made it to Burns. At 10 PM on February 10, 2016, he stepped off the plane at Portland International Airport, and a SWAT team surrounded him. Cliven was arrested and taken to the jail in downtown Portland, where his blood pressure was recorded at a sky-high 188 over 122.

Federal prosecutors in Nevada issued a thirty-two-page criminal complaint. The document contained a blow-by-blow account alleging that Cliven and four unnamed co-conspirators had "organized and led a massive armed assault against federal law enforcement officers" at Bundy Ranch in 2014. The charges, which included conspiracy to commit an offense against the United States, carried a possible sentence as long as thirty-five years.[*]

Twenty-two months had passed since the Battle of Bunkerville, and the government had finally struck back.

As Cliven was getting arrested, the FBI was closing in on the final four.

On the same day, Jeff Banta took a four-wheeler for a ride and encountered a group of FBI agents and armored vehicles. He sped back to Camp Finicum. A rough circle of armored vehicles with gun ports had moved in and surrounded the little camp on the refuge driveway. FBI tactical teams also had infiltrated the refuge buildings. The

---

[*] A superseding indictment issued a month later included sixteen counts with maximum sentences totaling eighty-six years.

FBI negotiators bumped up the pressure in a five-hour phone call that Franklin Graham joined. The evangelist prayed with the holdouts and told them that the standoff was over, that it was time to give up. The final four agreed to surrender the next day. Exhausted and paranoid, they wanted witnesses, both in person and on livestreams, to observe their arrests and ensure they wouldn't be assassinated.

Early the next morning, Franklin Graham, who was a pilot, flew to Burns. The FBI picked him up and whisked him to the refuge. Overnight, Fry had regained his resolve to hold out. Sometimes he was calm. Other times he was frantic. He'd found a bullhorn in one of the refuge buildings, and he screamed at the FBI through it.

After more hours of negotiation, the Andersons walked out of Camp Finicum to join the FBI. The husband and wife carried an American flag. Banta, who would have left days earlier if it weren't for Fry, kept trying to convince him to leave. Banta said he didn't think God wanted Fry to die there. He said he'd finally made a good friend in Fry and didn't want to lose him. Banta thought about simply dragging the smaller man out of the camp, but he knew Fry would never forgive him. Finally, reluctantly, Banta left too. The FBI took him to the Andersons and Graham at the top of the driveway. They hugged and prayed, and Banta wished he could leave the site. He didn't want to hear a gunshot from Camp Finicum.

More than 64,000 people, including Fry's father in Ohio, listened to the livestream as Fry continued to argue with Graham, the FBI negotiators, Sandy Anderson, and other supporters for another half hour. He was terrified of going to prison. YouTube commenters had taunted him for weeks, saying that he would be raped behind bars. He lay down on a sleeping bag and put a gun to his head.

"It's better to die with honor than to be forced to live dishonorably," he told the FBI negotiator. "You guys will probably have to kill me or watch me kill myself."

The FBI negotiator assured Fry that he'd be kept safe in prison, segregated from violent offenders. After weeks of conversation, Fry had come to believe the negotiator was a good person, that he meant what he said. Abruptly, Fry changed his mind and agreed to surrender peacefully. He had one condition, and it had nothing to do with the Hammonds or prison or the overreaching federal government.

"If everybody says, 'Hallelujah,'" Fry said, "I'll come out."

The negotiator eagerly agreed.

Fry lit a cigarette and walked out of the ramshackle tent city, moving toward the armored cars with his hands held high and clasping two cell phones, one of which was still livestreaming. Franklin Graham and FBI agents and Fry's three compatriots were at the top of the driveway, and everybody yelled: "Hallelujah! Hallelujah!"

"They're saying 'Hallelujah!'" Fry said, sounding amused.

A SWAT team member told Fry to keep his hands up, to turn around, to walk backward. The agent patted Fry down, took the cell phones away, and let him take a few more puffs of his cigarette before cuffing his hands behind his back. The forty-one-day occupation of Malheur was over.

Up the driveway, two FBI negotiators watched, weeping uncontrollably.

Chapter 10

UNITED STATES VERSUS BUNDY

For the next seven months, Ammon spent most of his days in a seven-by-twelve-foot cell in the Multnomah County Detention Center in Portland. It felt like being locked alone in a bathroom for nineteen hours a day—concrete walls, concrete floor and ceiling, a cot, and a toilet. Ammon read Scripture and wrote in a journal. He did jumping jacks and ran in place. He wore his jail-issued blue smock and pink T-shirt underneath. He was kept separate from Ryan, but the brothers sometimes found opportunities to slip each other a handwritten note. He was allowed out of the cell for five hours each day, and that's when he cleaned up, made phone calls, and met with attorneys. At 5:30 PM, Ammon used the "walking room" phones to place a fifteen-minute call to Lisa and the kids. They discussed the Scripture passages they'd read that day.

Most of Ammon's co-defendants had been released pending trial, but the Bundy brothers remained in jail. The judge who kept them there did not believe the Bundys would go on the run. Ammon and Ryan had each traveled out of the country only twice in their lives—once to Mexico and once to Canada. They had large families and were well connected to their communities. But they didn't respect the federal government's authority, and they had many followers who weren't afraid to take up arms. No, the Bundys weren't major flight risks, the judge believed, but it didn't seem far-fetched that they might hole up somewhere, surrounded by a private army, and refuse to return to court.

So Ammon sat in jail and prepared for two federal trials, one in Oregon and one in Nevada. In April, he flew in the custody of US marshals to Nevada for a court appearance, but mostly he prepared for the Oregon trial, which was scheduled first. Prosecutors had given the defense a staggering amount of evidence—six thousand hours of video, more than thirteen thousand photographs, a quarter-million pages of Facebook information, and forty thousand pages of FBI reports. Ammon wasn't allowed to review the documents electronically. He received hard copies of everything. For note taking, the jail gave him a few pieces of paper at a time and a special flexible pen that couldn't be used as a weapon. It was difficult to write legibly with the pen. Ammon could request up to six hours of access per week to the jail's law computer, a single touch-screen device that lacked internet capabilities but contained pre-loaded, searchable legal resources. Communicating with his lawyers was equally difficult. Calls were cut short or not connected due to lockdowns or other inmates using the phones. All the inmates shared two visiting rooms where they could meet with counsel, and if those rooms were in use, Ammon was often out of luck.

Outside the jail walls, things weren't much better. Ammon's cousin in Phoenix managed Valet Fleet Service for him, but the business suffered. Customers hadn't known what to make of Ammon's takeover of the refuge. And now US attorneys in two states had charged Ammon with felonies that could put him behind bars for the rest of his life. Customers who knew Ammon only as an amiable and fair businessman were now reading that he was not only the leader of an armed band of antigovernment militants, but that he had somehow become the guiding light of the entire Patriot movement. Most of his hundreds of customers abandoned Valet Fleet Service, and his staff dwindled from a peak of twenty-five to three.

Estimating that the Oregon case could cost between $400,000 and $1.5 million to defend, Ammon's attorney had launched a crowdfunding campaign the day after he was arrested. Over the subsequent six months, more than twelve thousand supporters pledged $95,076. Less famous defendants didn't receive the same largesse. In hopes of hiring a private attorney like Ammon had, Ryan Payne started his own campaign on the same website but received less than $4,000.

In all, twenty-six defendants were indicted on the charges of conspiracy to impede federal officers as well as five other charges involving theft, firearms, and destruction of government property.* There was Ken Medenbach, who had been arrested during the occupation for taking the refuge truck to Burns, plus the eight people arrested on the day LaVoy Finicum died. Three more had been taken into custody the next day while fleeing the refuge. Then, as the feds moved in and arrested the final four occupiers on February 11, federal agents in Nevada, Utah, Washington, Oregon, and California had arrested eight other defendants. The last two were picked up weeks later.

---

* Conspiracy to impede was the only charge lodged against all twenty-six defendants.

Some of the most militant-sounding and high-profile defendants agreed to plead guilty in exchange for lighter sentences, including Booda Cavalier, Blaine Cooper, Jon Ritzheimer, and Ryan Payne. Cooper told his attorney that he'd joined the Bundy movement because he felt like a nobody and the movement gave him purpose and fame. In Payne's case, the Oregon prosecutors agreed to recommend that he serve between forty-one and fifty-one months in prison. Payne indicated that he would likely plead guilty in the Nevada case as well. As the months passed, fourteen of the twenty-six indicted occupiers cut deals. The remaining defendants were divided into two trial groups. One group was mostly unknown to the public. The other included Ammon and Ryan Bundy, Ken Medenbach, Shawna Cox, Jeff Banta, David Fry, and, perhaps most surprisingly, Neil Wampler.

Wampler's inclusion was surprising because most of the defendants in this group had allegedly carried a gun or assumed a leadership role at the refuge, whereas Wampler had done neither. During the occupation, when a newspaper had revealed that he'd murdered his father in 1977, Wampler had headed home to Los Osos, California. He spent a couple days there, and then began traveling back toward the refuge. He stopped in Bly, Oregon, where he picked up a newspaper and read that Finicum was dead. While other former occupiers were holing up in safe houses, Wampler returned home and called the FBI. He told an agent that he'd helped take over the refuge and he wanted to turn himself in because he believed he was subject to the same charges as the occupiers they'd arrested. The agent asked what his role at the refuge had been, and Wampler said he'd been the cook. A week and a half later, the US attorney released a new indictment with his name on it. In addition to his kitchen duties, Wampler had given a video interview early in the occupation in which he fixed the camera with his distinctive glare and made some vaguely menacing statements about what would happen if the "*federales*" tried to take back the refuge. An FBI agent showed up to arrest him, and Wampler thought the agent seemed perplexed about why he was taking this disheveled sixty-eight-year-old man into custody. Wampler tried to educate the agent, scribbling out a list of constitutional experts he wanted him to check out. In the Portland jail, Wampler was put in the same unit as Ammon for a few days and got to know him better than he had during the occupation. A judge released Wampler pending trial. Wampler couldn't wait to make his stand in the courtroom with the Bundys. He was just delighted to be included.

Pete Santilli, however, was not. In the indictment, federal prosecutors said Santilli had used his YouTube show to incite people to join an illegal occupation. Santilli's attorney argued that his efforts to rally supporters were protected by the First Amendment. Furthermore, Santilli was an "unconventional news-gatherer" who opposed Ammon Bundy's tactics and had never stayed overnight at the refuge. The prosecutors knew the felony conspiracy case against Santilli was weak and that it could jeopardize the cases against his co-defendants. They offered him the chance to plead guilty to a reduced misdemeanor charge. Santilli rejected the offer. He spent eight months in jail, and then, the day before the trial was set to begin, prosecutors abruptly dismissed the case against him. Santilli remained behind bars, however, still facing serious charges in the Nevada case.

David Fry remained in jail, too, which wasn't as bad as he'd imagined in the fevered final days of the occupation. A forensic psychologist met with him three times, interviewed his relatives, and watched his YouTube videos. She diagnosed him with schizotypal personality disorder, a condition similar to schizophrenia but much less severe. Fry had eccentric beliefs, such as his fear of invasion from outer space. He experienced unusual perceptions, such as the female voice that told him Finicum was going to die in Oregon. He exhibited inappropriate social responses, such as his jovial game-show-host demeanor in the wake of Finicum's death. The judge declined to release him pending trial, and Fry lashed out: "You're a bigot and a liar, a racist."

Not long after his arrest, Ryan Bundy received a revelation that he should fire his court-appointed attorney and represent himself. Ryan was afraid, but the Lord promised that He would tell him what to say and send legal counselors. Ryan followed the instructions, and a half-dozen different advisers did show up, and they spent a tremendous amount of time on his case. Soon, Ryan was using language associated with the sovereign citizen ideology. In one pretrial hearing, he asked the judge if she was being paid by the detention center housing him or by the "United States of America Corporation." The judge said she was, in fact, paid by the federal government, though not by the county jail. "Do you understand that I am a living, breathing man, being warehoused in a commercial zone against my will?" Ryan asked. In a series of pleadings that employed sovereign turns of phrase and punctuation, Ryan said anyone who tried to take him to court would be charged $100 million. He wrote:

> i, ryan c, man, do not exist by the creation of the legislature
> of the UNITED STATES OF AMERICA; nor serve at the
> pleasure of the State of Oregon; nor the State of Nevada; nor
> am i subject to any statute or code of said State(s).

Ryan was equally defiant in jail. He tore bedsheets into strands and wove them together, fashioning a fifteen-foot rope that he hid under his mattress. Deputies found the rope and accused him of planning an escape; Ryan said he was practicing rope braiding, an essential ranching skill. In a different incident, he refused to be handcuffed, and it took several deputies to wrestle him down to the floor. He was moved to a higher-security disciplinary unit. Ryan also refused to let doctors remove the projectile that was still lodged in his arm. He believed it was evidence in the Finicum shooting, and he didn't want government hands on it.

THE DESCHUTES COUNTY TEAM INVESTIGATING THE FINICUM SHOOTING did not release the video Shawna Cox had taken inside Finicum's truck for several weeks, but they did review it, frame by frame. The video was crucial in helping them piece together events, and after a painstaking inquiry, the investigators concluded that law enforcement had fired a total of five bullets at the truck and three at Finicum after he exited the truck.*

First, a trooper had shot at the truck three times in an attempt to keep it from hitting the roadblock, which the investigators said was justified because the truck was a deadly weapon under the circumstances. Later, two troopers fired three more bullets that hit Finicum, and given his actions and movements, those shootings were justifiable as well, the investigators determined.

However, a mystery remained. As the Finicum family statement had pointed out, there were unaccounted-for shots fired at the truck after it plowed into the snowbank. The Shawna Cox video confirmed this—two shots rang out just as Finicum was getting out of the truck. One of the mystery bullets penetrated the roof of the truck, sending a small explosion of sparks and shrapnel flying, and either the bullet or a metallic chunk of shrapnel likely entered Ryan Bundy's shoulder. The investigators determined that neither of the mystery bullets had

---

* The evidence contradicted Victoria Sharp's statement that some 120 shots were fired altogether, which was a vast overinflation. However, between the gas rounds, the flash-bang grenades, and the actual bullets, the witnesses in Finicum's truck couldn't be faulted for believing they were under a barrage of gunfire.

hit Finicum, as his family had speculated. He was uninjured until the troopers shot him some twelve seconds later.

The Deschutes County team analyzed the flight of the bullet that caused Ryan's injury and determined it had come from the general area where several FBI agents were clustered near the roadblock, including the agent who'd nearly been flattened by the truck.

The problem was, in debriefings after the shooting, those FBI agents said they hadn't fired any shots. About six weeks after the shooting, the US Justice Department opened a criminal investigation into the incident, based on the work of the Deschutes investigators, who had concluded that one of the FBI agents must have fired the shots. The independent inquiry would probe whether Special Agent W. Joseph Astarita lied when he said he hadn't fired the two shots. It also would investigate whether the other four FBI agents at the scene had falsely backed Astarita's account.[*]

The revelation of potential federal duplicity sent the Patriot information networks into a frenzy. Infowars already had been reporting that Finicum had been shot nine times, that he'd been shot in the face, that the FBI had planted the gun found on Finicum. None of that information had turned out to be true, but for many, this fresh news justified every piece of baseless reporting. For many Patriots, the FBI's mystery gunshots took on the significance of the fire that killed seventy-five Branch Davidians and the FBI sniper bullet that killed Randy Weaver's wife.

"The whole thing was an ambush," an Infowars radio host said. "The whole thing was set up to stop a political protest."

---

[*] In August 2018, a federal jury acquitted Astarita of two counts of making a false statement and one count of obstruction of justice in the investigation of the Finicum shooting.

BEFORE THE OCCUPATION, SHERIFF WARD RARELY HAD CARRIED A GUN when he was off duty. It hadn't been worth the hassle. Sometimes he hadn't even used handcuffs when he arrested someone, just crooked his finger at the miscreant and said: *That's it, come with me.*

Now he carried a pistol in his jacket pocket everywhere he went, even at church, even on hot days when he didn't want to wear the extra layer. He felt supported by most Harney County residents, but he knew there were a few who wouldn't mind taking a shot at him. After the occupation and Finicum's death, this felt like a real possibility.

Like most everyone in Harney County, Ward had mulled over the Finicum shooting video. If Finicum was not injured, why did he lower his arms in such a fraught situation? The autopsy had ruled out the possibility that he was injured at that point. So was he struggling to draw the Ruger on the troopers? Was he faking a draw to force the troopers to shoot him, an attempt at martyrdom? Or was he simply stomping around in the snow, waving his arms, upset that the authorities had stopped him?

Ward believed the rancher was going for his gun, which meant the shooting was justified. To Ward, the tugging motion Finicum seemed to make on the video looked familiar. When Ward got dressed in the morning and dropped his Glock into the inside pocket of his jacket, the butt of the pistol tended to wedge itself down into the crease, making a quick draw difficult. At the end of the day, when Ward reached for the gun to put it away, the jacket tended to hamper his draw, which is how Finicum's movements captured on the video looked to Ward.

But the video was just ambiguous enough to allow for the possibility of many interpretations—it tended to reveal what people wanted it to reveal.

One thing was certain, however: in the days before January 26, Finicum had spoken about death often. He seemed to accept that

311

dying might be a consequence of his crusade, that death was preferable to being locked up. He also talked a great deal about Malheur being a peaceful occupation, about how the occupiers should never be the first to shoot.

Furthermore, Finicum had a genuine reverence for gunslingers and the mythos of the Old West. In the climax of *Only By Blood and Suffering*, when the hero faced off against three federal agents, Finicum described the scene this way:

> *A cowboy does not pack a six-shooter all his life and not know how to use it. My grandfather had taught me the fast draw as a child. Seldom had a week gone by in my life that I had not practiced.*
>
> *My right wrist flicked, and with a blur, my hand palmed the rosewood grips of my 44-40. In a flash, the old pistol cleared the leather holster with the hammer eared back. By reflex, I pulled the trigger, the hammer fell, and the gun bucked in my hand. The bullet took Zackary Williams between the eyes. Reflex, speed, and muscle memory, Zackary was still standing when my second bullet struck the agent to his right. It entered below the right eye. The agent on the left was barely raising his rifle when my third bullet clipped his chin and smashed through his throat.*

The hero spun the revolver on his finger, holstered it. But then he realized he was wounded.

> *The earth was slowly tipping. It started to tip faster. That was very strange . . . Suddenly the earth slammed into the side of my face and I plowed into the sandy wash . . . The sand of the wash bottom was cool as it pressed against my cheek . . . I'm tired. I think I'll sleep . . .*

FOR BUNDY SUPPORTERS, THE TRIAL OF THE BUNDY BROTHERS AND FIVE followers took place deep in enemy territory: downtown Portland, a city known as the greenest in the United States.

The occupiers' lawyers argued that jurors should be drawn equally from the two sides of the state, despite the long commute that would require for eastern Oregonians. The inland half of the state was overwhelmingly rural, suspicious of government, supportive of gun rights. The coastal side of the state was more urban, liberal, and supportive of the federal lands system. Most of the jurors who were eventually seated came from the Portland and Eugene areas, but the rest were from small towns scattered around the state.

Bundy supporters who were following the trial took over Lownsdale Square, a tree-covered park across the street from the federal courthouse, dubbing it Patriot Corner. When the supporters were in the courtroom, a homeless man held down the corner for them, waving an American flag. Lunchtimes resembled a tailgate party. One Sunday, they held a protest that included a parade of horses clopping down the city streets.

The courtroom action was just as unusual. Each day, the seven defendants and their lawyers crowded into the courtroom, and the defendants recited the Lord's Prayer before Judge Anna J. Brown took the bench. Judge Brown ordered Ken Medenbach to stop wearing a "Not Guilty" button into the courtroom. Ammon and Ryan petitioned the judge to allow them to wear boots and cowboy belts, and when she denied the request, Ammon insisted on wearing his blue jail scrubs. Some supporters took to wearing blue scrubs themselves. And there were many supporters, some flying in from as far away as North Carolina. The public gallery overflowed most days, so a live feed was set up in a spillover courtroom. Still, it was no Bunkerville-sized crowd, and Bundy supporters lamented their shrunken and dispirited numbers. Many had backed away from Ammon's movement.

313

"Ammon Bundy and his father basically handed their heads on the platter to the federal government," Stewart Rhodes of the Oath Keepers told the *New York Times*. "It was an 'Alice in Wonderland' viewpoint: 'This land is ours, now that we occupy it.'"

The government's challenge was to prove that the defendants conspired to prevent federal workers from doing their jobs. In his opening statement, an assistant US attorney outlined how the Bundys and their co-defendants established armed guards at the refuge's entrances and observation tower and used the buildings as residences.

"We are not prosecuting the defendants because they don't like the government," he said. "In Ammon Bundy's words, 'This was much more than a protest.' They were taking a 'hard stand.'"

Ammon's lawyer was a pugnacious Utahn named Marcus Mumford, who'd grown up on an Idaho dairy farm and who had, despite a severe stutter, worked for eight years at one of the country's biggest law firms before opening his own practice. In his opening statement, Mumford acknowledged that Ammon occupied the refuge but argued that his intent was to return the land to the people through adverse possession. Ammon was open about his intentions, Mumford said, and the feds were not.

"The government operated in the darkness," Mumford said. "Instead . . . instead of . . . instead . . . instead of going and confronting Mr. Bundy, they laid in wait as Mr. Bundy and others were going to a meeting in the next county. Instead of finding out whether or not Mr. Bundy was within his rights, they . . . they tried to arrest him, and they ended up shooting his friend."

For the next ten days of court, some three-dozen government witnesses chronicled the impact of the refuge occupation on Harney County. Sheriff Dave Ward was the government's star, the witness who had a front-row seat to the entire saga. When Ward walked into the courtroom and looked at the defendants, he was dubious about the prosecution's case. He firmly believed the Bundys and Payne had conspired to commit a crime. But Neil Wampler? David Fry? Would the jury believe they were part of a conspiracy?

Despite his misgivings, Ward took the stand and recounted his friendly early meetings with Ammon and their growing mutual suspicion. He described the flood of threatening emails he received from Bundy followers and the trickle of armed newcomers into his county. He told how the rally for the Hammonds mutated into the occupation when Ammon climbed onto a snowbank in the Safeway parking lot and rallied followers to take a "hard stand." He explained how Ammon rejected his offer of safe passage out of the county, how county residents repeatedly asked the occupiers to go home.

Butch Eaton reluctantly took the stand and recounted how the Patriots came to Burns and won him over, how he got swept into the advance team that drove to the refuge and cleared the buildings with rifles at the ready. How he realized what they were doing and got scared and walked out. Eaton was a government witness, but it was clear where his sympathies lay. When Marcus Mumford cross-examined him, Eaton said the occupiers were hardworking and peaceful.

"They're God-fearing men," Eaton said. "Better than me."

A parade of federal land agency employees described how the occupation disrupted their work. The Malheur refuge manager said the occupiers left the compound a mess—the post-occupation restoration had been completed only a month earlier, and the refuge was still not open to the public. A BLM district manager said his employees received threatening emails. A Fish and Wildlife biologist said her office was "completely trashed." A firefighter said the bunkhouse was a mess, that it reeked of cigarette smoke.

On cross-examination, Ryan Bundy questioned the firefighter about prescribed burns, asking if sometimes the fires burned more acreage than intended. The firefighter said yes.

"Were you ever prosecuted as a domestic terrorist for that?" Ryan asked.

Judge Brown told the jury to disregard the question.

Ryan was finding the words he needed to represent himself, as the Lord had assured him he would six months earlier when he decided to fire his court-appointed attorney. In his opening statement, he'd displayed a photo of his wife Angie and seven of their children. As testimony unfolded, he was usually the second person on the defense side to cross-examine the government witnesses, after Mumford, and he brought a relaxed style to the courtroom. Typically, his first question was friendly: "How ya doing today?" The rest of his questions were sharp and direct, as when he asked an FBI pilot who flew surveillance missions above the refuge: "So, do you spy on the American people a lot?" Sometimes his lack of legal education showed as he violated procedure, but often Judge Brown overruled the prosecutors' objections to his questions. Medenbach and Shawna Cox also followed Ryan's example and represented themselves, though their court-appointed standby counsel increasingly stepped in and took over as the two defendants struggled to conform to courtroom protocol.

The judge did bar questions about the issue Ammon most wanted to explore: the constitutionality of federal land ownership. The courts had already decided that matter, she said, and it had little to do with the trial's central question: whether the occupiers had conspired to prevent the refuge workers from doing their jobs.

Over and over, Ryan and Mumford also tried to slip in questions about the Finicum shooting. If federal agents lied about the pair of mystery shots fired at the traffic stop, Ryan argued, they might be lying about other things. But the prosecutors didn't call any of the FBI agents under investigation, and Judge Brown shut down the defense attempts to explore that topic with other witnesses, concluding that it, too, wasn't relevant. But Marcus Mumford kept bringing up the

Finicum shooting, with witness after witness, and he clashed repeatedly with the judge, who finally threatened to fine him $1,000 for each time he delved into the subject.

FBI agents described how it took a team of sixty-three federal investigators a dozen days to comb through the refuge and catalogue the disarray left behind after the occupation. Other investigators described their forays into the social media accounts of various occupiers, including David Fry's YouTube account and Ammon's Facebook page. They displayed pictures occupiers had posted with guns and inflammatory statements they'd made. But the prosecution lacked hard evidence that showed the defendants actually conspiring to impede federal employees. There were no emails, no texts, no videos that showed the defendants talking about the refuge employees they'd displaced.

So instead, the government built its case around guns and the implicit threat the refuge employees had felt. Four times, the jury watched a video of a line of occupiers leveling rifles and handguns near Malheur Lake and hammering thousands of rounds into the water. The prosecutors completed their case with a display of all the weaponry collected by investigators at the refuge after the occupation ended. One by one, an FBI agent held up twenty-two rifles and shotguns and twelve handguns and described where each was found. The firepower presentation was dramatic and lengthy, and Judge Brown objected when FBI agents then hauled into the courtroom fourteen black bins containing more than eighteen thousand rounds of spent and live ammunition.

"Do a summary, please, and let's get on with it," she said.

SIX DAYS AFTER THE GOVERNMENT RESTED ITS CASE, AMMON TOOK THE WITNESS stand carrying a well-used Bible and wearing blue jail scrubs. Over the government's objections, Judge Brown had allowed testimony and video from the Bunkerville standoff, saying it established Ammon's mindset as he decided to take up the Hammonds' cause and occupy the refuge. So, Ammon told the story of his life, from his childhood on Bundy Ranch to the moment when he was tased by federal officers. To the Bundys, Ammon said, the federal government had felt like an overwhelmingly powerful opponent.

"We can't do it against these people," he said. "They're too smart. They're too strong. They've got too many resources. And so we're begging the state and the counties to protect these rights that are ours and that have been in our family for hundreds of years. They're just being ripped away from us and just taken. And now they're taking it to the next level, where they're prosecuting. My dad and brothers are in jail right now." He began crying. "It's wrong. It's wrong."

After a direct examination that lasted most of three days, Mumford and Ammon ended with a moment of defiance.

"Mr. Bundy, one more question," Mumford said. "Your friend is dead. You and your brother have been in prison for eight and a half months. Is it still worth it?"

"Your Honor, I'm going to object to the relevance of the question," the prosecutor said.

Judge Brown sustained the objection and told Mumford to move on, but the lawyer kept going and pressed the point.

"Is it still worth it?" he repeated to Ammon.

"Absolutely," Ammon said.

"Mr. Mumford, I just sustained the objection," Judge Brown snapped.

Ammon ignored the judge and repeated his answer: "Absolutely."

IN A TRIAL FULL OF ODDITIES, ONE OF THE MOST UNUSUAL MOMENTS occurred when one Bundy brother cross-examined another. Ryan stayed seated at the defense table as he gave his customary casual opening question.

"Mr. Bundy, how ya doing?" Ryan said.

"Good," Ammon said from the witness box. "How you doing, brother?"

"How long have we known each other?" Ryan asked.

"Well, my whole life," Ammon said.

Observers in the courtroom laughed. Ryan nodded.

"We grew up in the same house?"

"Yes, we did," Ammon said.

"We worked, we played, we wrestled, we cared for each other all our lives?"

"That's correct," Ammon said.

When it was their turn, the prosecution barely cross-examined Ammon. The questions he did receive were mainly about his leadership.

"You are the leader of the group that took over the refuge, aren't you?" the prosecutor asked.

"No," Ammon said.

After additional questions, Ammon clarified how he saw his role: "I teach correct principles and let them govern themselves."

Ammon spent most of three days on the stand. The prosecutor spent less than fifteen minutes on his cross-examination.

EVER SINCE LAVOY FINICUM'S DEATH, TERRI LINNELL HAD BEEN TORN. She was angry and wanted to help her fellow Patriots, but she was terrified to reveal that she'd worked for the FBI.

Anger finally won. Three separate times, she reached out to different lawyers for the defense, ready to provide information even if she was exposed. Finally, one called her back, and she told him what she'd done and agreed to testify for the defense.

By now, everybody knew Linnell wasn't the only occupier who had been working for the feds. For Bundy followers observing the trial, one of the most intriguing and troubling developments was the unmasking of government informants who had spent time at the refuge. First, a state trooper had testified that Mark McConnell, who had been driving the Jeep Ammon was riding in, had tipped off the feds that the occupation leaders were heading to Grant County to meet with the sheriff. Even after being outed, however, McConnell continued to insist to Patriots that he wasn't an informant. Then, as the defense case drew to a close, a prosecutor revealed that no less than fifteen "confidential human sources" had fed information to the FBI about the occupation, including nine who had reported from inside the refuge itself. The defense wanted names, but Judge Brown declined to reveal additional informants.

Terri Linnell unmasked herself. When Linnell arrived in Portland to testify in the case, she told some of her compatriots about her role. The blowback was immediate and harsh. Vitriol poured onto her Facebook page.

When one friend wrote that everyone should lay off and let Linnell "do the right thing," another commenter wrote: "Suicide is the right thing. Actually, strap the fuck up and even the score with the federal government. Then suicide."

Another wrote: "How can she EVER be trusted again. Once a snitch always a snitch, she dug Lavoys grave and her own."

Gary Hunt, the Patriot journalist, weighed in: "It appears that many are rushing to judgement . . . Perhaps it might make more sense to wait until Terri has testified. It is quite possible that her testimony will help the defendants and hurt the government."

Linnell's testimony likely did not dramatically sway the jury in either direction. On cross-examination, the prosecutor read from reports Linnell had given to her FBI handler about the occupation's leaders, about the militia patrol shifts, about the sovereign citizens at the refuge. Linnell made no secret of where her allegiance lay as she repeatedly disputed how the prosecutor characterized her reports.

"So you don't recall reporting to the FBI that there was talk at the refuge about taking over another federal facility?" the prosecutor pressed.

"No, sir," Linnell said. "There . . . it was not taking over. This was a protest. If they chose to go anywhere, they were free to do so."

"That wasn't my question, ma'am," the prosecutor said.

Then, on the last day of testimony, the defense briefly grilled the man known as John Killman about his time at the refuge. Unlike Linnell, Killman had not volunteered to testify. In fact, Killman wasn't even his real name. Neil Wampler's defense attorney had tracked him down after another occupier gave her Killman's phone number, which she plugged into a reverse phone directory. As it turned out, Killman was Fabio Minoggio, a Las Vegas resident who had served in the Swiss army for two decades and was trained in psy-ops and marksmanship. At the refuge, he had run the shooting range for several days. Mumford made much of this fact, because the government had repeatedly shown the jury the video of occupiers firing assault rifles at the shooting range next to the lake.

"Do you realize there were more confidential informants at the refuge than we have defendants in this very courtroom?" Mumford told the jury in his closing argument. "They charged the cook, but not the guy running the shooting range. Because that's what the informant was there to do. The FBI hadn't gotten enough footage of scary people shooting guns."

PERHAPS BECAUSE THEY SENSED THE TRIAL WAS SLIPPING AWAY, THE PROSE-cutors reminded the jury in closing arguments that it was a simple, commonsense case. Ammon Bundy and his followers had conspired to take over a wildlife refuge that didn't belong to them.

Conversely, the defense attorneys stressed the complexity of the range wars. They said the occupiers took the sanctuary as a first step toward resolving, for once and for all, the question of who rightfully owned the land. They argued that the conspiracy charge was over-blown. In his closing, Ryan Bundy faced the jury and rapped his fist against his chest.

"I ask you to stand with us," he said. "Stand for freedom."

Eight days later, the jurors stood with the Bundys. Ammon rose and clasped his hands behind his back as Judge Brown read his verdict: "Not guilty."

Ammon smiled and laid his hand on Mumford's shoulder. Ryan mouthed to the jury: "Thank you."

One by one, all seven defendants were found not guilty of all charges except one: the jury could not agree on a theft count against Ryan for taking the government cameras, and the charge was later dropped. But the dramatics were not over. Judge Brown dismissed the jury and asked the defense if they had any further questions.

"Well, Your Honor, you're not keeping Mr. Ammon Bundy in custody, right?" Mumford asked.

"I said he is released . . ." the judge began.

"Okay, thank you," Mumford said.

". . . on this charge," the judge finished. "But he is still subject to hold by the District of Nevada."

"If they want to come, they know where to find him," Mumford said.

As he'd done throughout the trial, the chunky, middle-aged defense attorney raised his voice and began speaking over the judge. Bundy supporters, celebrating in the now half-empty audience seats, looked over.

"He's free, Your Honor," Mumford said.

"Mr. Mumford," the judge began.

"He has beaten these . . ."

A US marshal approached the attorney, saying: "Stand down." He told Mumford to come to the marshal's office if he wanted to see the Nevada court order to hold Ammon.

But Mumford continued to argue, his face reddening. A half-dozen deputy marshals moved closer to him.

"Mr. Mumford, step back," the judge ordered.

The deputy marshals grabbed the attorney, much like the BLM officers had grabbed Dave Bundy two and a half years earlier. And like Dave, Mumford resisted going down, so the scrum waltzed around the courtroom for a few chaotic moments, knocking chairs and the prosecution table out of place.

"No, I . . . I . . ." Mumford stuttered.

The marshals wrestled him to the floor as the attorney kept railing. One tried to put handcuffs on him.

"Whoa, whoa, whoa," Mumford said. "Wait. What are you guys doing?"

A deputy marshal pulled out a Taser. He was closer to Mumford than the BLM agents who had tased Ammon in Bunkerville, so the marshal didn't need to fire probes. The Taser was in dry-stun mode when the marshal put it against the attorney's body and pulled the trigger.

"Out!" Judge Brown yelled. "Everybody out!"

LATER, ONE JUROR EXCHANGED EMAILS WITH A REPORTER FROM THE *OREGO-nian*, responding to the nation's widespread disbelief over the verdicts. The juror's account depicted a judicious panel that took its mandate to apply the law seriously.

No, the juror said, the verdict was not a declaration of allegiance with the Patriot movement or a statement about the range wars. No, the jurors were not taken in by Ammon's charisma or emotional appeals during his three days on the stand. No, the jurors did not feel the occupiers were innocent of wrongdoing.

The government, this juror said, simply hadn't proven felony conspiracy. During the trial, the jury kept waiting for the prosecution to bring up evidence—emails, phone calls, testimony—that would prove the occupiers had intended to impede federal workers from doing their jobs. It never happened, the juror said. Throughout the occupation, Ammon had been consistently focused on the range wars, not on the federal workers he'd displaced at the refuge. He'd done wrong, the juror said, but there seemed to be no law that carried a serious penalty that could be applied in this case.

The juror said some members of the panel had changed their minds late in the trial when the extent of the government's infiltration of the refuge became clear. Other jurors didn't like the prosecution's repeated objections to defense attempts to read from the Constitution. Generally, the jury believed the federal prosecutors had overreached, which, after all, was exactly what the defendants were arguing.

"The air of triumphalism that the prosecution brought was not lost on any of us," the juror wrote, "nor was it warranted, given their burden of proof."

TWELVE DAYS AFTER THE VERDICT IN OREGON, DONALD TRUMP WAS elected president of the United States.

Cliven Bundy's feelings about Trump were complicated. Cliven had spent the previous nine months in a private prison in the desert near Pahrump, Nevada. Three television sets were bolted to the wall of his unit, and Cliven was disturbed by political advertisements that showed Trump speaking crudely about women and supposedly mimicking the movements of a disabled man. On the other hand, Donald Trump was a businessman, a producer, like Cliven. Trump supported the Second Amendment and exhibited disdain for the federal government. Cliven told his family to urge people to vote, and the Bundy Ranch blog posted a somewhat oblique Trump endorsement, a picture of Cliven on horseback hoisting the Stars and Stripes under the superimposed words: "Blow your 'Trumpence!' VOTE! VOTE! VOTE!"

Shortly after the 2016 election, the incoming and outgoing presidents began battling over the land Cliven still considered to be his ranch. On December 28, 2016, President Obama designated three hundred thousand acres in Gold Butte as a new national monument, a classification that carried protections similar to those that apply to national parks. The roughly rectangular monument ran from Lake Mead National Park to the Arizona/Nevada line and included Virgin Peak. It ended about nine miles south of Bundy ranch, just about where the mountain range begins to get steep. The majority of Cliven's cattle ranged to the north, but some of his water developments fell squarely within the new monument's territory.

Opponents called the designation a land grab, and some said the lame duck president did it as payback for the Bundys' defiance. But the move was in keeping with Obama's previous land policies—over his presidency, he'd designated 553 million acres as national monuments, more than any other president.

Trump had never shown much interest in the range wars and had said he opposed giving federal lands to states. But upon taking office he appointed a new Interior Department secretary, Ryan Zinke, who immediately began a review of twenty-seven monuments to determine whether protections should be rolled back at those locations, including Gold Butte.

AFTER THE VICTORY IN OREGON, AMMON AND RYAN BUNDY WERE SHIPPED to the prison near Pahrump, where they joined fifteen other defendants awaiting trial for the Bunkerville standoff. The other defendants included three Bundy men—Cliven, Mel, and Dave—as well as Pete Santilli, Booda Cavalier, Ryan Payne, and Eric Parker. Blaine Cooper and another defendant had already pleaded guilty, but the seventeen remaining defendants appeared determined to go to trial, especially after the Bundys' stunning win in Oregon.

As with the Oregon case, the defendants were split into different trial groups, three this time, organized by level of alleged culpability. The "leadership" group included Cliven, Ammon, Ryan, Santilli, and Payne. The "mid-level organizers" group included Mel and Dave. And the "gunmen" group, considered least culpable, included Eric Parker, the so-called Bundy Sniper.

A month after his arrest, Cliven had appeared before a federal magistrate court and refused to acknowledge the court's authority or enter a plea. Two months later, he sued numerous federal officials, including Senator Harry Reid and President Barack Obama, accusing them of plotting to steal his property. As the months passed, Cliven had deteriorated. After a lifetime in the desert, now he never saw the sun. He had been segregated from the general population for months, due to concern that the notoriety from his "Negro" speech would put him in danger. This meant he spent twenty-three hours a day in his cell and one hour in a larger room. His teeth decayed and several were pulled, making it hard to eat. He lost weight and grew despondent.

Periodically, Cliven called Bundy Ranch to check in, and the family could tell he was trying to hide his low spirits. Carol and Arden, the youngest son, who was now eighteen years old, were learning how to run the ranch, feeding the animals on the farm and then heading out on the range to check the water infrastructure. They sold more than one hundred cattle in the first six months after Cliven's arrest. With five Bundy families lacking their primary breadwinners, the family had ramped up fundraising efforts. The Bundy Ranch blog and Facebook page, which now had about two hundred thousand followers, contained PayPal links for donations. They also linked to an online merchandise store that contained various items stamped with the Bundy Ranch brand, including thirty-five-dollar brass-colored cowboy belt buckles and "Bye, Bye, BLM" bumper stickers. There was even a T-shirt with Cliven's signature phrase: "Whatever It Takes."

Some of the wives of the jailed Bundy men had to find jobs to pay the bills. In Idaho, Lisa never did, even as Valet Fleet Service business dried up. She continued raising the six kids, including the baby, who turned two in early 2017. She worried constantly, but people took care of them. Random acquaintances would drop off fruits and vegetables and meat at the house. Every month, someone sent a big Amazon package with food, batteries, toilet paper, lightbulbs, and Lisa never found out who it was.

THE "GUNMEN" WERE TRIED FIRST.

The feds had targeted this collection of defendants because they had made inflammatory remarks on social media or had carried rifles during the Toquop Wash standoff. Eric Parker was the most well-known of the gunmen defendants and the only one photographed actually pointing a rifle at the federal agents. He'd walked free for almost two years after the standoff. But then, a little less than a month after Cliven Bundy was arrested at the Portland airport, Parker had been driving down Main Street in Hailey, Idaho, on his way to work, when a bunch of FBI vehicles surrounded him and an agent put a pistol to his head through the window. On the same day, the feds swept up a dozen other Bunkerville defendants in six states. The defendants spent the next eleven months in the Pahrump prison.

The gunmen trial began in Las Vegas in February 2017. The government's case sustained an early blow when Judge Gloria Navarro forced prosecutors to release a federal ethics probe into alleged wrongdoing by the government's star witness, none other than the BLM's Dan Love.

Three years had passed since Love had supervised the roundup operation at Bundy Ranch. The special agent had become a lightning rod for all the strong emotions that swirled around the range wars, as well as the target of numerous death threats. Despite his notoriety, Love had received a promotion in 2016 to oversee security for BLM facilities nationwide. But then the Department of the Interior began looking into the behavior of the controversial agent. The resulting report said Love had used his position to obtain tickets to the Burning Man festival, that he bent rules to help a friend get hired, and that he bullied other BLM employees.

Rather than allow the defense to turn the case into a referendum on Dan Love, the prosecution chose not to call him as a witness. Instead, they called a number of BLM and Las Vegas Metro officers who testified that the face-off against the armed Bundy supporters ranked among the most terrifying experiences of their careers. Eric Parker spent two days on the stand, explaining to the jury how he saw the Santilli video and got caught up in the Bundys' plight, and then wound up on the bridge with his Saiga .223.

In his closing argument, Acting US Attorney Steven Myhre mocked the defendants, saying there was nothing noble or patriotic about their face-off against the feds.

"For what? For some cattle? For someone who hasn't paid grazing fees in twenty years?" Myhre bellowed. "Or to maybe feel like they're somebody for a moment in time."

Just as the Oregon defense attorneys had successfully argued, the gunmen's lawyers said the felony conspiracy charge was laughable.

The scene in Bunkerville was chaos. Little coordination existed, and each man acted independently, the defense argued.

The jury was less united than the Oregon panel had been. Jurors convicted two of the six defendants on some counts but deadlocked on fifty of the sixty total counts. Judge Navarro declared a mistrial, and the entire process began again. A second trial was set for summer 2017 for the four remaining gunmen, which pushed back the trial date for Ammon, Ryan, and Cliven, who'd by now been behind bars for almost fifteen months.

As they waited for trial, Ammon and Ryan clashed with their jailers in Pahrump. They were put in a segregation unit that mandated strip searches each time they entered or left the unit. Ammon sometimes refused, and once was taken to a hearing in his underwear. Ryan was forced to call in to one court hearing because he refused to be strip-searched, and he hung up on the judge. The brothers' defiance didn't endear them to the corrections officers, and they spent a lot of time in the "hole," which Lisa hated because Ammon couldn't call home and sing to the baby.

In May 2017, Ammon told a relative in a phone call that he'd been handcuffed in a jail bathroom for twelve hours. Word got around, and the Patriots swung into action once again. By now, it was almost routine. They headed for Pahrump and set up a new camp on a desolate stretch of desert just across the road from the detention center. For several weeks, tents, campers, and cars came and went from the spot, and the Patriots grilled meals, marched around the perimeter of the prison carrying flags, and shouted prayers to the prisoners through a loudspeaker system.

A new, less-militant set of activists was emerging as leaders in the Bundy movement, epitomized by John Lamb, a guileless, bear-sized

Amish father of eleven from Montana. Like many of his faith, Lamb had no Social Security number or birth certificate, believing that a number assigned to an individual at birth was the biblical mark of the beast. He'd grown up with the common Amish mistrust of government, an attitude heightened by the events of Waco and Ruby Ridge.

Despite his off-the-grid life, Lamb operated a successful construction company in Billings, and when one of his company's salesmen set up a Facebook account for the business, a new universe of information opened up to him. He became obsessed with the LaVoy Finicum shooting and when the Oregon trial began, he had left his wife and children on the farm and joined the Patriots in Portland. He'd barely missed a court date since then and had taken on an unlikely combination of roles for a forty-four-year-old Amish man: prison minister, community activist, and social-media guru. He began conducting regular livestreams using his smartphone. When the Oregon verdict had come down, Lamb broke the news to thousands of livestream viewers, sobbing the two words, over and over: "Not guilty! Not guilty! Not guilty!"

Now he was camping outside the Pahrump prison, and his days were filled with one task after another: painting protest signs, stirring pots of beans and ham, picking up trash. They called it Camp Liberty, same as the militia camp next to Bundy Ranch in 2014. But under the unofficial leadership of Lamb and a couple of others, the camp had taken on a decidedly less militant vibe. Specifically, fewer people were carrying handguns, and rifles were largely tucked out of sight. Lamb was a pacifist, and while he supported the right of others to bear arms, he didn't carry a gun himself. Other emerging leaders wanted the camp to present a mainstream image, and word had spread that open carry was frowned upon.

The new Camp Liberty was way too vanilla for Brand Nu

Thornton. If he had his way, he'd have a thousand militia members across the road from the prison, armed to the teeth, eyeing the security guards who drove past. But he also knew the decades-old Patriot math still applied: Beggars couldn't be choosers. The Patriots needed all the bodies they could get, and Thornton welcomed the new leadership. The last year had been tough on everybody, especially the revelation that fifteen so-called Patriots were turncoats. It wasn't easy, knowing that almost anyone could be a traitor. Thornton was now wary of some folks he'd once considered close friends. One woman he'd hung out with a lot at the refuge had recently texted him an oblique question about the Patriot command structure, which Thornton considered to be a tip-off. Despite Thornton's testimony for the defense in the Oregon trial, despite his high-risk support of the ex-occupiers in the safe houses in Utah, some people even suspected Thornton himself. After all, he hadn't been indicted for the Bunkerville standoff or the refuge takeover. Ever since the government had revealed the extent of its infiltration of the Bundy movement, just about anyone whose last name wasn't Bundy could be suspect. The most important thing, Thornton had learned, was to never, ever discuss anything illegal with anybody.

In July 2017, the remaining four gunmen went on trial again, and everybody moved back to Las Vegas. Thornton turned his Vegas apartment into a Patriot bachelor pad, hosting a half-dozen Bundy supporters. Patriots slept in the spare bedroom, on the couches under the mounted bighorn sheep trophies, even outside on the bare rocky patio. John Lamb curled up on the kitchen floor.

During the days, Lamb sat in the courtroom, taking assiduous notes for his livestreams, while others lounged in lawn chairs outside the federal courthouse, holding signs. Every so often, a Patriot drove by on Las Vegas Boulevard, honking and throwing up the Three Percenter salute out a truck window, and the crowd outside the courthouse flashed the sign back. Even Lamb threw up the three fingers sometimes, and then ducked his head and admitted: "I'm not really a Three Percenter."

After several weeks of testimony, the prosecution once again failed to convince the jury. Two of the defendants were acquitted on all charges. The other two defendants, including Eric Parker, were found not guilty on all but four charges; the jury was hung on those counts.

The US attorney decided to try a third time to convict Parker and his co-defendant. But he couldn't justify postponing the other defendants' trials again, so he lumped the two hard-to-convict "gunmen" defendants in with the "leaders" group that included Cliven, Ammon, Ryan, Pete Santilli, and Ryan Payne. A trial date was set for October 2017.

As the second gunmen trial had wound on, Interior Secretary Ryan Zinke hiked through Gold Butte and gazed at Native American rock art. Afterward, wearing a white cowboy hat at a press conference on Riverside Road in Bunkerville, he said that neither he nor President Trump advocated selling or transferring public land. But Zinke did believe that national monuments should cover only the specific objects they are designed to protect, which meant that he would recommend that some of the protected lands be reduced in size.

He refused to talk about what the BLM was going to do with Cliven Bundy's cattle, but he did offer praise for ranchers.

"The rancher is as much a part of the culture of these monuments as some of the objects," he said.

Six miles away at Bundy Ranch, Carol Bundy told reporters that she wished Zinke would answer her calls and emails.

"Why would you come to my front yard and not reach out to my family and hear our story, hear our plea?" she said.

TWELVE DAYS BEFORE THE NEVADA BUNDY TRIAL WAS SET TO BEGIN, A sixty-four-year-old man named Stephen Paddock entered a Mesquite store called Guns & Guitars and paid $600 for a .308 bolt-action Ruger rifle.

A forty-one-year-old gunsmith named Jonathan "Skipper" Speece ran the background check on Paddock and sold him the rifle. Speece lived on Bundy Ranch, in a camper about thirty yards from the main house. Speece had come to Bunkerville a couple days after the standoff and found he liked it better than Las Vegas, so he'd stayed. He thought of himself as less of a security guard than a witness. If the feds ever came for Cliven, he'd be there to tell what happened.

After Stephen Paddock bought the Ruger, he drove to the Mandalay Bay casino, where he had a hotel room on the thirty-second floor. Three days later, he used a small sledgehammer to break his hotel room's windows. Shortly after 10 PM, Paddock opened fire on a country music concert crowd on the Las Vegas Strip below, raining more than 1,100 rounds into the crowd in automatic-fire bursts from some of the fourteen AR-15 rifles and eight AR-10 rifles he'd stockpiled in the hotel room. Fifty-eight people died, and more than seven hundred were injured in the worst mass shooting in United States history.

Days later, Ryan Payne's attorney filed motions asking the judge to delay the start of the trial sixty days and to move it to Reno. It would be impossible, the motion argued, to pick a Las Vegas jury that would be fair to defendants accused of orchestrating a mass armed assault:

> Las Vegas is in mourning. The tragedy has affected the daily lives of every resident in this city. Thousands of people have lost friends and loved ones. This is not the time to pick a jury and commence a trial in this case.

Judge Navarro delayed the trial twenty days but kept it in Las Vegas.

For the prosecutors, the Bundy trial began to fall apart before it even got underway.

Trouble continued to dog the prosecution's would-be star witness, Dan Love. According to a new Interior Department report, Love had told a subordinate to take moqui marbles, spherical geological oddities stolen from a national park, from an evidence room to give to BLM employees and contractors as keepsakes. He also reportedly told an underling to "scrub" inappropriate or demeaning emails that could be used against him in an investigation. By October 2017, when he testified in a pretrial hearing in the Bundy case, Dan Love no longer worked for the BLM, though neither he nor the agency was giving specifics. The former special agent in charge of BLM law enforcement for all of Utah and Nevada would remain unemployed for months and suffered psychologically from the stress of the standoff in Toquop Wash and the many death threats he received afterward.

But the prosecution's problems didn't end with Dan Love. The defense team had come across photographs of bags of shredded documents from the BLM command post, and the lawyers demanded to know whether exculpatory evidence had been destroyed. The US attorney said the documents identified law-enforcement officers and had to be shredded, but after the Dan Love report that claimed the agent had mishandled evidence in other investigations, Judge Navarro began to take the issue more seriously.

Furthermore, the defense attorneys also asked to see the surveillance video of the Bundy home that had been recorded during the roundup. Myhre, the lead prosecutor, scoffed that this was a "fantastical fishing expedition." But when a retired National Park Service ranger confirmed that the FBI did in fact have cameras monitoring the Bundy house, the judge delayed the trial again, saying she wanted more information.

"It's difficult for the court to imagine there was a camera placed with no one watching it and making notes," she said.

Within weeks, Judge Navarro let both Ammon and Ryan walk out of jail. She said they could spend the rest of the trial in the home of a court-approved host, with GPS monitoring. She didn't explain the reversal. She offered the same arrangement to Cliven, but he refused, and his lawyer said he wouldn't accept unless he could walk out with no strings attached.

The trial proceeded in fits and starts, as the prosecution called only a handful of witnesses. Judge Navarro, a former public defender, kept finding evidence the prosecution had neglected to provide to the defense. Internal affairs documents about Dan Love. Threat assessments that deemed the Bundys unlikely to engage in a shootout. An FBI log that contained entries about snipers, which prosecutors had insisted the BLM had not employed during the roundup. All of the evidence would have been useful to the defense, the judge said.

The coup de grâce was a memo written by Larry Wooten, the lead BLM investigator in the Bundy case in Nevada. Wooten, who had been appalled by Dan Love's behavior during the roundup and afterward, wrote that he'd raised concerns in early 2017 that the government was withholding evidence that involved Love. In the memo, Wooten said he told the lead prosecutor, Myhre, about some of Dan Love's more inflammatory remarks and asked if the government would have to inform the defense about them.

Myhre's response, according to the memo, was: *We do now.*

Two days later, according to the memo, Wooten was removed from the investigation.

On December 20, 2017, after taking a lengthy break to investigate the withheld information, Judge Navarro declared a mistrial. She set a court date for January 8, 2018, and said she would decide then whether to dismiss the defendants' charges altogether.

Up in Oregon, most people in Harney County had learned to live with their feelings about the refuge occupation.* And most supported Sheriff Dave Ward's conduct during the crisis. Nine months after the occupation ended, 58 percent of Harney County voters had backed Ward to serve another term as sheriff. Still, Ward continued carrying a gun off duty, continued to feel like he was looking over his shoulder—majority support wasn't going to help him if some angry Bundy follower came looking to do him harm. It took only one unstable mind to wreak havoc, which was exactly the point Ward had kept trying to drive home to Ammon as the occupation was inflaming hearts and minds throughout the West.

On December 26, 2017, the long-simmering resentment of one Bundy stalwart finally boiled over. Nathaniel Macalevy, age forty-four, lived near Portland in Clackamas County, where he operated a heating and cooling company, but he also owned 160 acres in Harney County. Macalevy ran cattle on the Harney County property and visited a couple times a month to check on them. Ten years earlier, Ward had owned some property near Macalevy's, and the two men were casual friends. Ward sometimes put hay out for Macalevy's herd in the winter. Macalevy had strong constitutionalist views and was a survivalist, but Ward liked him and considered him a good neighbor.

Then, when Ammon Bundy took the refuge, Macalevy immersed himself in the occupation. The death of LaVoy Finicum, a fellow survivalist, embittered Macalevy toward the sheriff. Someone showed

---

* Many local residents were pleased in July 2018 when President Donald Trump pardoned Dwight and Steve Hammond, the Harney County ranchers whose conviction on arson charges sparked the refuge occupation. Trump said the pardon was warranted because evidence at the Hammond trial was conflicting and because the jury had acquitted the father and son on most charges.

Ward a vitriolic message from Macalevy. At that time, of course, Ward was getting hundreds of messages like this.

Macalevy's bitterness didn't dissipate. After the occupation, a neighbor told Ward that Macalevy was hosting militia members on his Harney County property, and they were doing a lot of shooting and talking about payback for Finicum's death. Ward passed the information along to other law enforcement in Harney and Clackamas counties. Macalevy's estranged wife told the sheriff that he'd become increasingly paranoid and violent after the occupation. Ward sent a deputy out to Macalevy's property to take a look, and the deputy reported that a sniper perch had been set up there. On Facebook, Macalevy posted pictures of himself flashing a Three Percenter hand sign. He displayed a new tattoo of Finicum's "LV" brand on his leg. He visited Carol Bundy and Skipper Speece at Bundy Ranch.

On Christmas Day 2017, Nathaniel Macalevy got drunk and went to his estranged wife's home in rural Clackamas County to see his thirteen-year-old daughter, violating a court order to stay away. He was wearing a camouflage ballistic vest and helmet and carrying an AR-15 and a handgun. His wife called police, and a SWAT team was dispatched to the home, but Macalevy was gone by the time officers arrived. A few hours later, a SWAT team member spotted Macalevy in his van. Several sheriff's patrol cars chased the van for a couple of miles before Macalevy pulled over and began firing, pinning down some deputies in a ditch. Seven police officers opened fire and a bullet struck Macalevy's spinal column, killing him instantly.

This shootout wasn't open to interpretation. Macalevy fired about thirty rounds at the police, and he was aiming to kill. Dashcam footage showed patrol-car windows shattering. Ward believes the deputies were lucky to make it out unscathed.

Ward believes his former neighbor probably would be alive if the Bundys hadn't come to Harney County. Paranoia and anger are contagious, and when they're fed by misinformation and misguided emotional appeals, everybody loses.

On January 8, 2018, a spectator ran out of Judge Navarro's courtroom into the hallway, yelling: "Dismissed with prejudice!"

A huge cheer went up, and the Patriots clapped. Prejudice, they'd recently learned, meant the defendants couldn't be tried again. The Bundys and Pete Santilli were free men. Ryan Payne still faced sentencing in Oregon, where he had pleaded guilty, but he was rid of the Nevada charges. Eric Parker and his co-defendant had already pleaded guilty to a misdemeanor and were free as well.

John Lamb cried again. Shawna Cox led a group prayer. Carol Bundy dabbed her eyes. Ammon hugged everyone.

"LaVoy is with us right now," a woman told Jeanette Finicum, who was preparing to file a $70 million wrongful-death lawsuit alleging a widespread federal conspiracy targeting Bundy supporters.

Outside, people gathered on the big plaza that had been built to help the federal courthouse withstand a McVeigh-sized car bomb. The Nevada sky was gray and leaky. When word came that Cliven had been processed and was on his way down, a semicircle of well-wishers crowded around the glass doors, an array of cell phones recording the moment.

Cliven came outside, doffed his Stetson, and merged into the throng. He'd been behind bars exactly seven hundred days. Someone gave him a brown-and-white sign, and he brandished it over his head, triumphantly: "First Amendment Area."

Terri Linnell was among the crowd that witnessed the seventy-one-year-old rancher's first moments of freedom on the courthouse plaza. Linnell had been attending fewer Patriot events as of late; many in the movement were suspicious of her since finding out that she'd worked for the feds. But she wasn't going to miss this moment. Besides, she believed that most of her friends had come around. The Bundys themselves seemed to have forgiven her. She posed for smiling photographs with Ammon and Ryan, and posted the shots repeatedly on her Facebook page, proof that she was still a Patriot, still Momma Bear.

She wrote: "Ryan even thanked me."

Ryan had been out of jail for almost two months, and he hadn't found it difficult to jump back into his life. He'd been eager to come home, and now he was home. Simple as that. The hardest thing for Ryan was being famous, everybody recognizing his singular face. Sometimes it put him on edge, because he could tell that people were always expecting his words to be profound. He was no prophet. And he was no lawyer either. Poring through legal documents wasn't something he had enjoyed, though people said he'd been pretty good at it. No, Ryan still wanted to be a rancher, as he always had.

But another idea had entered his thoughts recently, a way to turn his fame from a nuisance into a blessing. Ryan Bundy was thinking about running for governor of Nevada.*

AMMON'S RETURN TO FREEDOM WAS FAR MORE COMPLICATED.

Lisa and the kids had adapted to a life without him, and as much

---

* Ryan did run in 2018 as an independent but garnered only 1.4 percent of the vote. The top two items on his platform were his pledges to ensure that all lands within the state belonged to the people of Nevada and to "prevent unjust prosecutions by both the State and Federal courts." Clark County Commissioner Steve Sisolak, a pro-public lands Democrat, beat Republican state attorney general Adam Laxalt, who campaigned on transferring public lands from federal to local control.

as they wanted him home, his presence felt strange for awhile. After so many months in a bathroom-sized cell, it took Ammon time to adjust to bigger spaces. His digestive system wasn't used to real food: fresh fruits and vegetables and protein.

Ammon wanted to get back to work rebuilding Valet Fleet Service, but he couldn't bear to leave his family, so he hadn't yet traveled to Phoenix. One of his young sons didn't want to leave his father even to go to school for a few hours, so Ammon had begun homeschooling him.

Lisa knew life would never be the same. How could she ever be sure that the government had stopped chasing Ammon? How could she ever feel certain that Ammon would not receive another divine call to arms? She would always support Ammon for standing up for what he thought was right, but she also wanted him at home in Emmett, not in another standoff or prison cell or dead. She needed him to be a husband and a father, and she hoped that was what the future held. But after a lifetime of living with Ammon's revelations, she couldn't be sure.

Ammon knew how Lisa felt. So when Cliven walked out of the federal courthouse, Ammon stuck around for only a little while, talking to reporters and supporters, and then he hit the road, heading home. Vegas to Emmett was a ten-hour drive, and with any luck, he'd be home before the kids went to bed.

ON CLIVEN'S FIRST NIGHT HOME, MOST OF THE BUNDYS GATHERED AT THE ranch. Everyone else had burgers. Cliven had steak.

Two days later, Cliven got up early. He looked out at the morning and saw a half-moon hanging in the azure sky. The rain had stopped after almost two full days. The Virgin River was swollen, and the cottonwood leaves were dripping. The rain had washed away the desert dust, and everything gleamed. At this moment, Bundy Ranch was beautiful.

Bundy Ranch was freedom.

Cliven had a press conference planned for later in the day, on the plaza in front of the sheriff's office in Las Vegas. As always, Carol would stand by his side behind her big Jackie O–style sunglasses. There would be the skeptical and impassive faces of the reporters, the black camera lenses facing him, the smiles of his friends and family and acolytes, Neil Wampler and Brand Nu Thornton and Shawna Cox hanging on to his every word. His enemies would be nearby too—the sheriff inside the building, and the feds no doubt watching and listening.

Seven hundred days in jail. Cliven hadn't decided whether he was going to go after his enemies or forgive and forget. The Lord would tell him what to do.

EPILOGUE

Ivisited Cliven at Bundy Ranch in April 2018, almost four years to the day after the Battle of Bunkerville.

He'd been free for three months, and despite the initial pleasure he'd felt in being home after his release, he seemed like a man in turmoil. Carol was giving a speech with Jeanette Finicum in Salt Lake City, so he was alone that night. He ushered me into his small living room and graciously offered me a glass of ice water. Then he pounced, asking me what percentage of Nevada was owned by the federal government. When I said around 80 percent, he seemed ready to kick me out.

"If that's your story, there's not nothing else to say about it," he said.

I shouldn't have been surprised that Cliven was unwilling to submit to the usual rhythms of an interview. *He* chooses the questions, not some journalist. I'd watched him employ this tactic numerous times on video and in person. Often, his speeches were little more than a series of questions, which his audience rarely answered to his satisfaction. His method was more gotcha than Socratic.

Now, he railed for several minutes about how my belief that the federal government could own most of Nevada prevented us from even beginning a conversation.

"You can go to the law professors, you can go to all the different bureaucracies, you can go to the colleges, and they'll all back your position," he said, getting more and more worked up. "You got your story. Bundy just sits here, and he don't have nothing to say."

We sat for a long, silent moment in opposing leather recliners, glowering at each other.

It was my first real meeting with Cliven, but over the past year, I'd spent a good deal of time with other Bundys and their followers. I'd camped out with Patriots in the desert outside of Pahrump and chowed with them in Brand Nu Thornton's Las Vegas apartment. I'd joined them on jail visits and in an anniversary pilgrimage to Toquop Wash. I'd talked with Ryan Bundy for hours on two long car rides across the Mojave, and I'd sat with Ammon and Lisa in their living room in Idaho. In the wake of the FBI's Longbow deception, I'd encountered plenty of suspicion that I worked for the feds, including jibes about when I was heading back to Quantico. But I had yet to run into anyone who simply didn't want to talk about the cause or the events of recent years.

As it turned out, Cliven wanted to talk, too, once he'd wrested the conversation into his control. For the next four hours, as the sky outside gradually turned black and the living room darkened, Cliven didn't once move from his chair as he spoke about the ranch, the feds, his ancestors. I asked few questions, and he rarely answered the ones I did venture. He cycled through wave after wave of emotion. Sometimes he was relaxed and friendly, but then something would trigger his anger and his voice would rise until it creaked. Several times, especially when he spoke of the past, tears ran down his cheeks, and he didn't bother to wipe them away or seem to even be aware of them.

Deep into the evening, Cliven's son-in-law Clancy clomped in and looked around the living room in puzzlement.

"Any reason why it's so dark in here?" he asked.

Clancy turned on the lights and said he was done with the ranch chores. Using a Gold Butte vocabulary known only to Bundys at this point, the two men mumbled to each other for ten minutes about ranch business. Two calves were sick, one foaming at the mouth, and Clancy had penned them away from the others. The Nickel Creek water lines were plugged up. Some Mexicans wanted to buy a couple of Bundy bulls. The truck's four-wheel drive was balky.

Early the next morning, I returned to Bundy Ranch, and Cliven kept talking as he fed several dozen calves on the farm property, breaking apart a one-ton hay bale with a pitchfork and tossing loose sheaves toward the milling herd. At work, he seemed more relaxed and willing to have a real conversation. His eldest daughter, Shiree, came over to cook us pancakes, since Carol was away. Then Cliven and I headed up onto the range in his ramshackle Ford sedan on a dirt road that twisted higher and higher toward the base of Virgin Peak, all of it BLM land. The road was called Sheep Trail, and it was the same road the BLM convoy had come down just before Ammon got tased.

"Everything I do, almost from the time I step out of my front door, everything I do is against some federal law," Cliven said as he drove. "Even driving up this road right now is against their rules, because this is a non-designated road."

As we climbed, the vegetation changed and the land grew greener. Periodically, he stopped the car and we crossed some desert on foot to look at various water structures. We drank handfuls of mineral-rich springwater from the spout of one water tank. He showed me plants that he called by names not used by BLM botanists, ranchers' terms based on how the plant looked—fluff grass, bottlestopper, bladder brush. He gathered tufts of plants in his thick, gnarled fingers that were as brown as the desert crust. This country didn't look like much from Interstate 15, he said, but Bundy cattle turned this forage into usable protein.

The higher we climbed, the more he seemed to unclench. He'd spent a lifetime working these ridges, and no matter who owned them, this was his home. He had said he was going to church in Bunkerville at 11 AM, but that hour came and went, and Cliven didn't bring it up. Instead, he stopped to show me an ancient well.

"You're asking a lot of questions about my water rights," he said. "Well, I *own* this son of a bitch. My ancestors built this son of a bitch."

He bent over and deadlifted the weighty concrete well cover, seeming pleased with his enduring strength.

After nine rough miles, not far from the unmarked boundary of Gold Butte National Monument,* we turned around. Back at the house, we said goodbye, and I wished Cliven peace. He didn't respond, but tears filled his eyes again, trickling down the arid creases of his face, like a monsoon rain down Toquop Wash.

BY CONTRAST, AMMON BUNDY WAS EXCEEDINGLY EASY TO TALK TO, AS Sheriff Dave Ward had found. He was heartfelt and humorous and self-deprecating. He had well-practiced, bedrock talking points, but he was willing to scrutinize them. On the witness stand in Oregon, for instance, Ammon had insisted that the occupation had been worth it.

---

* In December 2017, President Donald Trump announced his decision to reduce the size of two national monuments in Utah, and Interior Secretary Ryan Zinke recommended that he also shrink two others, including Gold Butte. At the time of this writing, no action had been taken to shrink the Gold Butte monument lands.

In his living room, he reiterated that statement but acknowledged that the words might sound callous.

"It's pretty hard for the Finicum family to say it was worth it," he said. "I want to be careful and not insensitive here. But there are great sacrifices that have been made to keep us free. LaVoy made that sacrifice, and his death rung around the nation, and it probably wouldn't have if they hadn't killed him."

Ammon was correct that the Bunkerville standoff and the Malheur occupation had brought attention to the range wars. In the last few years, seemingly every major news outlet, including the late-to-the-game *New York Times*, has published lengthy features about the federal government's control of 47 percent of the landmass of the West, and almost every piece has been pegged to the Bundy movement. The prospect of the government relinquishing the public lands to states or individuals still seems as remote as county sheriffs disarming the feds, but at least people were talking about it.

"Going into the refuge, I felt that our job was to bring attention to these things, to give the American people a choice of where we're gonna go, to wake people up, to make them aware," he said. "Some people say the refuge was a failure. But it actually wasn't. Everything we went to do we accomplished." He paused and gestured at me. "Because you're here."

And for just a moment, his eyes seemed to be pleading with mine, and I wondered if he was not just trying to convince *me* that the whole thing had been worth it, but to convince himself. After all the death and turmoil and hardship, was Ammon Bundy capable of experiencing true doubt?

The moment passed, and his plaintive look vanished, and I thought maybe I'd just imagined his uncertainty. Pretty soon we were back on safe terrain, talking about the range wars and the Constitution and liberty, and he was Ammon Bundy again, absolutely convinced.

SOURCES

The bulk of the information in *Up in Arms* is drawn from author interviews with both participants and observers of the events as well as many hundreds of court documents and transcripts from USA v. Cliven D. Bundy, et al (case number 2:16-cr-46-GMN-PAL), in the US District of Nevada and USA v. Ammon Bundy, et al (case number 3:16-cr-00051-BR), in the US District of Oregon. Some key interview subjects included Cliven Bundy, Ammon Bundy, Lisa Bundy, Ryan Bundy, Jeanette Finicum, Terri Linnell, Neil Wampler, Brand Nu Thornton, Shawna Cox, David Fry, and Sheriff Dave Ward.

THE BOOK USED INFORMATION ORIGINALLY REVEALED BY THE MANY JOUR-nalists who covered the Bundy story as it unfolded. The book is especially indebted to the work of Maxine Bernstein and Les Zaitz for the *Oregonian*, Henry Brean for the *Las Vegas Review-Journal*, Ryan Lenz for the Southern Poverty Law Center, Sarah Childress for *Frontline* at PBS, Tay Wiles for the *High Country News*, and Leah Sottile for the *Washington Post*, Oregon Public Broadcasting, and *Outside* magazine.

THE BOOK ALSO DREW FROM NEWS AND IN-DEPTH COVERAGE OF THE BUNDY saga from the *Las Vegas Review-Journal*; the *Las Vegas Sun*; the *Spectrum* in St. George, Utah; *Range* magazine; the *Salt Lake Tribune*; and the *Los Angeles Times*. The organizations that covered the Bundys most closely have bundled years' worth of coverage on these web pages:

- *Las Vegas Review-Journal*: https://www.reviewjournal.com/news/bundy-blm/
- *Oregonian*: https://www.oregonlive.com/oregon-standoff/
- Oregon Public Broadcasting: https://www.opb.org/news/series/burns-oregon-standoff-bundy-militia-news-updates/
- *High Country News*: https://www.hcn.org/topics/cliven-bundy
- *Frontline* on PBS: https://www.pbs.org/wgbh/frontline/film/american-patriot-inside-the-armed-uprising-against-the-federal-government/
- Southern Poverty Law Center: https://www.splcenter.org/20140709/war-west-bundy-ranch-standoff-and-american-radical-right and https://www.splcenter.org/fighting-hate/intelligence-report/2016/670-days

THE FOLLOWING WEBSITES PROVIDED A PATRIOT-ORIENTED VIEW OF THE events:

- Outpost of Freedom: http://outpost-of-freedom.com/blog/
- Oath Keepers: https://oathkeepers.org/
- Bundy Ranch: http://bundyranch.blogspot.com/

THE FOLLOWING SOURCES SHED LIGHT ON RELATED BACKGROUND TOPICS. This is not a comprehensive accounting of the thousands of sources that informed the book but merely an attempt to categorize some of the most important references by topic, in roughly the order that those topics appear in the book.

Federal public lands in the western states

- Bui, Quoctrung and Margot Sanger-Katz. "Why the Government Owns So Much Land in the West." *New York Times,* January 5, 2016.

- Quammen, Betsy Gaines. "American Zion: Mormon Perspectives on Landscape from Zion National Park to the Bundy Family War." Doctoral dissertation. Montana State University, Bozeman, Montana, April 2017.

- Regan, Shawn. "Managing Conflicts Over Western Rangelands." Property and Environment Research Center, January 21, 2016. https://www.perc.org/2016/01/21/managing-conflicts-over-western-rangelands/.

- Vincent, Carol Hardy and Laura A. Hanson and Jerome P. Bjelopera. "Federal Land Ownership: Overview and Data." Congressional Research Service, December 29, 2014.

Dan Love's background

- Mozingo, Joe. "A Sting in the Desert." *Los Angeles Times,* September 21, 2014.

- Swenson, Kyle. "Pilfered artifacts, three suicides and the struggle over federal land in Utah." *Washington Post,* December 5, 2017.

Nephi Johnson and the Mountain Meadows Massacre

- Brooks, Juanita. *The Mountain Meadows Massacre, 3rd Edition.* Norman, Oklahoma: University of Oklahoma Press, 1991.
- Krakauer, Jon. *Under the Banner of Heaven.* New York: Random House, 2003.

Growing discord over public lands in the western states during the twentieth century

- Brooke, James. "In New Wild West, It's Cowboys vs. Radical Environmentalists." *New York Times*, September 20, 1998.
- Cawley, R. McGreggor. *Federal Land, Western Anger.* Lawrence, Kansas: University Press of Kansas, 1993.
- Christensen, Jon. "Nevada's Ugly Tug-of-War." *High Country News*, October 30, 1995.
- Danbom, David B. *Bridging the Distance.* Salt Lake City, Utah: University of Utah Press, 2015.
- DeVoto, Bernard. "The West Against Itself." *Harper's*, January 1947.
- Egan, Timothy. "Urban Sprawl Strains Western States." *New York Times*, December 29, 1996.
- Herbers, John. "West Taking South's Place as Most Alienated Area." *New York Times*, March 18, 1979.
- Kenworthy, Tom. "Angry Ranchers Across the West See Grounds for an Insurrection." *Washington Post*, February 21, 1995.
- Larson, Erik. "Unrest in the West: Nevada's Nye County." *Time*, Oct. 23, 1995.

- Mathews, Tom. "The Angry West vs. the Rest." *Newsweek*, September 17, 1979.

- Robbins, Jim. "Target Green." *Audubon*, July–August 1995.

- Siegel, Barry. "A Lone Ranger." *Los Angeles Times*, November 26, 1995.

- Taylor, Rob. "Rural Federal Workers Feel Heat from Neighbors." *Seattle Post-Intelligencer*, May 3, 1995.

- Taylor, Robert E. "Vitriol & Violence." *Government Executive*, July 1995.

- Turque, Bill. "The War for the West." *Newsweek*, September 30, 1991.

Desert tortoise conservation efforts

- "Desert Conservation Program: Multiple Species Habitat Conservation Plan." The Clark County Desert Conservation Program. http://www.clarkcountynv.gov/airquality/dcp/Pages/CurrentHCP.aspx.

The rise of the Patriot movement

- Coates, James. *Armed and Dangerous*. Toronto: Collins Publishers, 1987.

- Helvarg, David. *The War Against the Greens*. San Francisco: Sierra Club Books, 1994.

- Levitas, Daniel. *The Terrorist Next Door*. New York: St. Martin's Press, 2002.

- Mulloy, D. J. *American Extremism*. Abingdon, UK: Taylor & Francis, 2008.

The United States Constitution and federal land ownership

- Bartrum, Ian. "Searching for Cliven Bundy: The Constitution and Public Lands." *Nevada Law Journal Forum*, Vol. 2 (2018): Article 5.

Ryan Payne's background

- Brosseau, Carli. "Refuge occupation's co-leader disillusioned by Iraq finds purpose in Bundys' cause." *Oregonian*, January 22, 2016.
- McDermott, Ted. "Freedom Fighter." *Missoula Independent*, June 12, 2014.

Shawna Cox's background

- Cox, Shawna. *Last Rancher Standing*. Rochester, NY: Legends Library Publishing, 2016.

The FBI's "Longbow Productions" operation

- Devereaux, Ryan and Trevor Aaronson. "America Reloaded: The Bizarre Story Behind the FBI's Fake Documentary About the Bundy Family." *Intercept*, May 16, 2017. https://theintercept.com/2017/05/16/the-bizarre-story-behind-the-fbis-fake-documentary-about-the-bundy-family/.

The description of militia training activities led by "John Killman" at Malheur

- *No Man's Land*. Directed by David Byers. New York: Topic Studios and Warrior Poets, 2017.

ACKNOWLEDGMENTS

A heartfelt thanks to the many people who told me their stories or at least didn't kick me off their properties. Additionally, I'm grateful to the following individuals for lending their perspective and expertise to various portions of *Up in Arms*: Ian Bartrum, David Damore, and Michael Green of the University of Nevada, Las Vegas; Leisl Carr Childers of Colorado State University; Ryan Lenz of the Southern Poverty Law Center; and Shawn Regan of the Property and Environment Research Center. A special mention to Tony Swofford for helping me identify various weapons and better understand the world of snipers.

At West Virginia University's libraries, I am indebted to Judi McCracken, Jennifer Dubetz, Jessica Haught, and especially Penny Pugh for helping me track down and obtain various materials. As always, Maryanne Reed, my friend and dean at WVU's Reed College of Media, provided a great deal of support for this book.

I'm so glad this book landed with the amazing team at BenBella Books, including Sarah Avinger, Scott Calamar, Alicia Kania, Adrienne Lang, Jessika Rieck, Alexa Stevenson, Susan Welte, Leah Wilson, and Glenn Yeffeth. An extra measure of gratitude to publicist Lindsay

Marshall for her energy and imagination in spreading the word about the book, and to editor Laurel Leigh for being both meticulous and kind, as well as for her knack for brilliant narrative fixes.

Some special thanks are in order for the enthusiasm of my agent, Jacqueline Flynn at Joëlle Delbourgo Associates, and for the sage advice from the readers who tackled early drafts of *Up in Arms*, including my friend Elaine McMillion Sheldon; my mother, Loranne Temple; and my son Hank Temple.

And then there's my wife, Hollee Temple, who not only edited every page of the book, but then read the entire manuscript out loud ... and then listened to me read the whole thing again. Thank you for your relentless devotion to making this book better.

ABOUT THE
AUTHOR

Photo by Bunny Oldham

JOHN TEMPLE is a veteran investigative journalist whose books illuminate significant issues in American life. Temple's last book, *American Pain: How a Young Felon and His Ring of Doctors Unleashed America's Deadliest Drug Epidemic*, was named a *New York Post* "Favorite Book of 2015" and was an Edgar Allan Poe Award nominee. *American Pain* chronicles how two young felons built the largest pill mill in the United States and also explains the roots of the opioid epidemic. Temple also wrote *The Last Lawyer: The Fight to Save Death Row Inmates* (2009) and *Deadhouse: Life in a Coroner's Office* (2005). *The Last Lawyer* won the Scribes Book Award from the American Society of Legal Writers.

Temple is a tenured journalism professor at the Reed College of

Media at West Virginia University. He holds an MFA in nonfiction writing from the University of Pittsburgh. Prior to academia, Temple worked as a newspaper reporter. He currently lives in Morgantown, West Virginia, with his wife and two sons. More information can be found at www.johntemplebooks.com.